Inflection Journal
Volume 07 - Boundaries
November 2020

Inflection is published annually by the Melbourne School of Design at the University of Melbourne and Melbourne Books.

Editors:
Han Jiang, Louis O'Connor and Arinah Rizal

Collaborators:
Yuan Cao, Kate Donaldson, Ziqi Peng, Michaela Prunotto and Katja Wagner

Academic Advisor:
Dr. AnnMarie Brennan

Acknowledgements:
The editors would like to thank all those involved in the production of this journal for their generous assistance and support.

Special thanks are due to AnnMarie Brennan, whose continual support, guidance and encouragement has been invaluable.

We also acknowledge Ester Leung from the Sidney Myer Asia Centre for her help in translation for this issue.

For editorial enquiries contact:
editorial@inflectionjournal.com

For sales enquiries contact:
info@melbournebooks.com.au

inflectionjournal.com
facebook.com/inflectionjournal
instagram.com/inflectionjournal

ISSN 2199-8094

ISBN 9781925556636

Melbourne Books
Level 9, 100 Collins Street,
Melbourne, VIC 3000,
Australia
www.melbournebooks.com.au
info@melbournebooks.com.au

Cover image: DMC Constellation, UK-DMC2 image © Airbus Defence and Space Limited, 2016. Image reproduced with author's permission.

Inside cover: Studio Synthetic Crystallisation, Digital Landscape, Galapagos Islands, 2020. Image by Jaymin Saliya.

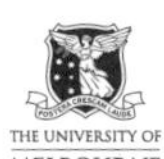

msd
Melbourne
School of Design

FACULTY OF
ARCHITECTURE,
BUILDING AND
PLANNING
www.msd.unimelb.edu.au

M
MELBOURNE BOOKS

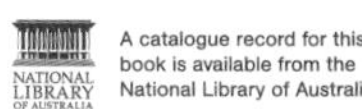
A catalogue record for this book is available from the National Library of Australia

CONTRIBUTORS

Anwyn Hocking
Hocking is an Ackman Trust Scholar in the MPhil of Architecture and Urban Studies at the University of Cambridge. Her research intersects psychology, sociology and architecture to explore the enactment of identity and collectivity in different socioeconomic contexts and typologies of collective dwelling. She is currently collaborating with London's Loneliness Lab to investigate loneliness in student accommodation, and is an editor of Cambridge Architecture Department's 2020 *Scroope Journal*.

Arinah Rizal
Rizal is an editor of *Inflection* Vol. 07. She is currently completing a Master of Architecture at the University of Melbourne and holds a Diploma in Music Performance. She was a copyeditor, curator and marketing manager for several books on contemporary Malaysian architecture, which include *The Tropical Malaysian House 1* by Robert Powell and Lin Ho (Atelier International, 2018). Having trained as an architectural assistant in London and Kuala Lumpur, Rizal continues to collaborate with community builders, musicians and designers based there.

Chatpong 'Chat' Chuenrudeemol
Chuenrudeemol is the principal of CHAT Architects based in Bangkok, Thailand. He also heads CHAT Lab, a research think tank aimed at discovering new Thai vernacular street typologies. He currently teaches a graduate studio at MIT School of Architecture and Planning on Thai coastal urbanism. In 2020, Chuenrudeemol received the prestigious *Silpathorn Award*, one of the highest honours for contributions to contemporary art and culture in Thailand.

Frank Burridge
Burridge is the co-steward and co-founder of the Victoria Chapter of The Architecture Lobby. He is a member of architecture collective *Makanbadawi* and has worked in several architecture practices in Melbourne. Burridge teaches history, theory and design studios in the architecture faculty at Monash University. He is currently completing a Master of Architecture at the University of Melbourne.

Han Jiang
Jiang is an editor for *Inflection* Vol. 07. She has worked for China Resources Limited, Shenzhen, as an assistant architecture manager on the Qianhai development project. Previously she worked for 'City of Lights' Studio, Tongji University Press, both as an editor and a free-lancer. She has broad interests in writing, publishing, economics and architecture. She is currently completing a Master of Architecture at the University of Melbourne.

Heather Mitcheltree
Mitcheltree is a graduate of the Melbourne School of Design where she currently teaches design. Having worked for over 15 years at the University of Melbourne across a range of teaching and research roles, she has a broad interdisciplinary research background. Her work focuses primarily on trauma-scapes, complex socio-spatial narratives, and the psychological impact of the built environment. In addition to research and teaching, she engages in private design work, art practice, creative design collaborations and research consultation.

Hsin Yeh
Yeh graduated from the Master of Architecture programme at the University of Melbourne, and is currently specialising in the residential sector. She is interested in issues surrounding Taiwanese cultural identity, politics in East Asian countries and the social value of close-knit communities.

Jennifer Ferng
Ferng is Senior Lecturer in Architecture and Postgraduate Director at the University of Sydney. She received her PhD from MIT. Her articles on immigration processing and detention centres have been published in *Architectural Theory Review*, *Asia Global Online*, and *the Journal of the Society of Architectural Historians*. She was awarded a Transregional Research fellowship from the Social Science Research Council (SSRC) and was a visiting scholar at the Harvard Asia Center in 2018.

Jonathan Russell
Russell is an architect and writer from Melbourne. A graduate of the Melbourne School of Design, he previously studied Urban Geography at Monash University and the University of California, Berkeley. Russell writes speculative architectural fiction and was a founding editor of *Inflection*.

Kenneth Wu
Wu is currently completing a Master of Architecture at the University of Melbourne and holds a Bachelor of Interior Architecture (Honours) from Monash University. He is interested in the intersection between these two professions and how they can be used as a means of empowerment.

Kim Bridgland and Aaron Roberts
Bridgland and Roberts founded Edition Office, an architecture studio based in Melbourne, in 2016. Through the execution of its built work and research, the practice seeks to continue a greater investigation into material, spatial and cultural practice. The studio has a considered awareness for the historical and cultural complexity that exists in within the sites that their projects occupy.

Léopold Lambert
Lambert is the editor-in-chief of *The Funambulist*, a print/online magazine and podcast dedicated to the politics of space and bodies. He is the author of three books examining the inherent violence of architecture and its political instrumentalisation, particularly in Palestine and France's *banlieues*: *Weaponized Architecture: The Impossibility of Innocence* (dpr-barcelona, 2012), *Topie Impitoyable: The Corporeal Politics of the Cloth, the Wall, and the Street* (punctum, 2015), and *La politique du bulldozer: La ruine palestinienne comme projet israélien* (B2, 2016). His forthcoming book is entitled *States of Emergency: A Spatial History of the French Colonial Continuum* (PMN, 2021).

Lorenzo Pezzani
Pezzani is an architect and researcher. He is currently Lecturer in Forensic Architecture at Goldsmiths, University of London. Since 2011, he has been working on Forensic Oceanography, a collaborative project that critically investigates the militarised border regime in the Mediterranean Sea, and has co-founded the WatchTheMed platform. His work has been used as evidence in courts of law, published across different media and academic outlets, as well as exhibited and screened internationally.

Louis O'Connor
O'Connor is an editor of *Inflection* Vol. 07. He is currently completing a Master of Architecture at the University of Melbourne and holds a Bachelor of Architectural Design and Bachelor of Engineering from Monash University. He has worked in residential practices in Melbourne and as a Research Assistant at the National University of Singapore, where he developed an interest in the city state's land reclamation projects and the trade of sand in South–East Asia.

Ma Yansong
Yansong is the founder and principal of MAD Architects. In 2006, he was awarded the Young Architects Award by the Architectural League of New York. In 2008, Yansong was selected as one of the 20 Most Influential Young Architects by *ICON* magazine and in 2010 he became the first architect from China to receive a RIBA fellowship. Parallel to his design practice, he has also been exploring with the public the cultural values of cities and architecture through domestic and international solo exhibitions, publications and art works.

Mitchell Ransome
Ransome is a graduate of the Melbourne School of Design where he currently teaches design and works in the Digital Fabrication Workshop. He has in-depth knowledge of experimental fabrication techniques as well as a variety of digital fields, such as 3 and 4 axis fabrication, sheet forming, and 3D scanning. Ransome's private work focuses on photography and the dislocation and exile of people and place. He has recently published a book, *The Opposite to Good but not Bad*.

Peggy Deamer
Deamer is Professor Emerita of the Yale School of Architecture and principal of Deamer, Studio. She is the founding member of the Architecture Lobby, a group advocating for the value of architectural labor. She is the editor of *Architecture and Capitalism: 1845 to the Present* and *The Architect as Worker: Immaterial Labor, the Creative Class, and the Politics of Design* and the author of *Architecture and Labor*.

Philippe Block
Block is Professor at the Institute of Technology in Architecture at ETH Zurich, where he directs the Block Research Group (BRG) together with Dr. Tom Van Mele. Professor Block is also the Director of the Swiss National Centre of Competence in Research (NCCR) in Digital Fabrication. Philippe studied architecture and structural engineering at the VUB in Belgium and MIT. Following the motto "strength through geometry", the BRG applies research into practice to address challenges posed by climate change.

Piper Bernbaum
Bernbaum is an Assistant Professor at the Azrieli School of Architecture and Urbanism at Carleton University in Canada. She is the recipient of the Prix de Rome for Emerging Practitioners and the Governor General's Academic Gold Medal. In recent years, Bernbaum has worked on international exhibitions of law, evidence and architecture—exhibiting work at the Venice Biennale in 2016, the Royal Ontario Museum in Toronto in 2017, and the Smithsonian Hirshhorn Museum in Washington in 2019.

Saba Innab
Innab is an architect, urban researcher, and artist practicing out of Amman and Beirut. She holds a Bachelor degree of Architectural Engineering from the Jordan University of Science and Technology (2004). In 2014, she received the visiting research fellowship initiated by Studio X Amman (Columbia GSAPP), and was listed for the Royal Academy Dorfman Award for Architecture, 2018. In 2019, Innab co-founded OPPA, an architecture and research collective.

Shamin Sahrum and Nur Nadhrah A.
Sahrum and Nadhrah A. are the founding partners of No-To-Scale*, a design-research platform responding to contemporary socio-political issues through architectural design and representation. Their works have been exhibited in Balai Seni Negara (The National Art Gallery of Malaysia) as part of the 'Kuala Lumpur Chair' exhibition in 2018, and have been featured in *Architecture Malaysia* and *Dezeen*. Sahrum is active in the Malaysian art scene, having exhibited in the 2019 Young Art Contemporaries show at Balai Seni Negara, and Nadrah is a past recipient of the *Malaysian Silver Medal Award* for architectural graduates.

Shatha Safi
Safi is an architect currently working as Co-Director of RIWAQ Centre for Architectural Conservation, Palestine, which she joined in 2008. She holds a Bachelor of Science in architectural engineering from Birzeit University and Master of Arts in World Heritage and Cultural Projects for Development from ITILO, Turin, Italy. Safi has been leading and working in different projects including the rehabilitation project of Beit Iksa, Hajjah and Birzeit, and Qalandiya.

Victoria King
King is a recent architectural graduate from the University of Melbourne. In 2019 King was awarded the RIBA Silver Medal for her graduating design thesis project *Surface Tension* which has since featured in publications including the *Sydney Morning Herald*, *RIBA Journal* and *Architecture AU*. She is interested in the potential of interdisciplinary design research to examine the complex relationship between our built and natural environments.

Wang Shu
Shu is the Dean of China Academy of Art. In 1997, he and his wife Lu Wenyu established Amateur Architecture Studio, devoted to the research of reconstructing Chinese contemporary architecture. This pursuit is reflected in his practice such as Ningbo Art Museum, Xiangshan Campus of China Academy of Art, and the comprehensive heritage renovation of the Southern Songyu Street in Hangzhou. In 2011, Shu won the Gold Medal from the French Academy of Architecture. In 2012, he won the Pritzker Architecture Prize.

CONTENTS

Corona Vision
Han Jiang, Louis O'Connor and Arinah Rizal 06

Lessons Along a Wire
Piper Bernbaum 12

Liquid Violence
Lorenzo Pezzani 24

Tomorrow, Poetry Will (Not) be the House of Life
Saba Innab 32

Bangkok Bastards
Chatpong Chuenrudeemol 40

Gentle Negotiations of the Civic Practitioner
Kenneth Wu and Hsin Yeh 48

Surface Tension
Victoria King 54

Contemplating the Void
Kim Bridgland and Aaron Roberts 64

The Territories of BIM
Peggy Deamer 70

Mistaken Identity
Frank Burridge 74

80 Strength Through Geometry
Philippe Block

86 Oneh
Shatha Safi

92 Representing the Colonial Continuum
Léopold Lambert

98 Partitioning Permanency
Anwyn Hocking

103 Kiewa: Encountering the Hydroelectric Margins
Jonathan Russell

110 Construction of the Garden and the People
Wang Shu

114 Refugee Space-Time
Jennifer Ferng

122 Contested States
Heather Mitcheltree and Mitchell Ransome

132 Welcome to ~~Uyghur~~ Wonderland
Nur Nadhrah A. and Shamin Sahrum

138 Hypernature
Ma Yansong

Han Jiang, Louis O'Connor & Arinah Rizal

In 1957, the CIA conducted a secretive military imaging reconnaissance programme, codenamed *CORONA*.[1] This project was part of an aspirational goal of the U.S. to join the space race and develop satellite technology for surveilling the Soviet Union by peaking over the Iron Curtain. With this historic example, we recognise that our current understanding of boundaries is, at times, derived from the wartime-military technology that has been transferred for use in the domestic realm.[2] We see how the advancements of military space technology during the Cold War has become a conventional navigation tool via Google Maps that we have grown dependent upon. Although these satellites are so remote and far beyond the capacity of our human senses, we cannot deny that the way their images are manipulated and presented governs how we distinguish boundaries and territories today. Imaginary lines, such as administrative zones and national borders that do not show up on remotely sensed images, reinforce the paradoxical nature of boundaries: they are both solid and intangible—or as ambiguous as they have ever been. It is with observations such as these that the editors of *Inflection* Vol. 07 ask, 'How should we understand the power of boundaries today?'

Contrary to man-made national boundaries, real cities are tangible and solid. The cover image of this journal is a satellite's view of the Hong Kong–Zhuhai–Macau Bridge (HZMB) that links three cities over a span of 55 kilometres. What appears as a tiny and delicate line captured from afar, is actually the longest cross-sea transport infrastructure in the world. It was built from 400,000 tonnes of steel, weighing an equivalent of 60 Eiffel towers. If we examine Hong Kong's border through Joshua Bolchover's concept of 'border ecology,' we can observe that the mobility of resources and exchange of materials between Hong Kong and mainland China has been dramatically increasing since Hong Kong's reunification in 1997.[3]

While the periphery of Hong Kong remains unchanged, the interwoven borders in the broader metropolitan area have become less clearly defined. Upon reunification, Hong Kong gradually opened six formal land border ports along its northern edge, using conservation parks as a buffer zone to engage with neighbouring Shenzhen. Tourists were then eligible to carry under HK$5,000 (around $900) across the border without being taxed. However, the transportation system of these two cities was separate, leaving travellers to pause their trips and transfer at the ports. In 2018, the Guangzhou-Shenzhen-Hong Kong Express Rail Link was opened, directly linking Hong Kong with 44 cities in mainland China and pushing the concept of ports deep into West Kowloon Station. The tendrils of the city spread out further into the mainland, enabling people to travel from the centre of a mainland city to the heart of Hong Kong, without the need to stop at territorial border ports, and enjoying the high travel speed without the expense of flying.

In the same year, the HZMB opened to the public, which allowed for the exchange of much larger goods and building-scale components. Some argue that the bridge serves as more of a political symbol than a generator of economic profit; helping the Chinese government link postcolonial Hong Kong and Macau with the mainland.[4] While the HZMB embodies its conception as a convenient transport connection, incrementally dissolving Hong Kong's border with the larger metropolitan area, the Y-shaped bridge also serves as a sociological barrier, excluding those without high economic means. For instance, private cars are permitted limited access to this megastructure, with special permits required to drive on it and proof of RMB 1 million (around $142,000) accumulated tax over three years.[5] It becomes harder to recognise the causal relationship between the

Opposite: The *CORONA* Programme satellite image of the Soviet Long-Range Aviation Airfield, 20 August, 1966.

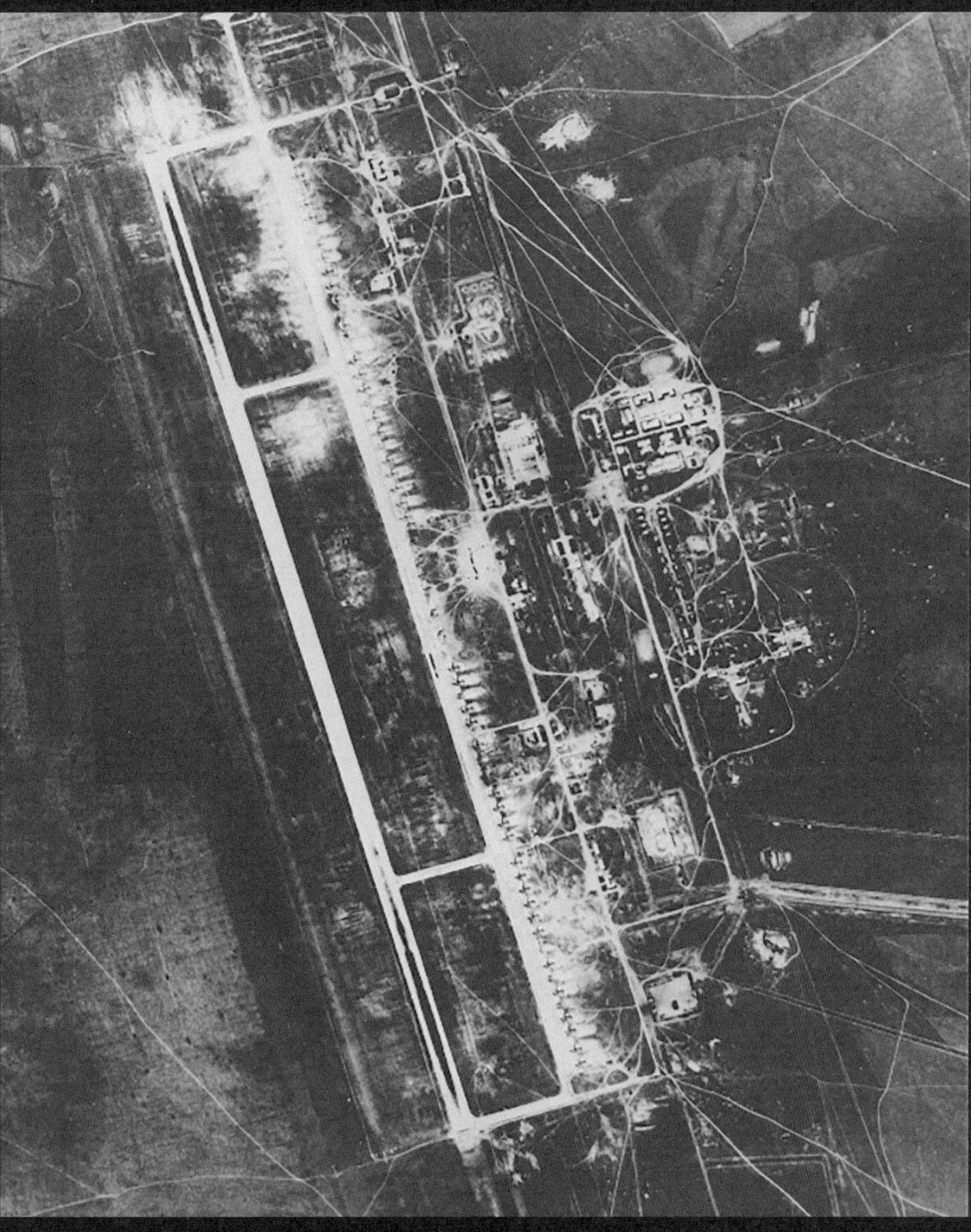

changing nature of the physical border, and its political and social systems. Is the HZMB, this incredible project, a harbinger of the future we aspire towards? By contending that physical and virtual boundaries are superimposed, the HZMB is equally layered with the flow of politics and capital. The scale of economic cost and the amount of material used, elevates modern mega projects from being purely an example of civil infrastructure, but rather a vital means of facilitating the larger dynamics of sociological, economical and political consequences.

Transport infrastructure has been popularly represented as a form of convenient connection since the world embraced globalisation. They are as influential, powerful, and costly as the ancient citadels, fortresses and castles that were defended by fortified boundaries. In the 21st century, the renewed focus on the penetrability of national borders demonstrates a common pursuit for tightly closed and protective sovereignty. Half of all border-barriers constructed since World War II were built after 2000, forming 20,000 kilometres of concrete, steel, sand, stone, and wire.[6]

The symbolic value of boundaries was reinforced by United States President Donald Trump when he described his U.S.-Mexico border wall as "physical, tall, powerful and beautiful."[7] Such adjectives are more suited to a monument than a border wall, questioning whether these structures serve more effectively as a political declaration that provides a psychological sense of security for Americans. Yet, when examining the architecture of boundaries, we are confronted with a series of contradictions—more boundaries are created by the forces that appear to overcome them.

International transit and digitised communications make it harder to prevent the flow of people, capital and information, which seems to undermine the purpose of expensive impenetrable barriers. But the flow of humans cannot be virtualised in the same way as money, commodities and information—hence border walls built to impede migration illustrates the hidden disconnections brought about by globalisation. Technologies such as 'Smart Walls' developed by Israeli weapons company, Elbit Systems™, make it possible to identify potential targets kilometres away, transforming the overt boundary line into a covert surveillance zone. Regardless of how 'smart' these boundaries have become, their stealth design only adds to the growing difficulty of locating their tendencies and their logic.

Therefore, we assert that when the Berlin Wall came down in 1989, the ideological limits it had originally created did not disappear: they became less tangible, less spatial, less easily defined, and more permeable. The symbolism of the wall remains, and its associated attitudes and beliefs continue to play out socially as divisive powers.

While architectural practice has always been in a position of crossing territories, the boundary between global and local is further blurred when international architects are commissioned to design cultural landmarks in cultural contexts foreign to them. Local buildings take on a global character, elevated to iconography through worldwide media consumption. One may question whether this is celebration of cultural diversity or a new aesthetic of globalisation. On a sociological level, significance leans heavily towards the simplification of local cultures as an added value for global cities. Rather than prompting the complex nature of civilizations, it sets up intangible boundaries by assigning different accessibility to public spaces. More often than not, those with greatest influence over the built environment of the public realm are developers and the government, rather than architects or designers. Today, the ability of architects to attract potential clients and buyers, is facilitated by the digital technologies and networked communication which allow firms to transcend geographical frontiers. Within the architectural profession itself, professional subdivisions are created by the wider use of digital tools, making it harder to recognise the core skills of architectural workers. This overfocus on efficiency and profit undermines the profession's capacity to affect meaningful change.[8]

Two weeks before the completion of this journal, the State of Victoria officially declared 'a state of disaster' to control the spread of coronavirus. Restrictions implemented across metropolitan Melbourne allowed for an activity range no further than a five-kilometre radius of one's home with a nightly curfew. Being constrained to our places of dwelling, our observations are also constrained to a screen. We look from the inside, out to a world available to our observation that is slightly more remote than usual. When our physical experience is largely replaced by the telematic space of our phones or laptops, it sparks worries that digital surveillance through contact tracking apps imposed by governments may function beyond pandemic control measures, threatening the privacy of citizens.

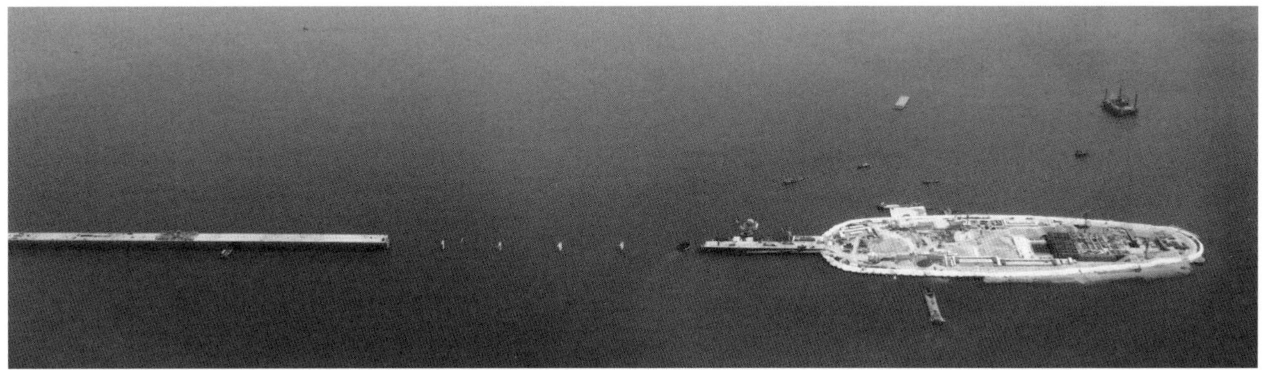

Like the classified *CORONA* Satellite Programme, which was only known to the public 40 years later, the most significant shifts take place outside of the public's focus. On platforms such as Facebook, Tik Tok, or Amazon, algorithms have long been deciding what information or products people should consume. In a way, the mediascape, nicely designed to cater to our taste, makes the promise of connection by providing people with similar opinions, ideas or visualisation styles, but it also separates the ideologies people embrace, making people gradually less tolerant to different opinions.

The parallels between the current pandemic and the *CORONA* Satellite Programme during the Cold War, constitutes another privileged view of the world, and magnifies the physical and ideological disonnections that technologies have advanced through stealth. This 'corona vision,' through which we experience life certainly underscores the invisible forces that both undermine and reinforce boundaries.

At this juncture, *Inflection* Vol. 07 offers another space for critical discourse, and reasserts the value of the printed word. Through the diverse and valuable perspectives of authors from around the globe, it carefully addresses a multitude of issues. In a profession built on the promise of permanence, how can architecture accommodate the transient and those displaced by conflict and crisis? How might designers respond to existing and impending states of emergency? How can we assert local values within a system that routinely preferences global ambitions and universal aesthetics?

Inflection welcomes you to investigate the expansive power of boundaries, and its forms of control and exchange within these pages, and beyond.

01 Francis Gary Powers Jr., "Foreword: From the U-2 to Corona," *CORONA: Between the Sun and the Earth: The First NRO Reconnaissance Eye in Space*, ed. R.A. McDonald (Bethesda: American Society for Photogrammetry & Remote Sensing, 1997), vii-ix.

02 AnnMarie Brennan, "Forecast," *Cold War Hothouses: Inventing Postwar Culture, from Cockpit to Playboy* (Princeton Architectural Press, 2004), 56.

03 Joshua Bolchover and Peter Hasdell, *Border Ecologies: Hong Kong's Mainland Frontier* (Boston: Birkhauser, 2017), 89.

04 Ben Blackledge, "The HK-Zhuhai-Macau bridge: An economic excuse for a political gamble?," *Hong Kong Free Press*, 2016. https://hongkongfp.com/2016/12/06/the-hk-zhuhai-macau-bridge-an-economic-excuse-for-a-political-gamble.

05 Guangdong Provincial Public Security Department, 《11月18日起，可重新申请经港珠澳大桥口岸通行的粤港两地车牌》, Guangdong Province, 2019. http://gdga.gd.gov.cn/bsfw/bmts/content/post_2654285.html.

06 Ron E. Hassner and Jason Wittenberg, "Barriers to Entry: Who Builds Fortified Boundaries and Why?," *International Security* 40, no.1 (2015): 157, doi: 10.1162/ISEC_a_00206. Theo Deutinger, *Handbook of Tyranny* (Zurich: Lars Müller Publishers, 2018), 37.

07 Rishi Iyengar. "Read Donald Trump's Speech on Immigration," *Time*. https://time.com/4475349/donald-trumps-speech-immigration-transcript/. "On day one, we will begin working on an impenetrable, physical, tall, power[ful] [and] beautiful southern border wall."

08 Peggy Deamer, "The Territories of BIM," *Inflection Journal*, Vol. 07 Boundaries (Melbourne Books, November 2020), 72.

The Hong Kong-Zuhai-Macau Bridge under construction, June 2014. Image courtesy of James Wong on Wikimedia Commons.

Next Page: View of the Hong Kong-Zhuhai-Macau Bridge from the northern edge of Macau. ©视觉中国, Visual China Group.

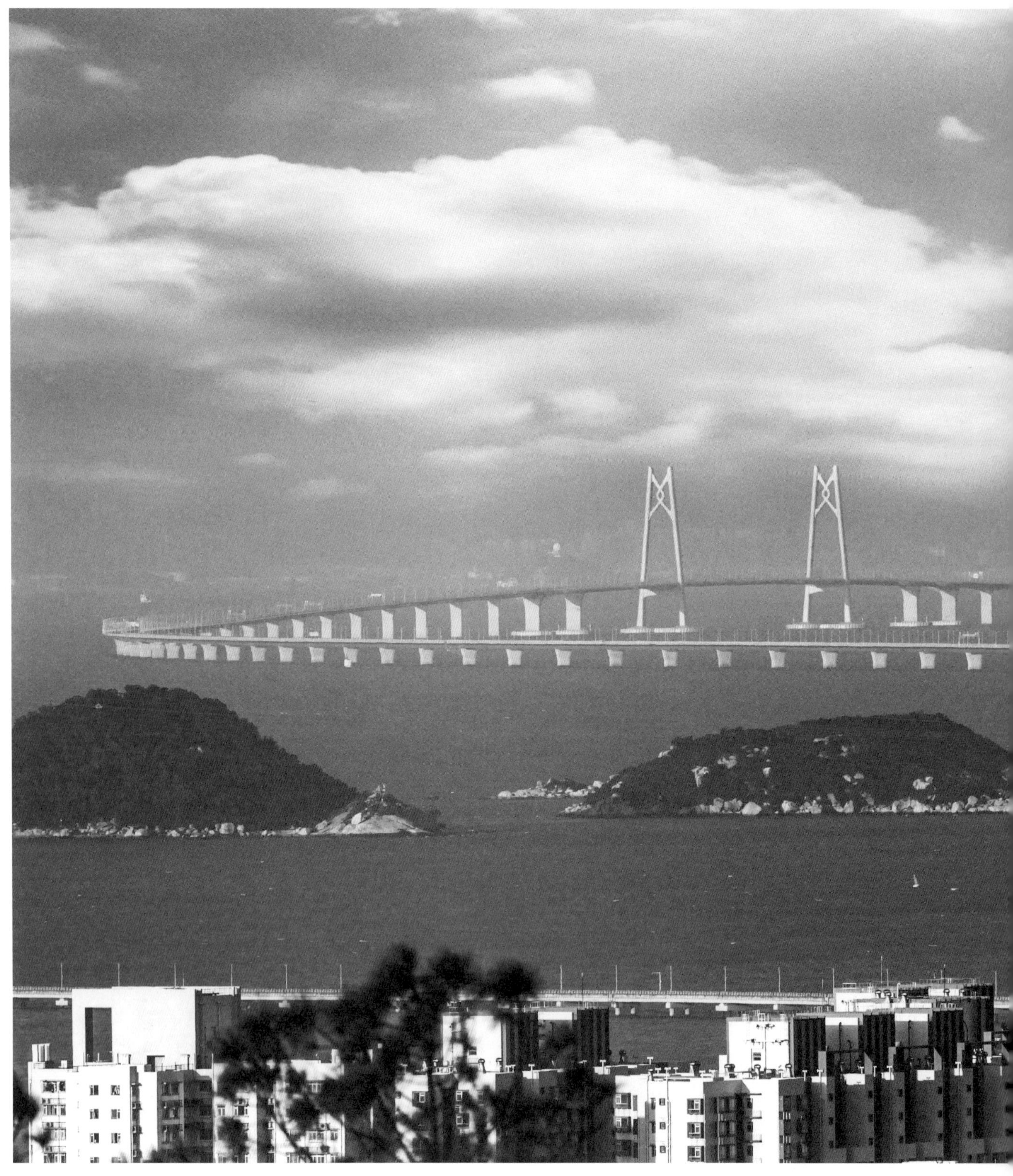

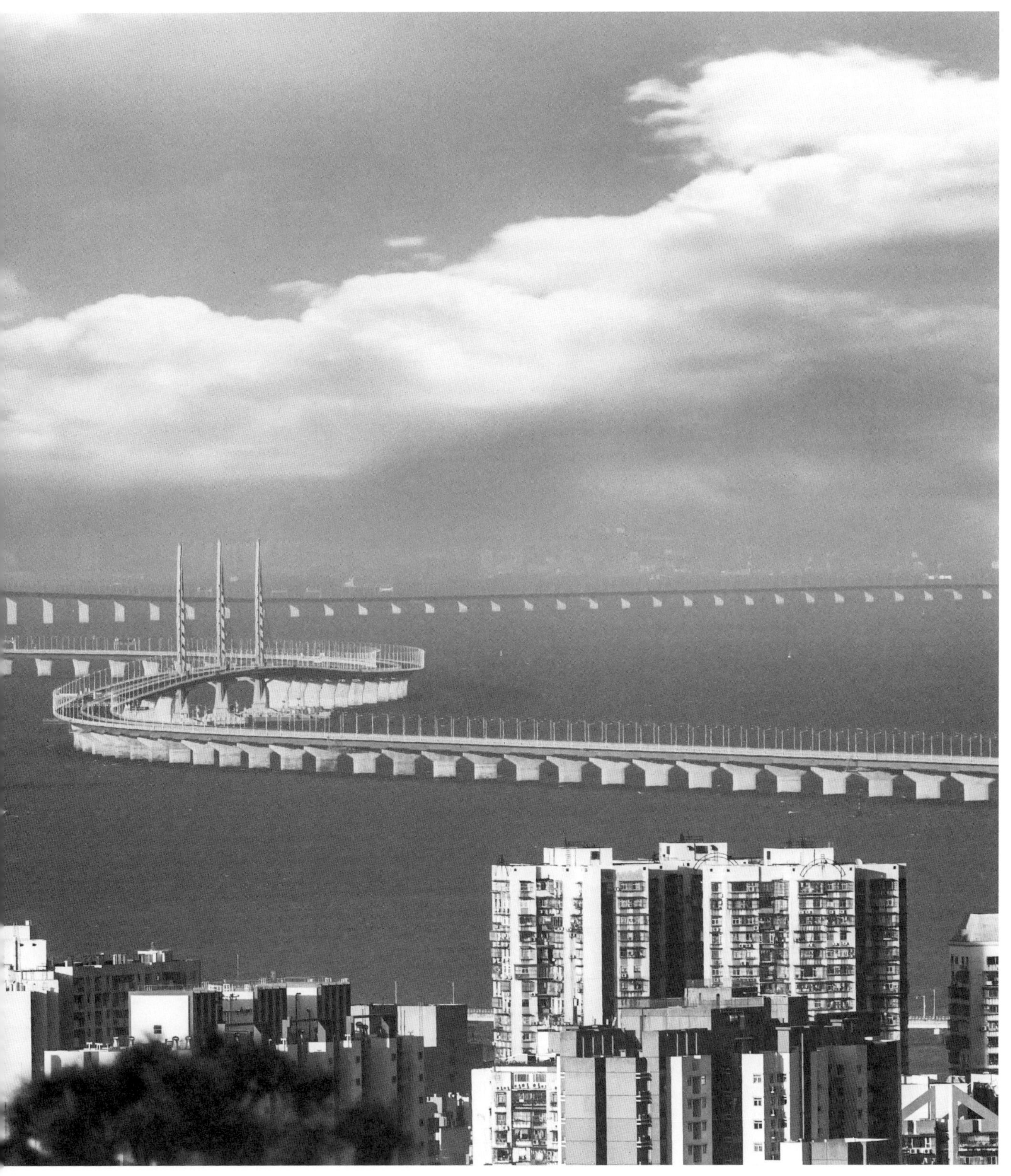

LESSONS ALONG A WIRE

SEEKING, FINDING AND UNDERSTANDING THE JEWISH ERUV: AN ARCHITECTURE OF MINGLING

Piper Bernbaum

Since 2015, I have spent time travelling to the outskirts of cities—tracing imaginary lines—in search of an elusive and subtle construct: the Jewish eruv. The Jewish eruv defines a physical area, symbolically extending the 'home' beyond its traditional walls and into the community. Written into the Talmud and acknowledged as a 'legal-fiction' (an assertion accepted as true), the eruv (plural eruvin) transforms space, providing leniencies to Orthodox Jewish communities by creating symbolic private realms within public urban space.[1] The eruv permits the performance of daily activities otherwise forbidden on the Sabbath.[2] However, the implications are much greater; Jewish citizens can participate in their communities and cities while also maintaining identity and traditions. Commonplace materials such as fishing wire, timber, existing walls and telephone posts are often used to construct the eruv. As a result, the boundary blends into its surroundings, encompassing portions, or even entire cities, while remaining virtually invisible to those unaware of its sacredness.

Redefining Boundaries

Prior to stumbling upon an article written by architects Manuel Herz and Eyal Weizman, titled 'Between City and Desert,' I was completely unaware of the eruv.[3] Detailing its historical value and purpose, Herz and Weizman theorise and describe the eruv as a transitory space, bridging the two primary states of existence found in the *Torah*; the desert and the city, or placelessness and kingdom. At the time, the essay was one of the first and only descriptions of the eruv as a critical form of architecture and urbanism. 'Between City and Desert' describes the capacity of the eruv to transform the public realm into a symbolic, privatised space representative of the Temple of Jerusalem; making the 'dweller' of the eruv a wanderer. 'Between City and Desert' elaborates upon the eruv as a symbolic threshold, a layered symbolism that gives multiplicity to space. In addition to its thorough overview of the eruv, the article redefines possible preconceptions of boundaries. Herz and Weizman describe the eruv boundary as a limit where the material and the metaphoric encounter one another in a city—a visible artifact portraying an intangible experience.[4] The article introduced me to the symbolic and physical nature of the eruv; an occupation of the public domain in the contemporary city. Still built today, and existing primarily in North American cities to serve diaspora communities, the eruv seems to contradict what I understood as traditional pluralistic public space. It was simultaneously a practice for a specific religion and inclusive to all people; a traversable, sometimes unrecognisable boundary for many.

As my understanding of the eruv grew, questions remained. I wanted to know more about the decision-making behind the establishment of these communities: where, why and how was the boundary formed? How does the eruv negotiate its existence with the complex attitudes of a city? With only the North London eruv described in detail, I decided to elaborate upon Herz and Weizman's work, comparing eruvin at multiple scales; exploring their meaning within already established communities and cities.[7]

To further my understanding and attempt to answer the above questions, I undertook a series of fieldwork investigations, documenting eruvin through sketches, mapping, writing and photography. This article details my research investigations into the eruv performed over the past five years. The work focuses on the conception of the boundary as a symbolic threshold of mingling and inclusion. The ongoing research is currently titled 'The Atlas of Legal Fictions.' With more than 50 eruvin visited and documented to date, the story of the eruv has also become my story. The eruv has a plurality unto itself: it is diverse in its form and shape in what it represents and what it allows, what it provides and how it acts, how it is made and how it reads its surroundings. It is both a boundary and a home; an edge to

Opposite: Williamsburg Eruv, New York.
All images by the author.

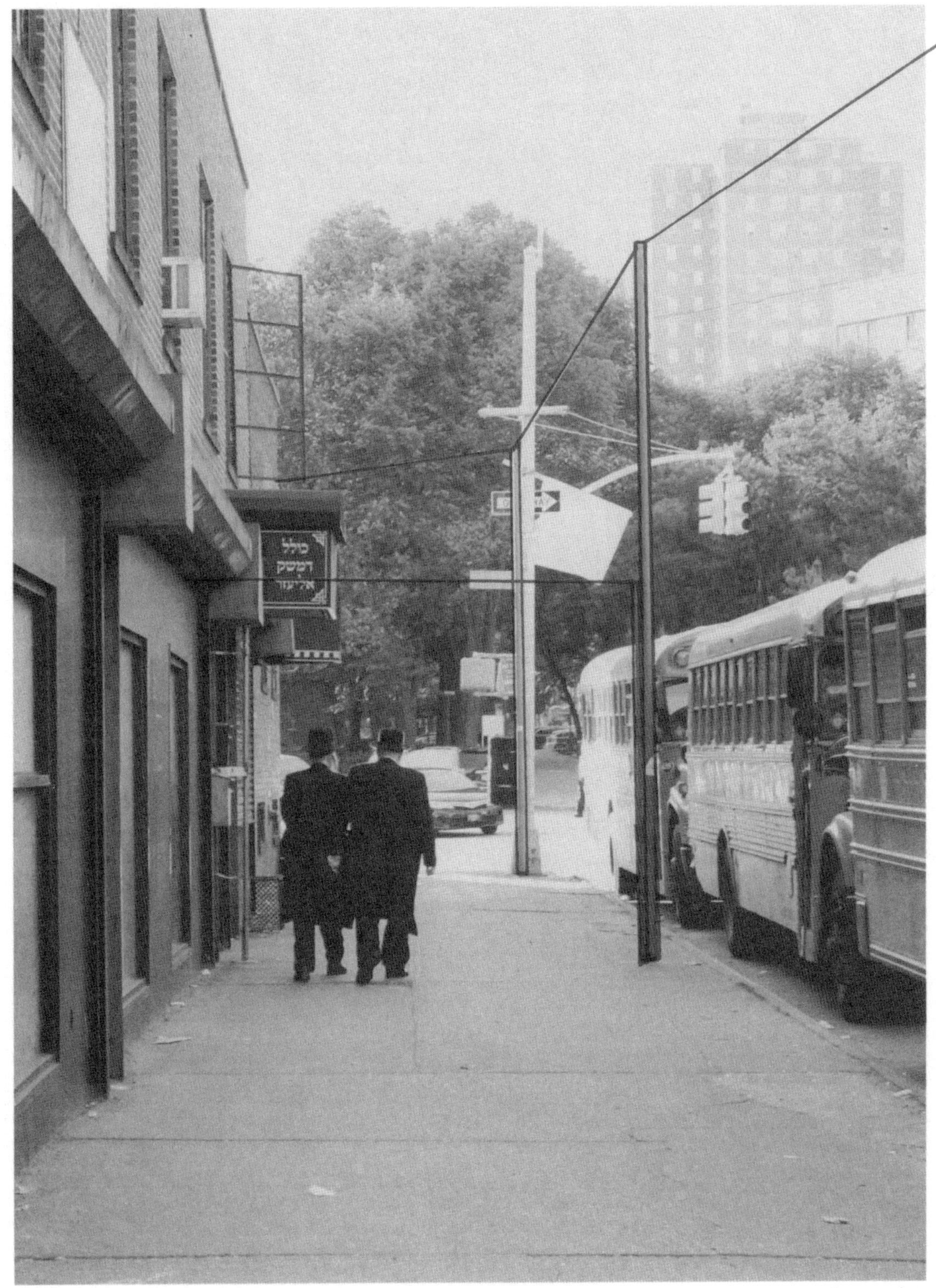

WILLIAMSBURG ERUV - BROOKLYN, NY JUNE/15

the outside and a threshold to the inside. Most importantly, the eruv becomes a manifesto for the contextual urban politics in which it is embedded.

Eruv Hunting

I began my research and fieldwork in Kitchener, Ontario, seeking out the closest publicly recorded eruv to my home just east in Cambridge. I had a map of the eruv (a re-scanned print of a road map with pink and yellow highlighter) downloaded from the synagogue's website.[7] The map showed the boundary edge, so I drove to the city confident I would easily find the eruv. Much to my surprise, I walked the snowy streets with no such luck. I searched for timber posts and fishing line standing proud from the typical street setting. Instead, I saw nothing different. No fishing line, no timber posts, no eruv? I photographed everything, hoping I was missing something. Upon reviewing my photographs, I quickly realised this was the case. In the photographs 'two-by-fours' revealed themselves—affixed to the base of lamp posts—about a metre high, zip-tied.[7] They seemed out of place, yet hardly noticeable; hiding in plain sight. With further research I discovered this was called a *lechi* or doorpost used on the corners of streets where the eruv would bend; subtly identifying an enclosure and its entrances.

Kitchener became a quick lesson about the eruv; the boundary embeds itself in its surroundings. It is resourceful, it is simple and it is accessible. I thought back to the map that originally led me to the boundary; a poorly scanned map marked up with highlighters. The eruv is not an architecture due to its sophistication. Its significance is found in its existence and the spatial continuity it provides, however modest it may be. These boundaries are fabricated by the community who uses them, and therein, represents the values of the community in their making. The disconnect between *my* understanding of urban architecture and eruv urban architecture became apparent in my fieldwork. Its simplicity allows it to exist without hierarchy or privilege, and to be constructed without complex tools or materials.

The required components to fabricate an eruv all represent parts of a house. These include 'walls' referred to as *Mechitsot* and are typically made of posts or existing boundaries (fences, walls, etc.). *Tzurat Hapesach* are 'doorways' into the community acting as operable gates; two posts and a fishing line strung between, high enough to pass under. *Lechi* identify doorposts and are represented with small wood posts or paint added to the base of walls or lampposts. Lastly, and most importantly, the *Korah* is the lintel; the fishing line that brings together

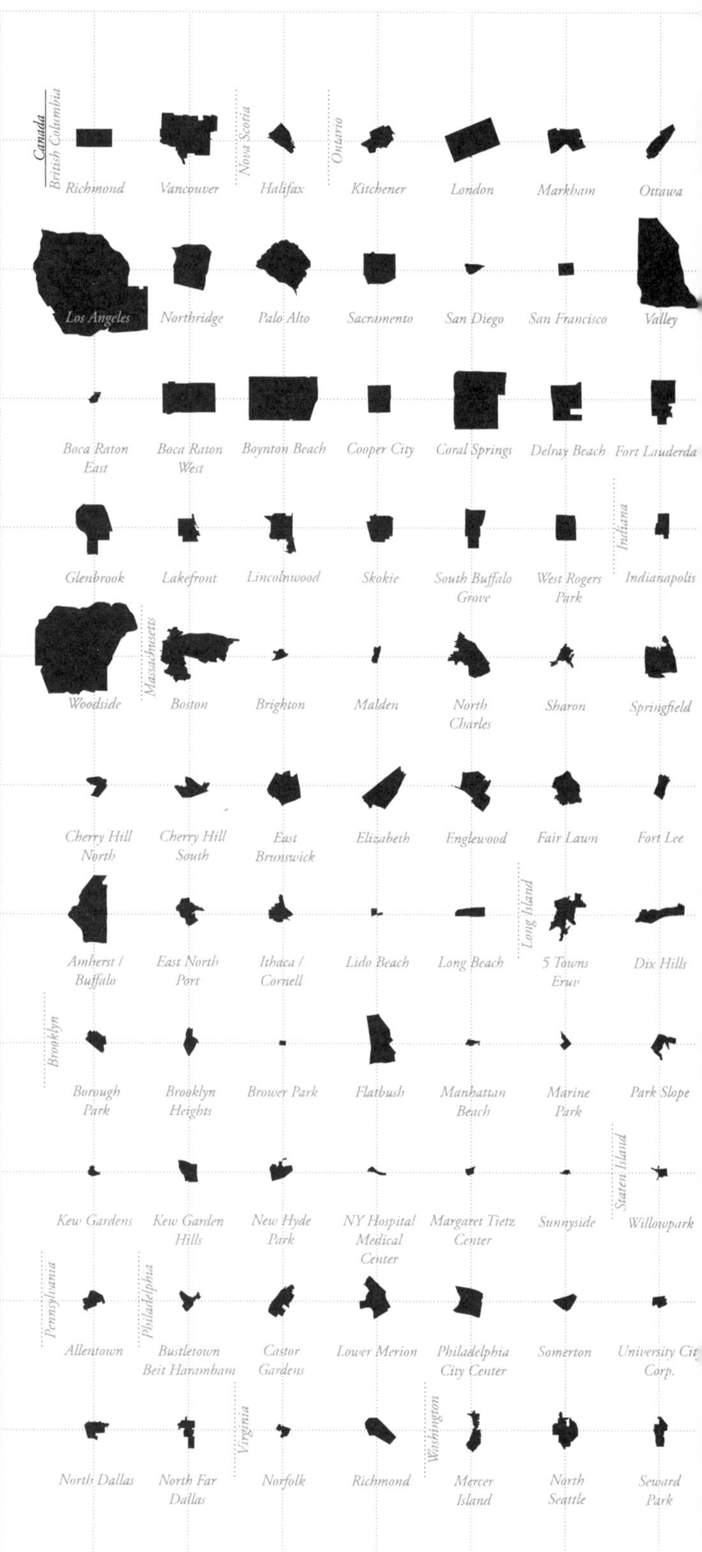

The Incomplete Atlas of Eruvin in North America, 2016.

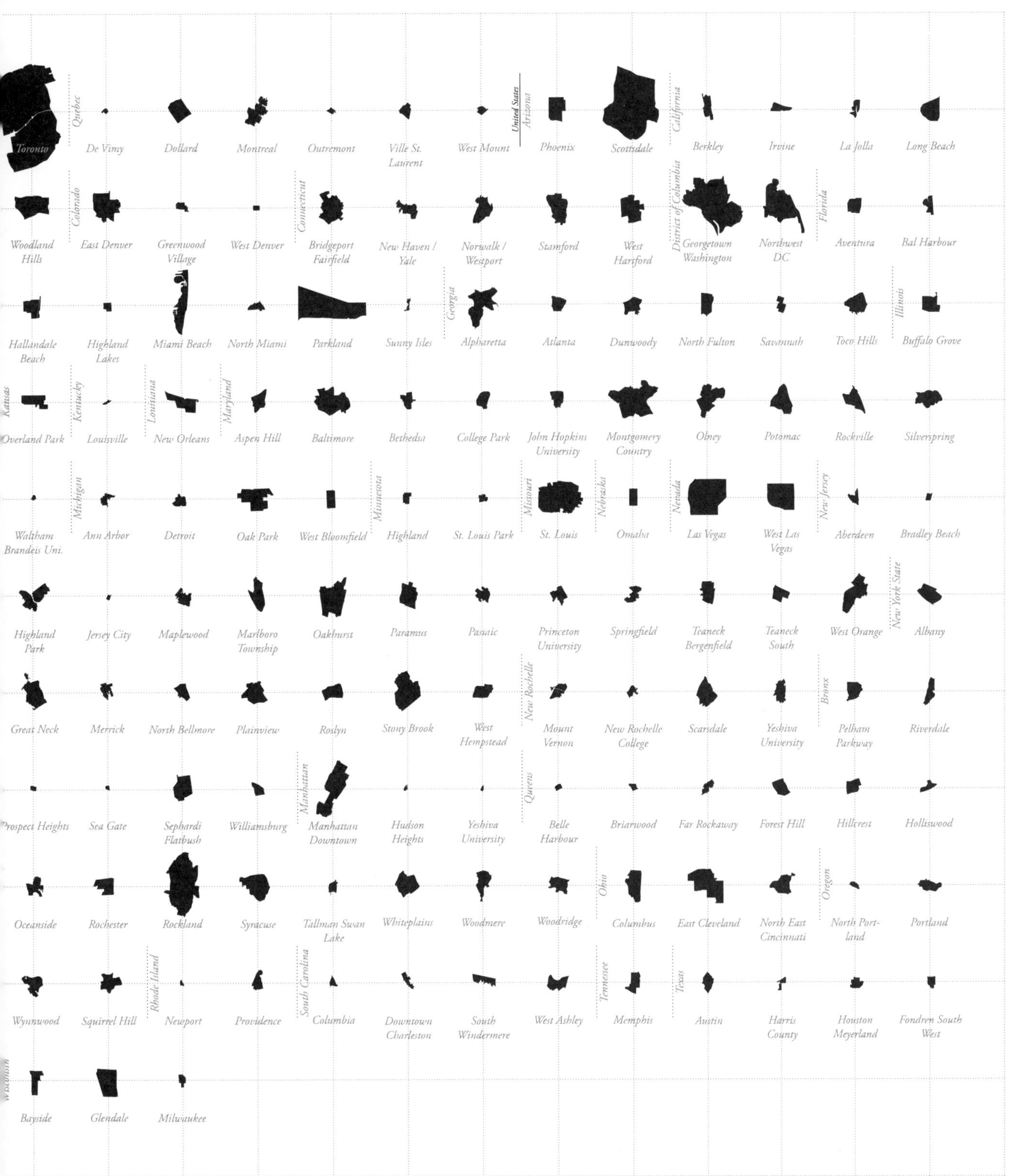
Toronto
Quebec
De Vimy
Dollard
Montreal
Outremont
Ville St. Laurent
West Mount
United States
Arizona
Phoenix
Scottsdale
California
Berkley
Irvine
La Jolla
Long Beach
Woodland Hills
Colorado
East Denver
Greenwood Village
West Denver
Connecticut
Bridgeport Fairfield
New Haven / Yale
Norwalk / Westport
Stamford
West Hartford
District of Columbia
Georgetown Washington
Northwest DC
Florida
Aventura
Bal Harbour
Hallandale Beach
Highland Lakes
Miami Beach
North Miami
Parkland
Sunny Isles
Georgia
Alpharetta
Atlanta
Dunwoody
North Fulton
Savannah
Toco Hills
Illinois
Buffalo Grove
Kansas
Overland Park
Kentucky
Louisville
Louisiana
New Orleans
Maryland
Aspen Hill
Baltimore
Bethedsa
College Park
John Hopkins University
Montgomery Country
Olney
Potomac
Rockville
Silverspring
Waltham Brandeis Uni.
Michigan
Ann Arbor
Detroit
Oak Park
West Bloomfield
Minnesota
Highland
St. Louis Park
Missouri
St. Louis
Nebraska
Omaha
Nevada
Las Vegas
West Las Vegas
New Jersey
Aberdeen
Bradley Beach
Highland Park
Jersey City
Maplewood
Marlboro Township
Oakhurst
Paramus
Passaic
Princeton University
Springfield
Teaneck Bergenfield
Teaneck South
West Orange
New York State
Albany
Great Neck
Merrick
North Bellmore
Plainview
Roslyn
Stony Brook
West Hempstead
New Rochelle
Mount Vernon
New Rochelle College
Scarsdale
Yeshiva University
Bronx
Pelham Parkway
Riverdale
Prospect Heights
Sea Gate
Sephardi Flatbush
Williamsburg
Manhattan
Manhattan Downtown
Hudson Heights
Yeshiva University
Queens
Belle Harbour
Briarwood
Far Rockaway
Forest Hill
Hillcrest
Holliswood
Oceanside
Rochester
Rockland
Syracuse
Tallman Swan Lake
Whiteplains
Woodmere
Woodridge
Ohio
Columbus
East Cleveland
North East Cincinnati
Oregon
North Port- land
Portland
Wynnwood
Squirrel Hill
Rhode Island
Newport
Providence
South Carolina
Columbia
Downtown Charleston
South Windermere
West Ashley
Tennessee
Memphis
Texas
Austin
Harris County
Houston Meyerland
Fondren South West
Wisconsin
Bayside
Glendale
Milwaukee

all of the components, connecting the 'house.' The *Korah* is the roof under which the community dwells, where space is shared and where the symbolic components of the eruv are given physical spatial value.[8]

The eruv differs from common Western conceptions of home, which purposefully separate space for private inhabitation. Along the eruv, there is no apparent inside or outside, and no substantial threshold that signifies change from common to spiritual territory, or public to private space. The city becomes the home.[9] The eruv, in its physical and spiritual form, is an architecture of bare essentials. Acting as a refuge, the eruv requires both material and emotional commitment.[10]

Mingling Space

The word eruv (עירוב) is a transliterated Hebrew word meaning literally 'mixture' or 'blending,' and is further defined as a 'mingling,' or more appropriately, an 'amalgamation.' From the way it is built, to who builds it and to who dwells in it, eruvin are mingling spaces of many people and the unique contexts of these communities.

After my time in Kitchener, the desire to continue to learn more about the eruv as a response to varying and diverse contexts continued. In some cities, the eruv is a large area that has expanded over time to include and encompass new communities and migrating populations (such as in Toronto or Boston). In contrast, some cities have many eruvin, likely out of a desire among individual communities to have control over their own space and practice apart from other sects or groups (such as in Brooklyn or Montreal).

As the Atlas continued to develop and more eruvin were visited, it became clear the eruv was a morphology rather than a replicable template. Regardless of the size or scale of the eruv, its shape is always informed by the existing city. Although the eruv is territory overlaid on the traditional civic fabric, it is both the physical constraints and the legal limitations of a place that influence the location of the eruv. But how is it legally built? In Buffalo, New York, Rabbi Taub explained that the eruv is not classified by entitled ownership.[11] To justify the use of public space for such a unique community need, Rabbinic authorities included in Talmudic Law a necessity to approach public space as a private realm. In other words, the eruv is rented space through contract, rather than owned or entitled property of a synagogue or Jewish community. It is through municipal agreement with 'outsiders' (anyone who does not participate in Jewish practice or the eruv) that the eruv can be built.

Opposite: *Tzurat Hapesach* (doorways).

This permission is required for construction and involves formal submission to the governing city planning department, and a lease drafted and signed by both parties. Once the agreement is signed, the space and its existing infrastructure are available for appropriation or modification as required.[12] The eruv is the signifier of a transaction between the Jewish community, through the synagogue, and the city as the proprietor.

Returning to the translation of the word eruv, 'mingling' gains further significance through the cooperation required to enact such a boundary. Mixing becomes more than a symbolic overlay of public and private realms, by formalising the cohabitation of communities and beliefs within this signified urban territory. The Talmudic mandate of renting space embraces the eruv's pluralism within the required contract. This means an eruv cannot be established without the permission and consent of the non-Jewish neighbour, and eruvin are not erected in secret.[13] Consequently, the role of the eruv and its relationship to the city is defined by what it produces, not its property.[14]

Bricolage and Plurality

The purpose of the eruv can be understood as an extended space of lenience; a negotiating urban layer whose purpose appears to reach further than its original Talmudic intent. As both symbolic and physical space, the eruv is a form of urbanism. 'Eruv Urbanism' is a reinterpretation of space, and a reappropriation of the physical environment. In a separate article written about the sacred vernaculars in Jerusalem, Eyal Weizman identifies this as a new reading of existing public space and symbols:

> The Eruv, like a giant-scale act of urban bricolage, incorporates and uses the existing boundaries of urban scars . . . : fences, walls, concrete decks, metal handrails, rock faces, house facades, water reservoir[s], a railway line, a deep valley to mark its boundary, saving the use of poles and string . . . Seeing the city as an object, the Eruv reinterprets and reuses its props and imbues them with another meaning.[15]

Bricolage, in this case, refers to using what is available in the urban environment for construction purposes, a collage of objects whose arrangement enacts symbolic space.[16] However, Weizman's description can be extended. The eruv is a bricolage of artefacts for construction, and a bricolage of communities—their inherent laws, forms and character included in the activation of space. The eruv is an imprint of contextual urban politics of a city and its citizens. Knowing that the eruv is constructed by the people who use it as they

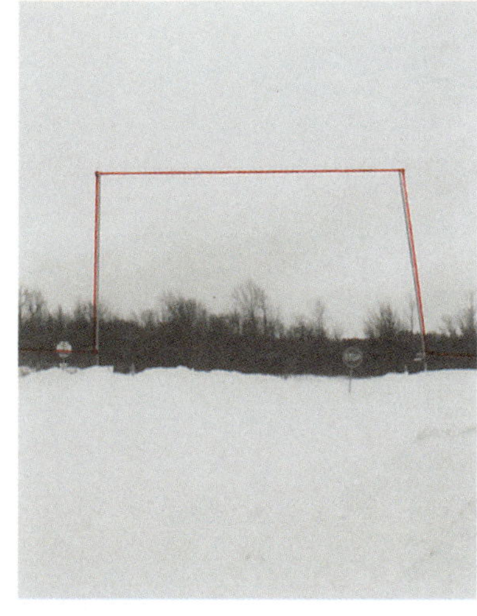

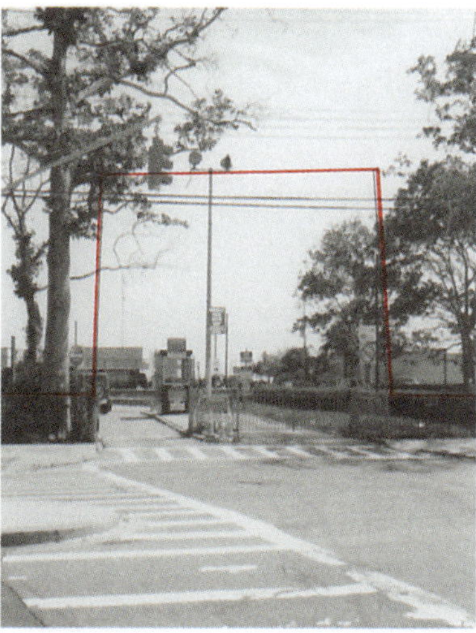

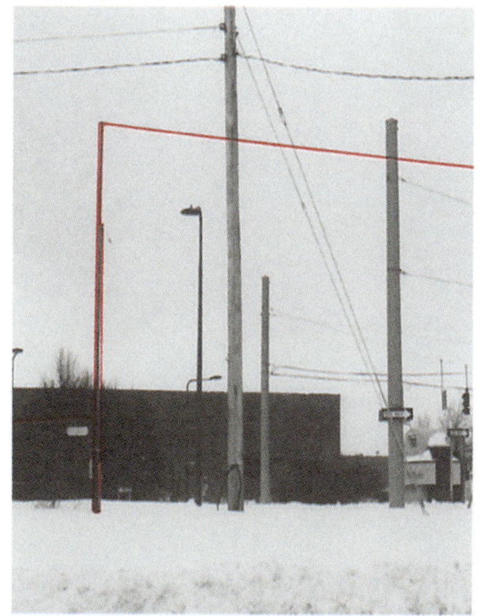

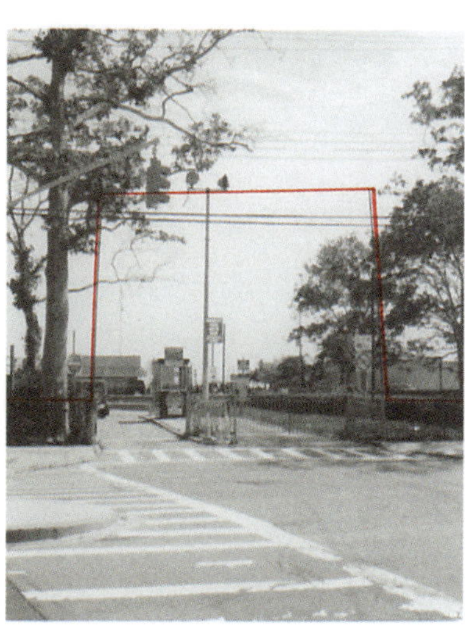

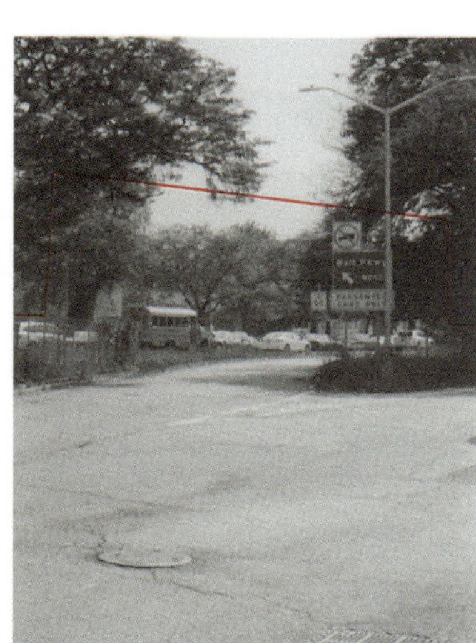

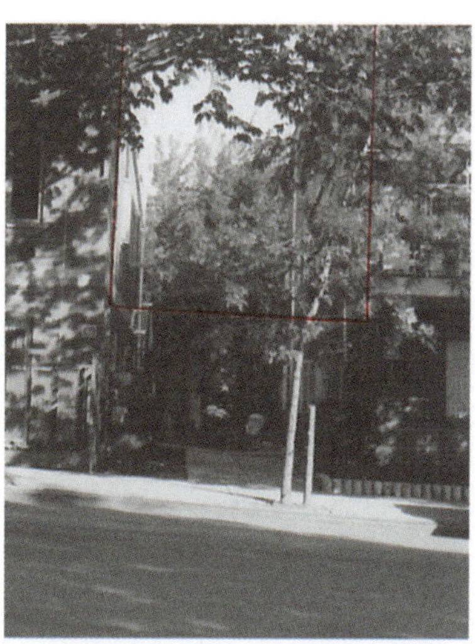

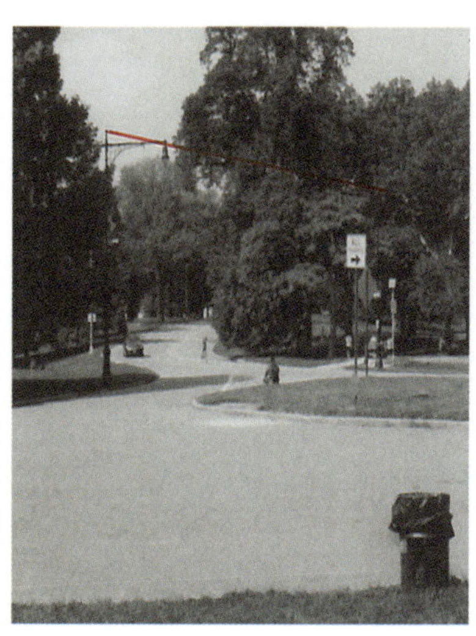

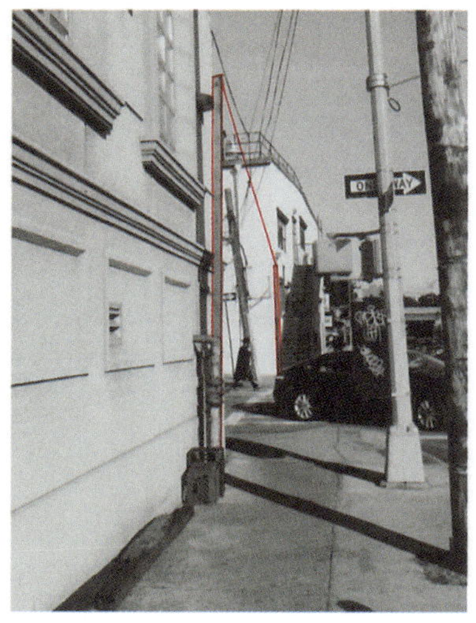

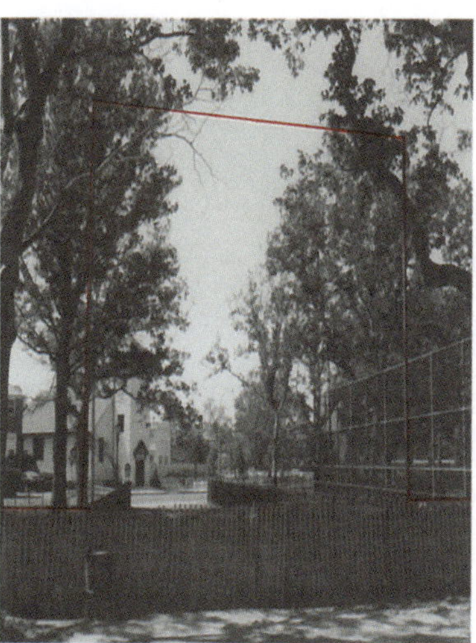

build boundaries for their congregation, the question is: What would they decide to include in their community? In addition, when considering these inclusions and exclusions, can the eruv be considered a boundary of pluralism?

The best place to assess these questions of plurality and spatial evolution is New York City. Manhattan's eruv is one of the oldest in the United States; initially established to serve the first Jewish immigrant families that arrived in North America as diaspora, it originated in the Lower East Side, Garment District of Manhattan. As the city and its Jewish population has changed and grown, so has the eruv. To serve the needs of multiple communities, the eruv slowly absorbed and made obsolete previously existing boundary lines.[17] The Manhattan eruv was established in 1905 and included the entire east side of the borough, making use of the above ground rail line that once ran north–south through the centre of the city, and the East River as its boundaries.[18] The rail line and river edge that defined the eruv required no alterations or additional components. They were chosen primarily out of convenience due to lack of funds; creating a natural, enclosed 'wall' around the Jewish community.

The continued industrialisation and trade expansion of the early 20th century led to the construction of additional docks and bridges along the east edge of Manhattan. The demolition of river walls and increased access to the city from Brooklyn, Long Island and out of state indicated a more permeable eruv boundary. These infrastructural transformations privileged new modes of transport, and the majority of above ground rail lines were dismantled. As a consequence of these greater urban transformations, a reconsideration of the eruv was necessary as the influx in population questioned the viability of the eruv as privatised space. The Manhattan eruv continued to change with the city and with Rabbinic debate. In 1949, the boundary encompassed the entire island, using only the waterways as its boundaries. In 1968, it was redesigned again, forming an inset border using the streets of the city to its advantage. Since 1968, the eruv has periodically changed, reflecting the conditions of the metropolis in balance with the views of the Jewish community.[19]

In addition to the storied history of its bounds, the Manhattan eruv is also a symbolic space of incredible scale. The eruv serves many different synagogues and areas of the city, covering approximately 60 percent of the land available on the island. Although a rigorous urban grid with consistent infrastructural elements defines Manhattan, the eruv does not exist as a simple and efficient rectilinear object.

Opposite: *Korah* (roof).

Manhattan's eruv weaves back and forth through city blocks, as the shape of the line illuminates the idiosyncrasies of the agreement with the city. These moments, unusual jogs in the eruv boundary pattern, reveal moments of negotiation of local, contextual politics.

Inside and Outside

New York City is a metropolis of boroughs, and Manhattan itself has strong neighbourhood identities. These distinct enclaves, such as Harlem, Chelsea, Hell's Kitchen and the Lower East Side, have developed their own character and taken claim to space in entirely unique ways. Manhattan's eruv reflects that. The intricacies of the Manhattan eruv plan, the unusual bends in the boundary line, are caused by a multiplicity of area-specific conditions, moments of control, inclusion and exclusion. The following conditions explore the eruv, elaborating on the legalities of certain boundary locations, and speculating on how one creates a neighbourhood within an already established city.

At the time of my fieldwork in 2016, the north and south boundaries of the Manhattan eruv showed clear exclusionary practices.[20] Tracing the line, the north end of the eruv just above Central Park has a noticeable extension along the Upper West Side, reaching up to 126th Street along the edge of the park, before jutting back down to 111th Street where it moves past Morningside Heights towards East Harlem. These moves are purposeful; the eruv decisively jumps and extends in order to include Columbia University's campus and student housing, while excluding East Harlem. This certainly could be out of community need—the eruv may have been designed to serve those attending Columbia, while assuming very few Orthodox Jewish Families live in East Harlem and that universities are all-inclusive spaces. However, it could also be seen as a means to define where Rabbinic authorities wish for their community members to live—including safer communities such as Morningside Heights, and excluding historically higher crime areas such as East Harlem.

These maps provoke the question, does the eruv indicate where community members *currently* live? Or does the eruv act as an edge guiding where community members *should* live? Which came first? It is likely both. However, we do know that the eruv is a powerful tool, decisively defining how and where Jewish Orthodox people may be influenced to settle within a city. Although symbolic, the boundary of the eruv indicates the space in which individuals dwell, invest their time and money, and where they socialise. The edge, although permeable, is a means of control, and a means of closeness. Safety and concern over what is within the community boundary is considered carefully.

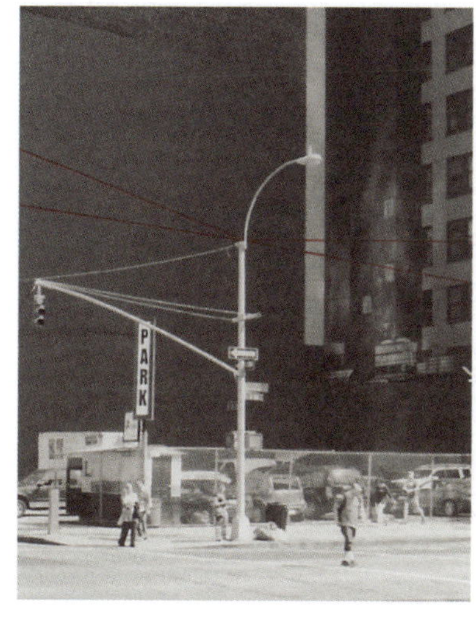
PARK

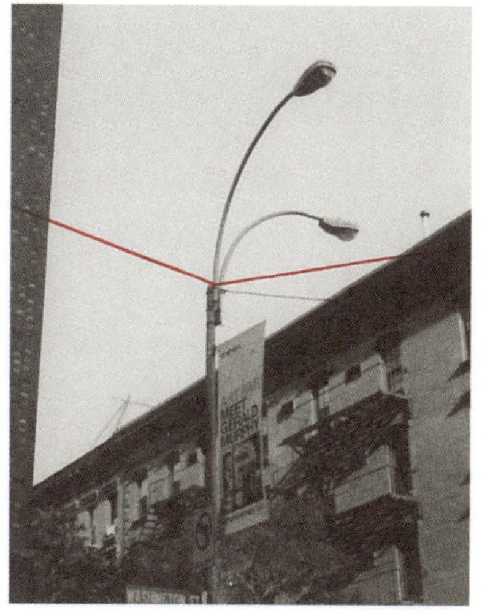

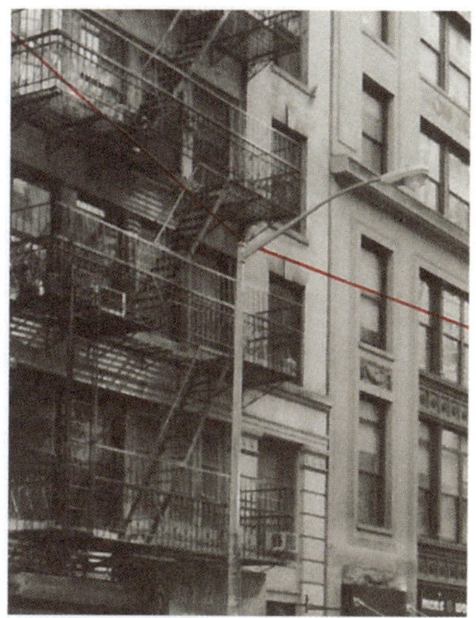

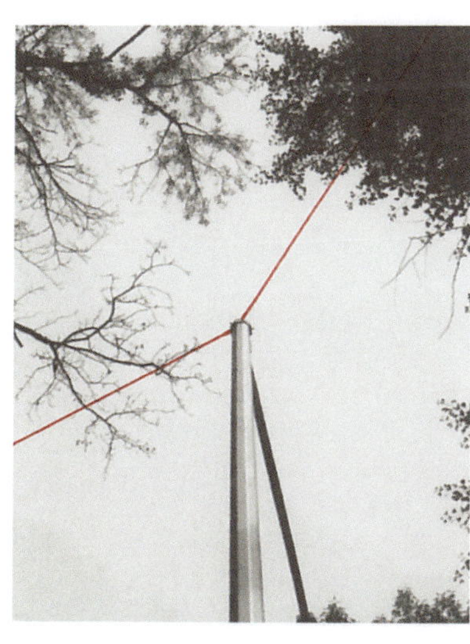

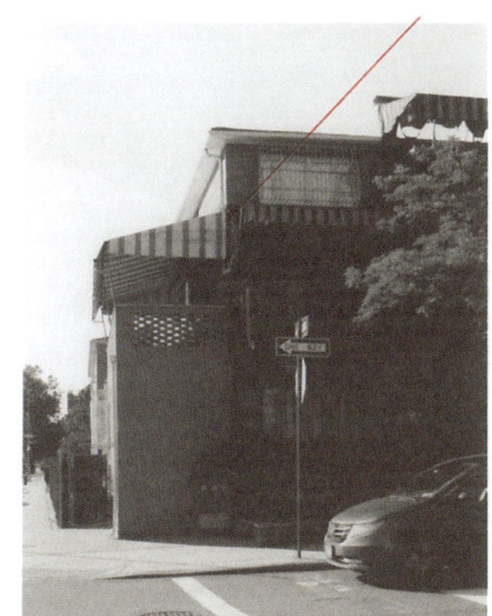

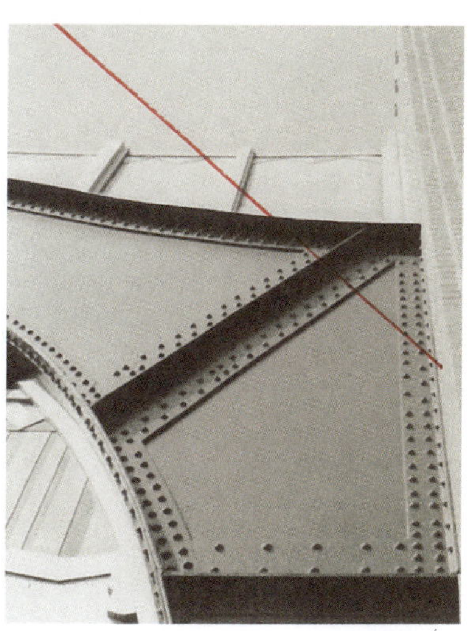

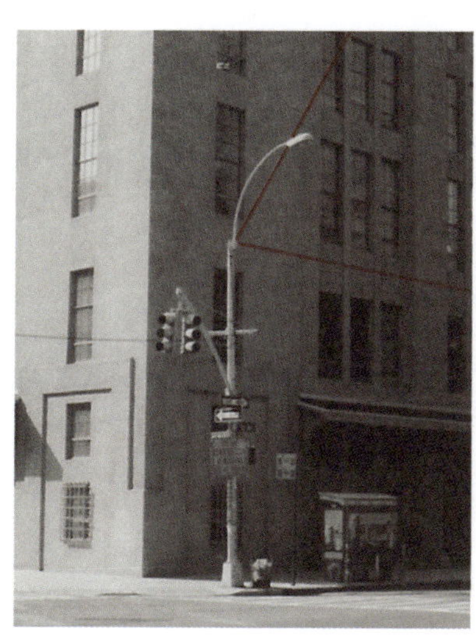

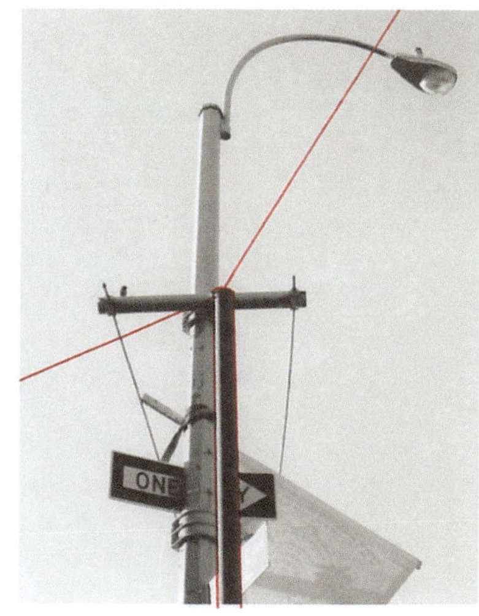
ONE

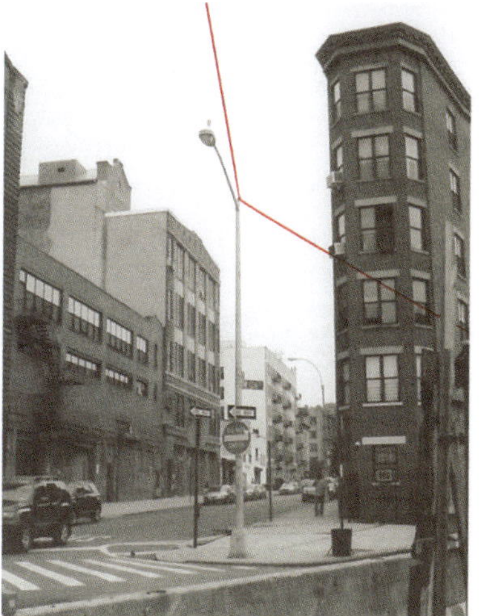

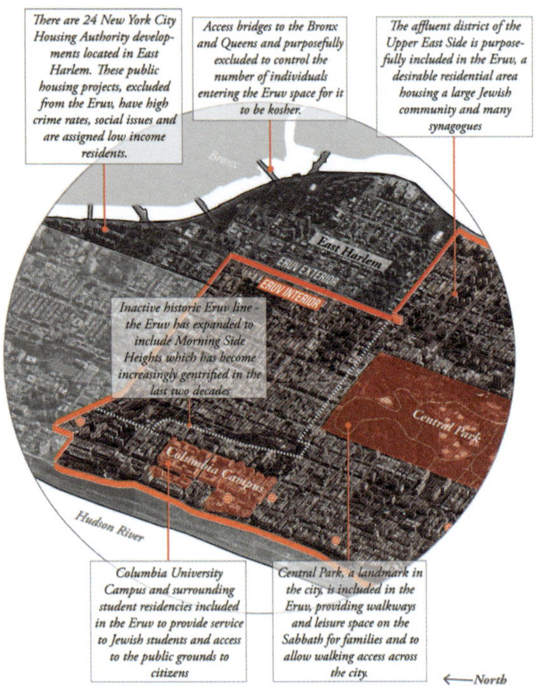

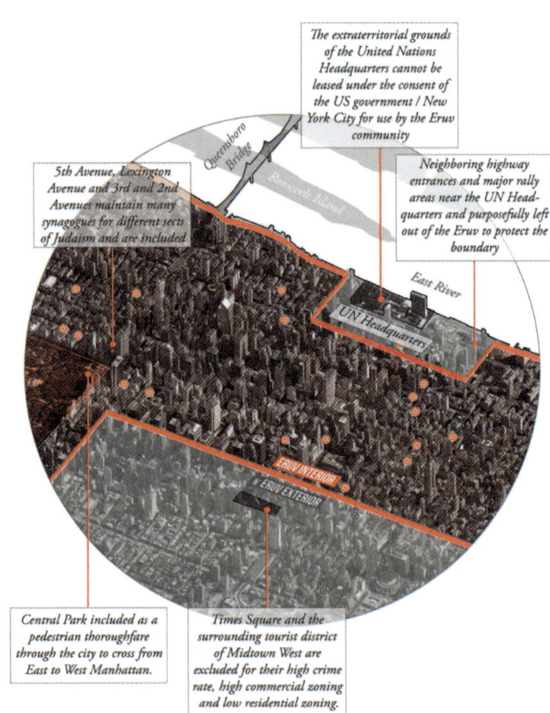

Similar to the decision to include Columbia University, the south edge of the eruv excludes certain territory. The eruv cuts across Houston Street and Noho, excluding the Southern tip of Manhattan Island. The answer for this is less ambiguous. The district excluded is the Financial District, including Wall Street, a substantial place of business and work. Although the eruv is an intricate form of urbanism, its mandate is tied to the Sabbath, the day of rest. The Financial District, including Wall Street, the New York Stock Exchange and more, is inherently associated with work. As the eruv is a space of dwellinge for Jewish community members on the day of rest, the Financial District is considered non-essential and therefore unnecessary to include within the boundary.

These included and excluded districts in Manhattan are rooted in some of the longstanding institutions and neighbourhoods in the city, but what about public spaces? Central Park, for a period of time, was excluded from the eruv. It was eventually integrated into the boundary as it eased movement for community members by foot. Additionally, it addressed a need for places of relaxation and leisure on the Sabbath. It allowed for families to enjoy the Sabbath, to play in the park and spend time outdoors. It is an amenity to the city, and also an amenity for the eruv. A similar shift in the Manhattan eruv boundary appeared in 2016 when the eruv boundary was modified to include a portion of the historic Meatpacking District on the Lower West Side of the island. The new boundary line traces a familiar edge in the city—the new Highline Park by James Corner Field Operations, Diller Scofidio + Renfro and Piet Oudolf. A revitalisation of an abandoned elevated rail line, the park has transformed the Meatpacking District into one of the most expensive neighbourhoods on the island. Such a place of leisure and luxury is a desirable place to have within the eruv. It too is a valuable public amenity similar to Central Park, and so the eruv changes its way as the city is transformed, including such valuable public domain. The development of the eruv is tied to the development of the city—the shift from using infrastructure as an exclusionary boundary (in 1905), to a space of inclusion with the Highline Park (in 2016) suggests that the eruv also responds to the larger trends of post-industrial reuse in New York's urban environments.

The eruv also respects existing rules of property, territory, and public domain. Although it is a new layer on top of the city, it takes an imprint of the streets. The last example of contextual politics that influence the eruv is the small notch of space excluded from the eruv on Manhattan's East Side near 42nd Street. Here, the eruv bends to exclude the United

Left: Eruv in Upper Manhattan, New York.

Right: Eruv near the United Nations, New York.

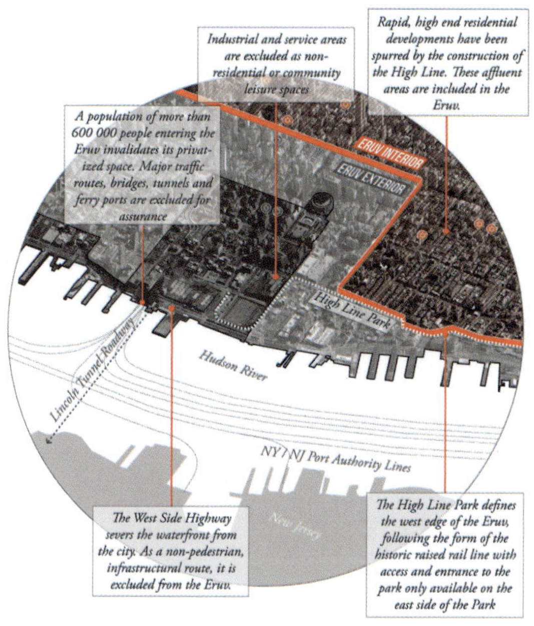

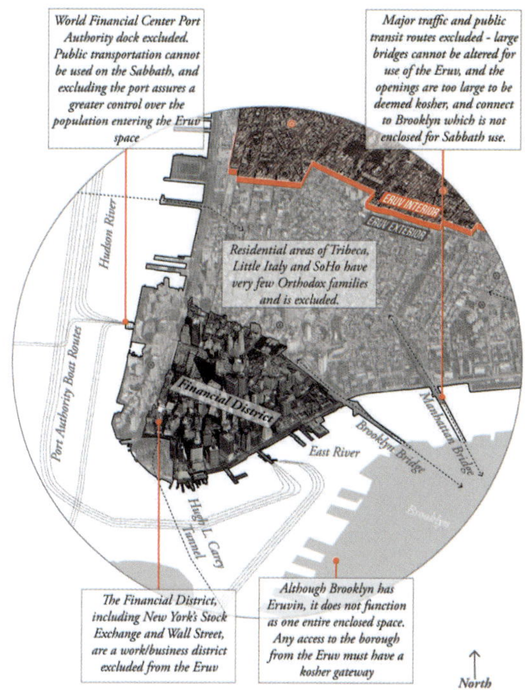

Nations Headquarters, and its surrounding blocks. The UN Headquarters, although situated in New York City, occupies land under sole administration by the United Nations, not the US government. The UN is technically extraterritorial through a treaty agreement, existing as international ground. Due to this, the city is unable to include this territory in the signed agreement with the Rabbinic authorities. The eruv respects these limits of space, and the limits of its own laws consequently diverge.

The eruv in Manhattan encourages further questions: How do we build strong communities that we desire? What space do we wish to provide for our citizens? And, in subtle ways, the eruv, with its power as a border, answers these; spatial belonging as a community is just as important. The eruv's power is found in the formalised bricolage of various communities that make up an entirely new community. The multiplicity of people, neighbourhoods and politics embraced within the eruv boundary create a unique type of border, uniquely established out of plurality.[21]

I found myself consistently humbled by the eruv—seamlessly, carefully and consciously—it remains and always will remain an open and permeable boundary. However, it is a remarkable tool; the eruv provides a sense of control, a threshold to space, and becomes the foundations of a new place, over existing places. As a layer to the city, those who build it have the ability to redefine their community edge, to build a neighbourhood, to govern what is inside and break the other existing spatial boundaries. There is an important condition of control with the eruv; it is a negotiation of city space, but in many ways, it is also a critique. The eruv excludes and includes purposefully and with care. By doing so, it creates a place of security and dependence. Although the eruv is by definition an allowance, it originates from a place of restriction. The Sabbath is a day of rest, and of limitation. Although the eruv is permeable and open to the diversity of society, it is not always represented in such a way to the members of the community who use it. To these communities, the eruv is a lenience, yet still an edge. It controls if one can leave the house, where one can go, and by consequence, with whom and with what one can interact. For one day a week, the community using the boundary will not leave its midst, they will abide by it, they will not wander beyond it. Like Herz and Weizman said, the wanderer does become the dweller.[22] Although only used one day a week, the eruv exists all the time, quietly forming new relationships within a city's neighbourhoods.

Left: Eruv in the Lower West Side, New York.

Right: Eruv in the Financial District, New York.

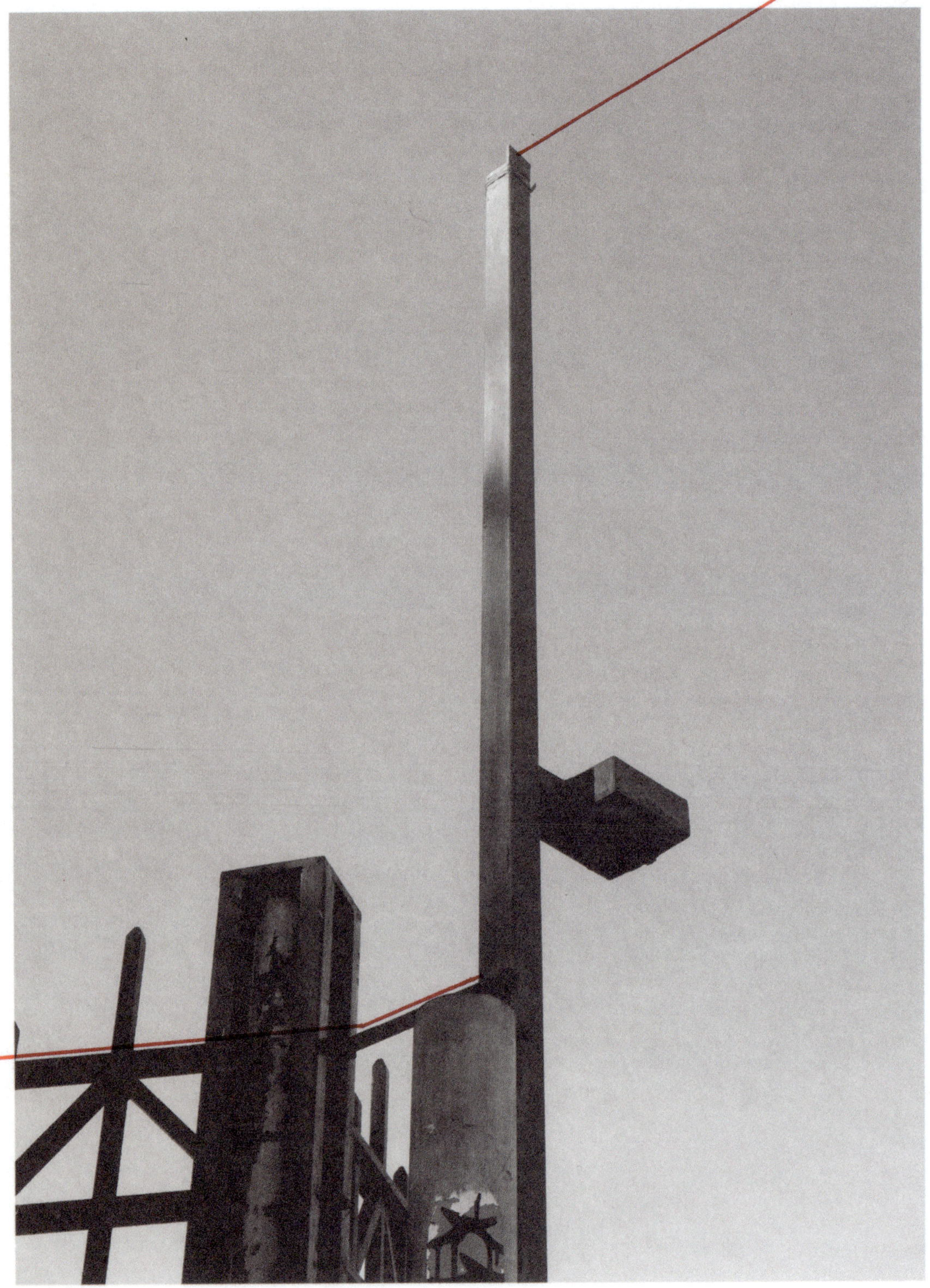

WILLIAMSBURG ERUV - BROOKLYN, NY JUNE/15

Herz and Weizman describe the eruv as a symbolic threshold that grounds the Jewish community in collective memory, in the act of wandering, in placelessness and in longing; building a symbolic connection to reach the Holy Land. Although the symbolic connotations of the eruv and its value as a transformative threshold is undeniable, its strength, survival and grounding is found in the contexts upon which it is embedded, rather than its allusions. From my time walking the line of the eruv, from city to city—specifically through North American Diaspora communities—it was the contextual support, exchange and embrace that grounded the eruv's existence. These spaces are granted through the already built communities, people, and cities—a line of reciprocity—only transformative through what has been negotiated, sacrificed and maintained by the community within its context. The eruv is not just a space made of symbolism, it is fabricated through humanism. Herz and Weizman state that the building of the eruv is a temporary resurrection of the temple in the modern city, which through this metaphoric existence "registers in the visible world the outcome of an encounter that would otherwise remain intangible."[24] The eruv builds relationships—symbolic, yes—but very real spatial relationships as spaces of action. The eruv now relies less on its symbolism, and more on its negotiation and its role as a mingling space. These eruvin require commitment to a pre-existing community, and the result is a spatial denotation of acceptance, significant meaning beyond a symbolic response to placelessness from memory. Plurality prevails here, where the eruv's existence and success comes from the community that builds it, the neighbours that allow it, and the city's identity embracing it. It is endlessly fascinating to read the edge of the eruv, to have walked in it, to speculate upon it as an active space, and to see a city through a new lens.

My work on the eruv is far from complete, building an atlas and continuing the fieldwork will likely be a lifelong obsession. There are years ahead of walking the edges of these sacred spaces. The eruv is another urban artefact in our world; a line that is meaningless to some, but sacred to others. There is great power in knowing such thresholds exist, and that in traversing seemingly banal urban contexts, we may momentarily be crossing into sacred symbolic space.

01 The Talmud, or *Mishnah*, is a code of laws perhaps best understood as a series of amendments and debates; a written re-evaluation of ancient rituals and practices inscribed in the Jewish faith through the Torah. Marcus Jastrow, *Sefer Ha-milim: Dictionary of the Targumim, Talmud Bavli, Talmud Yerushalmi, and Midrashic Literature* (New York: Judaica Treasury, 2004), 1075.

02 *Shabbat* (Hebrew), *Shabbos* (Yiddish), *Sabbath* (English) are interchangeable terms in the Jewish faith used to describe Judaism's day of rest on the seventh day of the week.

03 Manuel Herz and Eyal Weizman, "Between City and Desert," *AA Files* 34 (1997): 68-76.

04 Ibid., 76.

05 Piper Bernbaum, "Atlas of Legal-Fictions: Discovering the Implicit and Invisible Boundaries of the Jewish Eruv," (Master's Thesis, University of Waterloo, 2016), xxviii.

06 "The Kitchener Eruv," digital map, *Beth Jacob Congregation of Kitchener-Waterloo*, accessed 2020, https://www.bethjacobkw.ca/eruv-.html.

07 'Two-by-fours' is a dimensional standard timber section, measuring 38 x 89 mm.

08 Yosef Gavriel Bechhofer, *The Contemporary Eruv: Eruvin in Modern Metropolitan Areas* (Jerusalem: Feldheim, 1998), 67-73.

09 Sophie Calle, *Sophie Calle: Eruv* (Jerusalem: Jerusalem Center for the Visual Arts, 1996), 1.

10 Piper Bernbaum, "Atlas of Legal-Fictions: Discovering the Implicit and Invisible Boundaries of the Jewish Eruv," 41-54.

11 Rabbi Moshe Taub, in personal conversation in Buffalo, New York, February 2015.

12 Bechhofer, *The Contemporary Eruv*, 98.

13 Liza Stoltz Hanson, "The Theoretical Symbolism of Eruvin: A Model of Dual-Identity and Sacred Space," (Master's thesis, University of Denver, 2012), 14.

14 Piper Bernbaum, "Atlas of Legal-Fictions: Discovering the Implicit and Invisible Boundaries of the Jewish Eruv," 89.

15 Eyal Weizman, "The Subversion of Jerusalem's Sacred Vernaculars: Four New Planning Tools for a Holy Environment," in *The Next Jerusalem: Sharing the Divided City*, ed. by Michael Sorkin, (New York, NY: Monacelli Press, 2002), 122.

16 'Bricolage' is a construction achieved by using materials at hand.

17 Adam Mintz, "Halakhah in America: The History of City Eruvin, 1894-1962," (PhD diss., New York University, 2011), 229-282.

18 Ibid., 370-373.

19 "The Manhattan Eruv," *Fifth Avenue Synagogue*, accessed February 11, 2015, http://www.5as.org/index.php/manhattan-eruv-information.

20 This details the boundary of the Manhattan eruv of 2016, when fieldwork was completed, prior to the late 2019 expansion to the eruv boundaries.

21 In regard to plurality and the consideration of spaces of action, see Hannah Arendt, *The Human Condition* (Chicago: University of Chicago Press, 1958).

22 Herz and Weizman, "Between City and Desert," 70.

23 Ibid., 76.

Opposite: Williamsburg Eruv, New York.

LIQUID VIOLENCE

Lorenzo Pezzani

Since 2011, in a project called Forensic Oceanography, I have critically investigated the militarised border regime imposed by European states across the Mediterranean Sea, through the analysis of political, spatial and aesthetic conditions that have led to more than thirty thousand migrant deaths recorded over the last thirty years.[1] With my colleague Charles Heller and a wide network of NGOs, lawyers, scientists, journalists and activists, we have produced maps, videos, visualisations and human rights reports that attempt to document and challenge the transformation of the Mediterranean into the deadliest crossing in the world: the epicentre of those 'landscapes of deaths' represented by global borders.[2] In these works, we have argued that while the sea might already, in some way, constitute a 'natural boundary' due to its geophysical characteristics, it is through very specific practices, protocols and laws that these characteristics have been weaponised against specific categories of people and along with an environment rendered hostile to them.

Complex and overlapping jurisdictions at sea play a fundamental role in creating the conditions that structurally lead to the death of migrants. Sea-border crossing is a process that can last several days and extends across an uneven and heterogeneous territory that sits outside the exclusive reach of any single polity. As soon as a migrant boat sets off, it passes through the many jurisdictional regimes that crisscross the Mediterranean: from the various areas defined in the UN Convention on the Law of the Sea (UNCLOS) to Search and Rescue regions (SAR), from ecological and archaeological protection zones to areas of maritime surveillance. At the same time, these very same boats are caught between legal regimes that depend on: the juridical status applied to those onboard (refugees, economic migrants, illegals), the rationale of the operations that involve them (rescue or interception), and many other factors such as the flag and insurance agreements of the rescuing vessel.

These overlapping jurisdictions, conflicts of delimitation, and differing interpretations are structural characteristics of the maritime frontier that have allowed states to simultaneously extend their sovereign privileges through forms of mobile government and elude the responsibilities that come with it.[3] For instance, the strategic mobilisation of the notion of 'rescue' has allowed coastal states to justify police operations on the high seas, yet the overlapping and conflicting SAR regions have also led to recurrent cases of non-assistance to migrants in distress.[4] In contrast to the trope of the sea as a lawless zone, whose liquidity would make it impossible to draw stable boundaries, the proliferation and spatial entanglement of different legal regimes across the maritime border has created what Keller Easterling calls a 'disposition': a powerful form of obscure agency that possesses "unfolding potential," or an "inherent agency [that] makes certain things possible and other things impossible," ultimately producing large-scale violence.[5]

While these conditions have created the overall context in which migrant deaths occur on a structural basis, the sea has been made more or less deadly through specific operational shifts. In particular, operational areas of different maritime activities (border control operations such as those conducted by Frontex, the European Border and Coast Guard Agency, or the anti-smuggling operations of the European Union Naval Force Mediterranean) have been drawn and redrawn over the course of the last few years. For instance, in late 2014, Italy discontinued its military-humanitarian Mare Nostrum mission, which had rescued thousands of passengers over the previous 12 months. In response, EU agencies sought to use the shrinking of rescue capacities and the resulting increased risk for migrants as a means of deterrence—even though it was well aware that this would have led to an increased number of fatalities.[6] In addition, media and sensing technologies play an essential role in the transformation of the sea into a hostile terrain by creating selective conditions of (dis)appearance, (in)audibility, and (in)

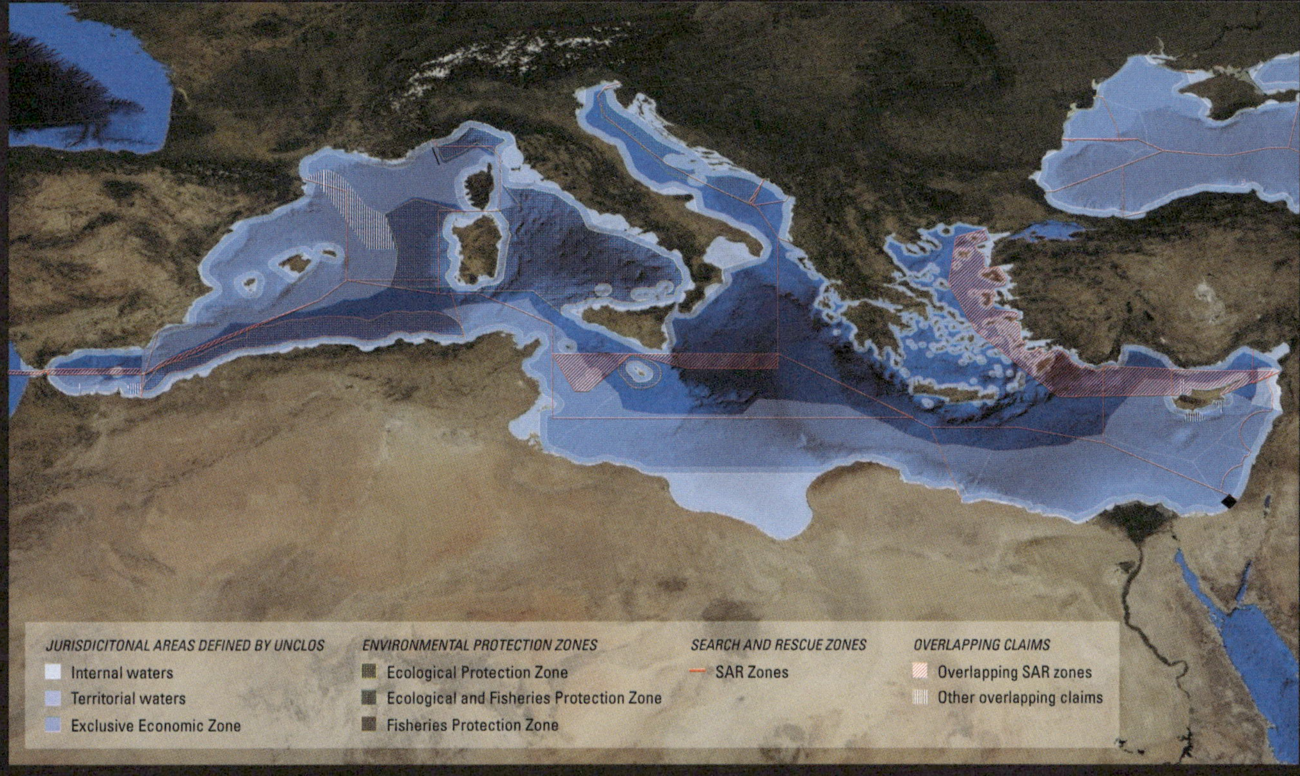

visibility. By focusing on what a security consultancy company called CIVIPOL has defined in a report to the European Commission as 'focal routes,' i.e. areas where the crossing is easier thanks to geographical proximity, the vast surveillance apparatus that polices cross-Mediterranean migration funnels migrants towards longer and more perilous areas.[7] These different practices disclose a specific form of *liquid violence* that operates at the European Union's maritime frontier—one that operates in an indirect way, not only *at* sea but *through* the sea, with the latter mediating between state policies and practices on the one hand and the bodies and lives of migrants on the other.[8]

The work of Forensic Oceanography has attempted to challenge this state of affairs. For instance, we have tried to reverse the process by which surveillance technologies are used to weaponise terrains—using them instead to challenge the deadly effects of border control. This is perhaps most clearly exemplified in the ways we used satellite imagery and drift modelling in the frame of our investigation of the 'left-to-die boat' case.[9] In this incident, 72 passengers were left to drift for 14 days despite repeated contacts with ships and helicopters in an area closely monitored by tens of military assets deployed in the context of the 2011 military intervention in Libya. This led to the slow death of 63 people.[10] By combining a satellite image taken at the time of the event with a spatial model that mapped the trajectory of the drifting on the basis of wind and current data recorded by various meteorological and oceanographic sensors, we were able to establish that the bright pixels in the image were large ships located in the vicinity of the migrants' boat just as it had run out of fuel. We also established that the migrants' boat had always remained within the boundaries of NATO-established maritime surveillance areas. All military and non-military vessels in the area had been informed of the distress of the migrants as well as the boat's position and could have easily rescued them—yet all chose not to intervene. Instead, they abandoned them to the wind and currents. While their act of non-intervention transformed the sea into an unwilling killer, our project sought to turn it into a witness of sorts.

Map of maritime jurisdictions in the Mediterranean, based on data compiled by Marineplan (www.marineplan.es) and the International Maritime Organization.

Courtesy of Forensic Oceanography.

The Design of Hostility

The relation between practices of border control and environments has been perhaps most explicitly theorised in relation to the US-Mexico border, where the notion of 'prevention through deterrence' was adopted by US border guards as early as 1994.[11] Similar to the already described bordering practices in the Mediterranean, this enforcement strategy calls for the deployment of massive numbers of agents as well as so-called 'tactical infrastructure' (e.g. surveillance technologies, sections of walls or fences) along the sections of the border that are easiest to cross, usually around urban areas. These concentrations, in turn, lead migrants to attempt to cross in areas such as the Sonoran Desert that are much more inhospitable and, therefore, more difficult to traverse, often leading to cases of death. The declared aim of this tactic is to facilitate border enforcement by deterring potential migrants from attempting the perilous crossing and by pushing others into places where they are slower; thereby dramatically lowering their chance of survival.

'Prevention through deterrence' demonstrates the ways nonhuman actors—plants, animals, and biophysical processes—constitute boundary making, in the same ways as border guards, national and international institutions, legal frameworks and surveillance systems.[12] The term 'geopower,' coined by Elisabeth Grosz, underlines how geographic environments are endowed with "forces contained in matter that precede, enable, facilitate, provoke and restrict 'life.'"[13] While many other examples could be mentioned of enlisting geopower as a crucial mechanism of border control, what emerges in all of them is the process of design at work in the becoming hostile of deserts, oceans, and mountain ranges as borderlands.

Emphasising the way in which legal geographies, surveillance technologies, and bureaucratic protocols have turned certain environments into rugged borders, is also a critical antidote to (neo-)colonial narratives that continue to imagine them as always *already* empty, remote, and unlivable. This vision willfully—and culpably—erases not only centuries of indigenous inhabitation and trans-regional exchange, but also the extractive and developmental processes that in many cases have indeed turned those areas into toxic sacrifice zones.[14] Paying attention to these processes allows simplistic accounts of the nexus between environment and migration to be complicated beyond some of the narratives which have crystallized around the iconic, and by-now ubiquitous figure of the 'environmental refugee.' The introduction of this notion has raised public awareness on the harmful impacts of the environmental crisis and opened up an important space to imagine new (para-)legal instruments for defending vulnerable populations. Yet, it has also become part and parcel of a technocratic discourse that, by instituting a mechanical relationship between environmental degradation and migration, paints apocalyptic scenarios of mass displacement. It should not come as a surprise, then, that the very expression 'environmental refugee' was initially formulated in the context of neo-Malthusian debates on population growth and resource scarcity in the wake of the 1973 oil crisis.[15] Since then, the alarmist tones of many mainstream discussions about environmental refugees have fueled an approach that sees migration as a key threat to global stability, and one to be tackled from a security perspective.

A form of 'accumulation by displacement' is visible in many contemporary border zones whose contested political ecologies are deeply intertwined with histories of dispossession and migration.[16] Take, for instance, the fragile ecologies of the Rio Grande Valley, which marks the easternmost section of the US-Mexico land border. As Avi Varma writes:

> From the dispossession of Native and Hispanic inhabitants to the establishment of water-intensive agricultural settlements, conflicts around water have fundamentally shaped this landscape and the regimes of mobility that traverse it. As an agent of bordering, the hydrological body of the Rio Grande river has always proved an unstable and highly ungovernable ally, which continues to shift and change course at both geological and seasonal timescales. Moreover, in the transition from indigenous land use to ranching and finally intensive farming, water has been forcibly redirected from zones deemed non-productive towards those deemed profitable, partitioning the South of Texas into a chequerboard of water-rich regions and sacrifice zones on which migrant detention centers, like the infamous Tornillo tent city, have been built. In the words of feminist and Chicana author Gloria Anzaldúa, the the 'tragic valley' of the Rio Grande river is a 'serpent nailed to the fence' of the border, its waters serving less as a source of life and connection than as a marker of their absence.[17]

Against this 'naturalisation of causes,' it is imperative to foreground the complex structures of causality that connect, in non-linear ways, individual desires with complex social, cultural, and economic conditions, and ultimately lead to decisions about whether or not stay or move.[18] Here, climate itself is "difficult to tease apart from other variables (cultural, political, economic) . . . not simply because these factors are

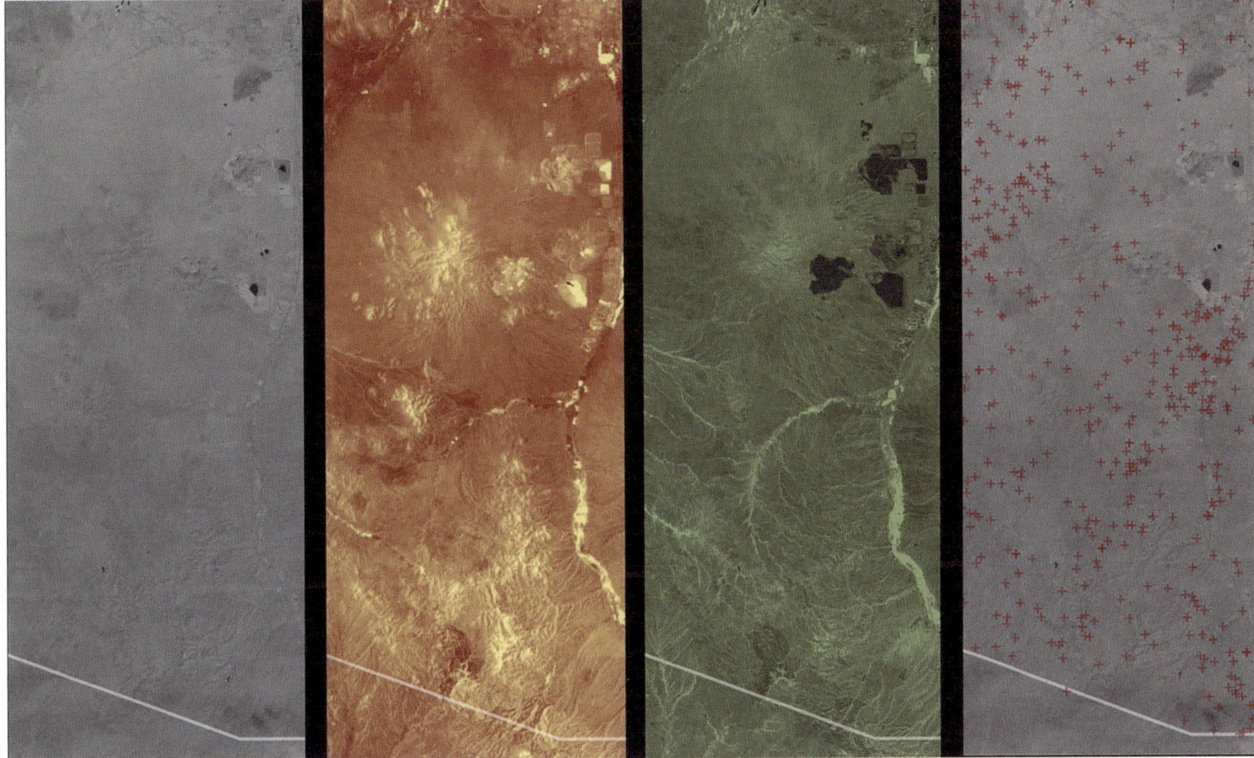

entangled, but because all these aspects of collective life always already bear the trace of climatic and environmental change," and are thus "even more deeply implicated with politics, ethics and culture than we usually imagine."[19] At the same time, it is also paramount to foreground the very geo-historical conditions that have made the global environmental crisis not only possible but inevitable. This means going deeper into the roots that connect neocolonial extractive practices and migration as part of the same historical continuum.[20] It means thinking about displacement, as Rob Nixon has suggested, not simply as "the movement of people from their places of belonging," but also as "the loss of the land and resources beneath them, a loss that leaves communities stranded in a place stripped of the very characteristics that made it inhabitable."

Environmental Governmentality

On the 14th of June, 2018, Lord Bassam of Brighton stated that he had never associated the term 'hostile environment' with his own country because it "conjures up notions of a war zone, of environmental degradation or an inhospitable climatic event, perhaps an earthquake—something stark and unpleasant, like a scene from a World War I killing field."[22] Beyond their obvious differences, the bordering practices at work across the Mediterranean, the arid regions on the US-Mexico border, and urban life in the United Kingdom all appear to be the expression of a similar form of power, one that does not operate by disciplining specific subjects but rather by intervening in the environment they inhabit or traverse.[23] This resonates with the kind of governance that Michel Foucault had started to write about in some of his later work on biopolitics: what he called, echoing his notion of governmentality, 'environmentality.' In a few scattered notes, the French philosopher described the then-budding forms of neoliberalism as 'an environmental type of intervention,' rather than a subject-based or population-based distribution of governance.[24] While the notion of environmentality has been taken up predominantly in the context of environmental studies, Jennifer Gabrys usefully reconceptualises it as "a spatial-material distribution and

The Altar Valley desert corridor in Arizona, north of the US-Mexico border, where No More Deaths/*No Más Muertes* strategically stations caches of water jugs along known migrant paths. Screenshots from an animation, from left to right: satellite image; ground temperature; vegetation density; and the location of recovered human remains, 2001-2019. Realised by the author as part of the exhibition 'Hostile Environment(s)' at ar/ge kunst, Bozen/Bolzano. Based on GIS analysis produced by Geoffrey Alan Boyce, Samuel N. Chambers, and Sarah Launius. Projection development and 3D model by Tom James. Physical model by Kamil Dalkir.

relationality of power through environments, technologies, and ways of life," expanding the concept to include "those distributions of power that influence not just life, but also how to live."[25]

In this sense, a hostile environment could be understood as a space in which certain ways of life have been made unviable. In May 2012, the United Kingdom's Home Secretary, Theresa May, announced in an interview the introduction of new, groundbreaking legislation in the field of immigration control. The aim of these new measures, she declared in language that was described as "uncharacteristically vivid," was "to create here in Britain a really hostile environment for illegal migration."[26] "Work is underway," she further explained, "to deny illegal immigrants access to work, housing, and services, even bank accounts."[27]

Albeit not always easy to document, the consequences of these measures as well as the subsequent immigration acts, passed in 2014 and 2016, have been disastrous, and have culminated in the 2018 so-called Windrush scandal. Thousands of people who had come to the UK from former colonies in the aftermath of World War II were asked to prove their right to stay, despite having entered the country legally and having lived there for decades. At least 83 of them were wrongly deported, and many more lost their homes, livelihoods, and basic rights in ways that even the UK High Court has ruled to be racially discriminatory.[28] The NGO Corporate Watch effectively captured this aspect in regards to the situation in the UK, when it argued that the rationale of May's policies could be summarised as follows: "if the government can't actually seal tight the external borders, it can push unwanted 'illegals' to leave, or deter others from coming in the first place, by making it near impossible to live a normal life."[29] May's hostile environment policies have conjured up a diffused 'atmosphere of surveillance' that has infiltrated the most elementary infrastructures of living, a form of racialised violence that has become, in terms proposed by Christina Sharpe, as pervasive as the weather.[30]

Corporate Watch also foregrounds another important aspect on this form of bordering, which has acknowledged what many critical scholars have said for years: that, despite continuous claims of the contrary, borders do not simply *keep* people *out* (and often fail to do so), but rather *manage* them *inside* and *across* territories. Paraphrasing anthropologist Ghassan Hage, we might say that hostile environments exist at the intersection of two sets of laws: one aiming to contain and restrict people's movement to their respective nation-states, and the other seeking to govern their social disintegration.[31] The Windrush scandal is quite revealing in this sense, as it shows that those racialised as outsiders can never quite exist entirely inside, even when residing legally. Contrary to how this event has been discussed in the press, the tragedy it revealed was not how deserving citizens were treated like undeserving aliens, but that certain categories of people can never become fully part of the national community, regardless of their juridical status.
By exposing the racial nature of borders, the Windrush scandal thus threw into sharp relief the mechanics of a regime of global apartheid, one that is better understood, as suggested again by Hage, as:

> [T]wo separate realities that coexist within the same global space: on the one hand, . . . a world where a 'third-world looking' transnational working class and underclass citizens . . . are made to feel that national borders are exceptionally important and difficult to cross; . . . and another experienced as open . . . by the largely White upper classes.[32]

This spatial arrangement is less reminiscent of the image of the fortress or that of the wall, which have often been mobilised to emphasise the exclusionary nature of borders, rather, it is the eloquent representation described in China Miéville's dystopian novel *The City and the City*, where two distinct yet overlapping cities are kept apart by their citizens' ability to 'unsee' those from the other city.

Building Spaces of Sanctuary

It is urgent to imagine what shape practices of solidarity could take in this age of intensified hostility. If the creation of hostile environments involves the denial of basic services and provisions, then a crucial task becomes building life-sustaining infrastructures of support. The notion of sanctuary, whose genealogy extends back to the use of religious buildings as spaces of refuge, might provide a useful lens to think about this task. In the last few years, the term, which first emerged in the US, has been used to define a diffused and multifarious movement of municipalities, religious congregations, and many other initiatives all around the world that support migrants regardless of their status. The aim of this loose network is to "stabilise access to substantive rights and provisions" that federal and national legislation would want to curtail. As Ana Naomi Paik writes about the US, "the fact that practices [of criminalising immigrants and other marginalised communities] are so pervasive means that the connections for building . . . a radical movement that challenges different forms of domination already exist."[33]
In this sense, "sanctuary provides an expansive archive of social movements that we might not otherwise see as being connected."[34]

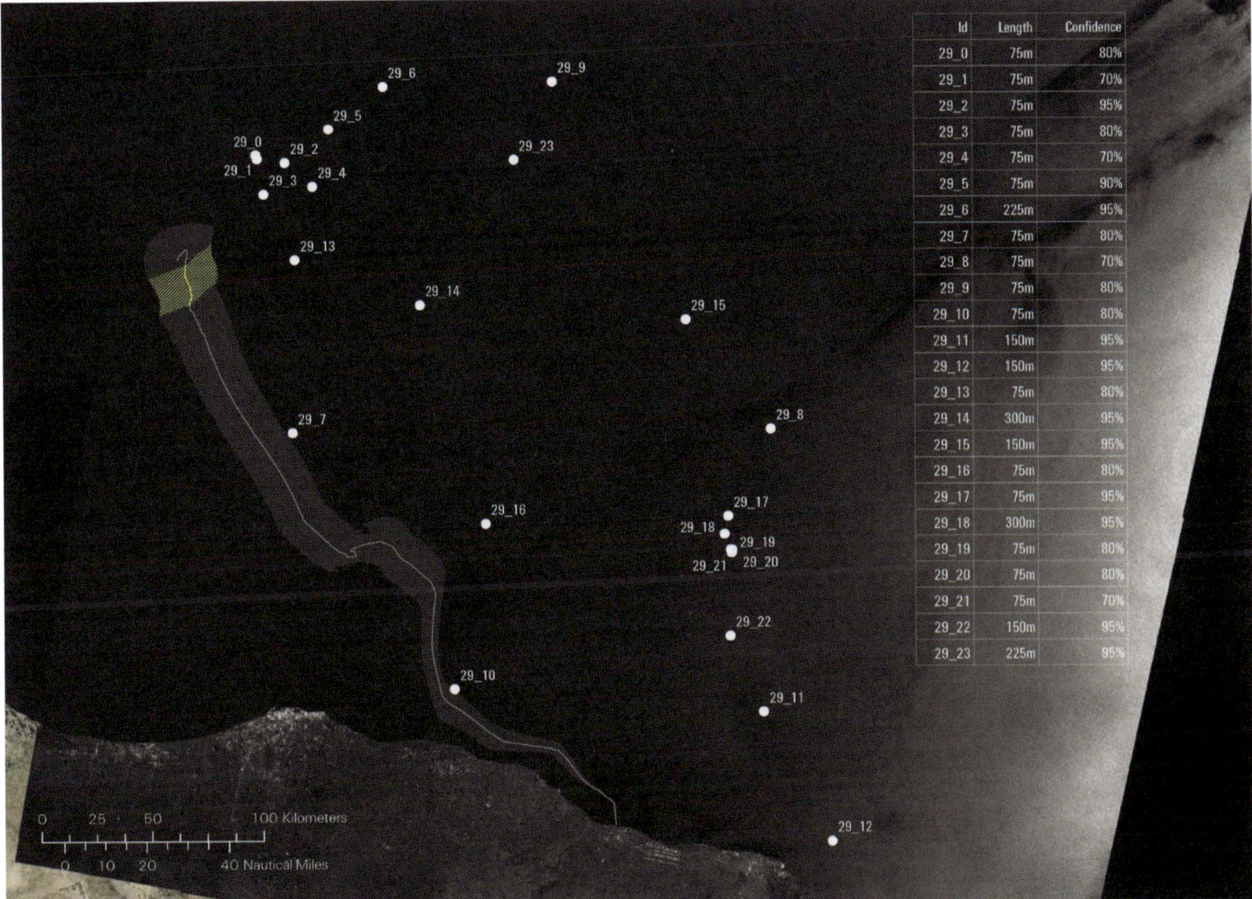

Id	Length	Confidence
29_0	75m	80%
29_1	75m	70%
29_2	75m	95%
29_3	75m	80%
29_4	75m	70%
29_5	75m	90%
29_6	225m	95%
29_7	75m	80%
29_8	75m	70%
29_9	75m	80%
29_10	75m	80%
29_11	150m	95%
29_12	150m	95%
29_13	75m	80%
29_14	300m	95%
29_15	150m	95%
29_16	75m	80%
29_17	75m	95%
29_18	300m	95%
29_19	75m	80%
29_20	75m	80%
29_21	75m	70%
29_22	150m	95%
29_23	225m	95%

In the UK, this multitudinous front of struggle includes groups like Uni Resists Border Controls, Docs Not Cops, Against Borders for Children, and Homes Not Borders: alliances of academics, healthcare workers, parents, landlords, and renters who directly resist their own enlistment as border controllers, all the while supporting those targeted by hostile environment policies. Examples also abound across those harsh terrains traversed by migrants, where spaces of sanctuary take the form of networks supporting unauthorised movement in ways that more or less explicitly recall the experience of the American Civil War-era underground railroad. These includes initiatives like the Alarm Phone, an activist-run emergency hotline for migrants in distress at sea; the 'civil fleet' of rescue vessels in the Mediterranean, which has taken to the sea in response to state authorities' curtailing of search and rescue missions; solidarity groups that provide food, shelter, basic information, and legal support to migrants from Palermo to Calais, from the Alps to the Balkans; or groups like No More Deaths/*No Más Muertes,* which has been providing water and first aid across the treacherous deserts into which migrants have been funneled at the US-Mexico border. These forms of 'pirate care' open up spaces of resistant sociality often by intervening in the grey areas at the margins of various bureaucratic practices, laws, and technologies.[35] They rub scales of intervention against each other, fighting global borders through municipal jurisdictions and affirming a planetary 'right to the world' through local networks of mutual support.[36]

Faced with expulsions and ecological crisis, the right to mobility and the possibility of escaping toxic milieus must be reaffirmed. At the same time, resistance to hostile environments must involve the rethinking care as the practice of "maintain[ing] and repair[ing] a world so that

Analysis of March 29, 2011, Envisat satellite image showing the modeled position of the "left-to-die boat" (yellow diagonal hatch) and the nearby presence of several military vessels that did not intervene to rescue the migrants. Courtesy of Forensic Oceanography and SITU Research, report on the "left-to-die boat" case.

humans and non-humans can live in it as well as possible in a complex life-sustaining web."[37] As marginalised communities have known all too well and for far too long, hostile environments do not only differentially infiltrate our social lives. They also penetrate our bodies, blurring the very distinction between an inside and an outside that our skin gives us the illusion to uphold. They are the food we eat, the water we drink, the air we breathe. Thus, fighting them implies struggling against what Malini Ranganathan calls 'environmental unfreedoms': all those "threats to our water, air, food, land, schools, and homes [that] mark contemporary racialised environments [and] constrain our individual and collective potential."[38]

The current pandemic has possibly made our entanglement with the environments we inhabit even more acutely clear. While the response to this public health crisis has been overwhelmingly framed in nationalist tones (with each state taking care of its own national citizens), the spreading of the virus, its obliviousness to the widespread closing of borders, has revealed our interconnectedness in an even stronger way. As Heather Davis put it in text that, while written before the pandemic, could not read more topical:

> [W]e are radically open, inherently constituted by the molecular outside. We breathe in each other's air, and despite air conditioning and all the attenuating accoutrements of the wealthy, there is no way to shield against our collective molecular becoming. This radical openness to the outside is both what links us to the world and what threatens us.[39]

This condition of radical openness demands, as Miriam Ticktin has powerfully suggested, "a commitment to—rather than freedom from—others."[40] In the current conjuncture, this involves, amongst many other things, also a radical redistribution of the ability and the privilege to move and stay put, especially in a context in which marginalised groups are disproportionately hit by the pandemic, as noted by the activists participating in the current global uprisings against anti-Black racism. In the face of negationist governments putting the lives of nurses, cleaners, teachers, logistics, call centres and factory workers at risk by imposing the continuation of business as usual, subtracting one's mobility and demanding the possibility to safely self-isolate for everyone has become, in certain situations, also a form of care. This, too, has now become yet another fundamental facet of the wider struggle to affirm a "universal right to breathe" in the toxic atmospheres of hostile environments.[41]

01 See the list of migrant deaths at the European borders established by UNITED for Intercultural Action: http://unitedagainstrefugeedeaths.eu/about-the-campaign/about-the-united-list-of-deaths.

02 Joseph Nevins, *Operation Gatekeeper: The Rise of the "Illegal Alien" and the Making of the US-Mexico Boundary* (New York: Routledge, 2002), 144. Forensic Oceanography's work can be accessed here: https://forensic-architecture.org/category/forensic-oceanography.

03 Philip E. Steinberg, *The Social Construction of the Ocean* (Cambridge, UK: Cambridge University Press, 2001); Thomas Gammeltoft-Hansen and Tanja E. Alberts, "Sovereignty at Sea: The Law and Politics of Saving Lives in the Mare Liberum," DIIS Working Paper (2010): 1-31.

04 Ruben Andersson, "A Game of Risk: Boat Migration and the Business of Bordering Europe," *Anthropology Today* 28, no. 6 (December 2012): 7-11.

05 Keller Easterling, *Extrastatecraft: The Power of Infrastructure Space* (New York: Verso Books, 2014), 14.

06 As explicitly stated in a document produced by Frontex, the European Border and Coast Guard Agency, cutting back rescue operations "could become a deterrence for facilitation networks and migrants . . . taking into account that the boat must now navigate for several days before being rescued or intercepted." See our 2016 report "Death by Rescue": https://www.forensic-architecture.org/case/death-by-rescue.

07 CIVIPOL, "Feasibility Study on the Control of the European Union's Maritime Borders," European Commission, April 7, 2003, http://www.ifmer.org/assets /documents/files/documents_ifm/st11490-re01en03.pdf.

08 Charles Heller and Lorenzo Pezzani, "Liquid Violence: Migrant Deaths at Sea and the Responsibility of European States," *Transit: Art, Mobility and Migration in the Age of Globalisation,* ed. Sabine Dahl Nielsen (Aalborg: Aalborg University Press, 2019).

09 See: https://forensic-architecture.org/investigation/the-left-to-die-boat

10 Charles Heller and Lorenzo Pezzani, "Liquid Traces: Investigating the Deaths of Migrants at the EU's Maritime Frontier," in *Forensis: The Architecture of Public Truth,* ed. Anselm Franke and Eyal Weizman (Berlin: Sternberg Press, 2014), 656-684.

11 Geoffrey Alan Boyce, Samuel N. Chambers, and Sarah Launius, "Bodily Inertia and the Weaponization of the Sonoran Desert in US Boundary Enforcement: A GIS Modeling of Migration Routes through Arizona's Altar Valley," *Journal on Migration and Human Security* 7, no. 1 (March 2019): 23-35; Tara Plath, "An Elusive Viewshed: An Investigation of United States' Border Patrol Rescue Beacons in Arizona's Western Desert," forthcoming in *PLOT(S)*, Vol. 07.

12 Juanita Sundberg, "Diabolic Caminos in the Desert and Cat Fights on the Río: A Posthumanist Political Ecology of Boundary Enforcement in the

United States-Mexico Borderlands," *Annals of the Association of American Geographers* 101, no. 2 (March 16, 2011): 318-36.

13 Duncan Depledge, "Geopolitical Material: Assemblages of Geopower and the Constitution 45, no. 2 (2015): 91-92.

14 Steve Lerner, *Sacrifice Zones: The Front Lines of Toxic Chemical Exposure in the United States* (Cambridge: MIT Press, 2010).

15 James Morrissey, "Environmental Change and Forced Migration: A State of the Art Review" (Refugee Studies Centre, University of Oxford, January 2009).

16 Farshad Araghi, "Accumulation by Displacement: Global Enclosures, Food Crisis, and the Ecological Contradictions of Capitalism," *Review (Fernand Braudel Center)* 32, no. 1 (2009): 113-46.

17 A slightly edited version of this text appears in the "Atlas of Critical Habitats" guide that I have edited with Tara Plath and that was designed by Tom Joyes and Hanna Rullman in the context of the exhibition 'Hostile Environment(s),' commissioned by ar/ge kunst, Bozen/Bolzano and co-produced with Z33 House for Contemporary Art, Hasselt.

18 Marco Armiero and Richard Tucker, eds., *Environmental History of Modern Migrations,* 1st edition (London; New York, NY: Routledge, 2017). See also: Giovanni Bettini, "Climate Barbarians at the Gate? A Critique of Apocalyptic Narratives on 'Climate Refugees,'" *Geoforum* 45 (March 2013): 63-72.

19 Nigel Clark, "Strangers on a Strange Planet: On Hospitality and Holocene Climate Change," in *Life Adrift: Climate Change, Migration, Critique,* ed. Andrew Baldwin and Giovanni Bettini (London; New York: Rowman & Littlefield International, 2017), 131-50.

20 Nadine El-Enany, *(B)Ordering Britain: Law, Race and Empire* (Manchester: Manchester University Press, 2020).

21 Rob Nixon, *Slow Violence and the Environmentalism of the Poor* (Cambridge, MA: Harvard University Press, 2011), 19.

22 Dan Hicks and Sarah Mallet, *Lande: The Calais "Jungle" and Beyond* (Bristol: Bristol University Press, 2019).

23 Michel Foucault, *Security, Territory, Population: Lectures at the Collège de France,* 1977-78 (New York: Palgrave Macmillan, 2007), 20-23.

24 Ibid., 22-23.

25 Jennifer Gabrys, *Program Earth: Environmental Sensing Technology and the Making of a Computational Planet* (Minneapolis: University of Minnesota Press, 2016), 191.

26 An earlier version of this article was published on e-flux in a series edited by Nick Axel, Jan Boelen, Charlotte Dumoncel d'Argence, Nikolaus Hirsch: https://www.e-flux.com/architecture/at-the-border/325761/hostile-environments/. Parts of this article have also previously appeared in an essay co-authored with Charles Heller and published in: Laura Kurgan and Dare Brawley, eds., *Ways of Knowing Cities* (New York: Columbia Books on Architecture and the City, 2019).

27 James Kirkup and Robert Winnett, "Theresa May Interview: 'We're Going to Give Illegal Migrants a Really Hostile Reception,'" Telegraph, May 25, 2012, https://www.telegraph.co.uk/news/uknews/immigration/9291483/Theresa-May-interview-Were-going-to-give-illegal-migrants-a-really-hostile-reception.html.

28 The specific rule that was brought to court is the so-called 'right to rent' scheme, which forces landlords to carry out immigration checks on potential tenants. Despite this ruling, the UK Home Office has recently won an appeal for upholding the rule. See https://www.theguardian.com/politics/2020/apr/21/right-to-rent-rule-justified-finds-uk-appeal-court.

29 See "The Hostile Environment: Turning the UK into a Nation of Border Cops," April 8, 2017, https://corporatewatch.org/the-hostile-environment-turning-the-uk-into-a-nation-of-border-cops-2.

30 Darren Ellis, Ian Tucker and David Harper, "The Affective Atmospheres of Surveillance," *Theory and Psychology* 23, no. 6 (December 2013): 716-731; Christina Elizabeth Sharpe, *In the Wake: On Blackness and Being* (Durham, NC: Duke University Press, 2016).

31 Ghassan Hage, *Is Racism an Environmental Threat?* (Malden, MA: Polity Press, 2017), 36-37.

32 Ibid., 38.

33 A. Naomi Paik, "Abolitionist Futures and the US Sanctuary Movement," *Race & Class 59,* no. 2 (October 2017): 3-25, 17.

34 A. Naomi Paik, Jason Ruiz, and Rebecca M. Schreiber, "Sanctuary's Radical Networks," *Radical History Review 2019,* no. 135 (October 1, 2019): 1-13, 3.

35 "Introduction," *Pirate Care Syllabus,* https://syllabus.pirate.care/topic/piratecareintroduction/#on-the-concept-of-pirate-care

36 Joseph Nevins, "The Right to the World," *Antipode* 49, no. 5 (November 2017): 1349-67.

37 María Puig de la Bellacasa, *Matters of Care: Speculative Ethics in More than Human Worlds* (Minneapolis; London: University of Minnesota Press, 2017), p. 62.

38 Malini Ranganathan, "The Environment as Freedom: A Decolonial Reimagining," *Items: Insights from the Social Sciences,* June 13, 2017, https://items.ssrc.org/the-environment-as-freedom-a-decolonial-reimagining.

39 Heather Davis, "Molecular Intimacy," in *Climates: Architecture and the Planetary Imaginary,* ed. James Graham (New York: Columbia Books on Architecture and the City, 2016), 205-11.

40 Miriam Ticktin, "No Borders in the Time of COVID-19," *American Anthropologist Blog* (blog), July 2, 2020, http://www.americananthropologist.org/2020/07/02/no-borders-in-the-time-of-covid-19/.

41 Achille Mbembe, "The Universal Right to Breathe," *In the Moment* (blog), April 13 2020, https://critinq.wordpress.com/2020/04/13/the-universal-right-to-breathe/. Léopold Lambert, "Introduction," *The Funambulist,* No. 14 Toxic Atmospheres (November-December 2017).

TOMORROW, POETRY WILL (NOT) BE THE HOUSE OF LIFE

Saba Innab

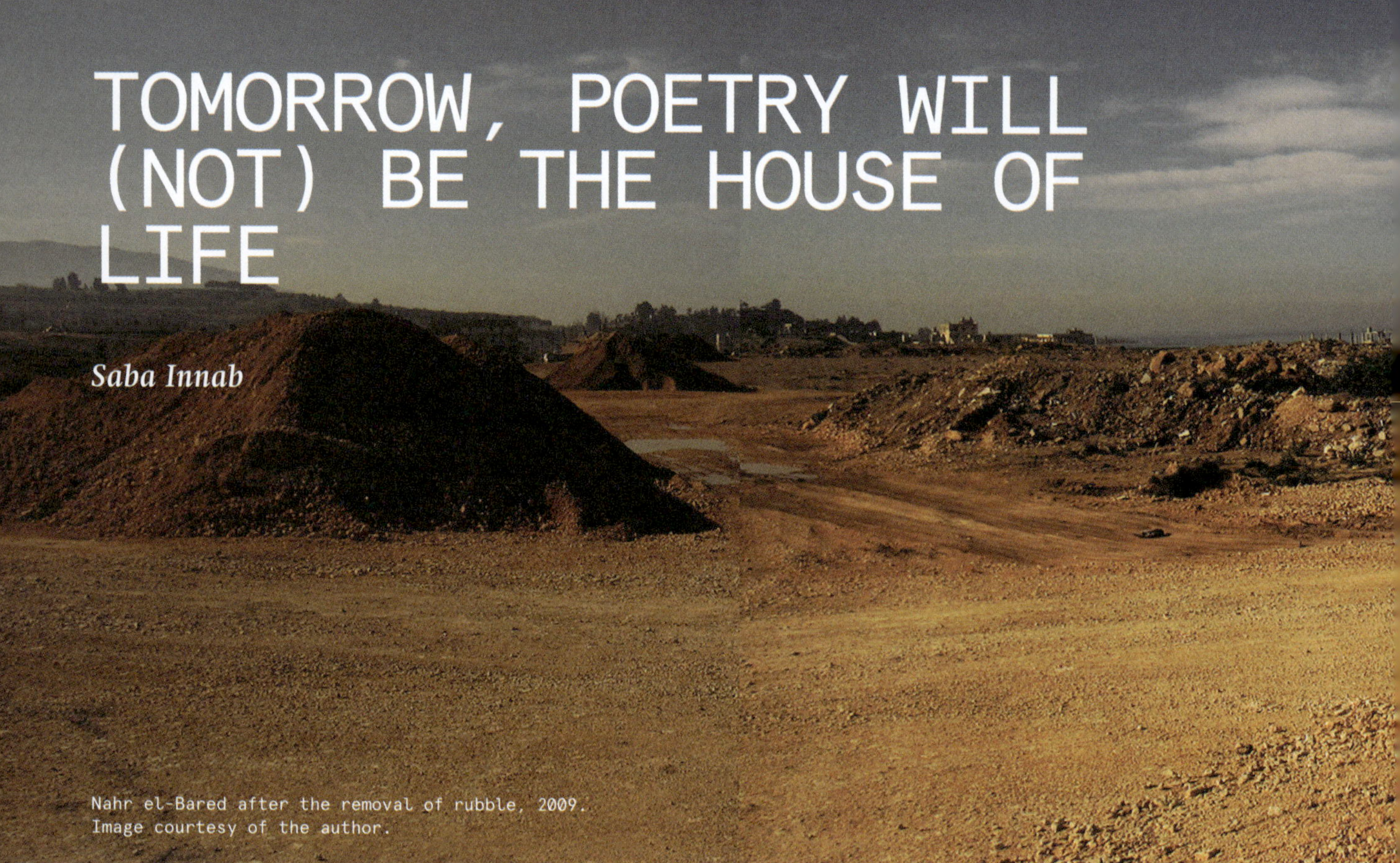

Nahr el-Bared after the removal of rubble, 2009. Image courtesy of the author.

'Walking Through Someone Else's Dream' was the curatorial framework for the first edition of the Biennale d'Architecture d'Orléans, a Biennale organised by the Frac Centre-Val de Loire in 2017. The title invited propositions that sought to contextualise contemporary practices in other contexts, especially historical moments derived from the Centre's archive. In my proposition for this Biennale, a new reading was suggested for Constant Nieuwenhuys' 'New Babylon.' This was situated within my ongoing research into the meaning of dwelling and building in the perpetual state of impermanence, in reference to the Palestinian context.

At a meeting of avant-garde artists in 1956 in Alba, Italy, Constant delivered a lecture entitled '*Demain la poésie logera le vie*' (Tomorrow Poetry Will Be the House of Life), which marked the beginning of his seminal project 'New Babylon.' The meeting in Alba was instrumental in setting up the Situationist International (SI). A central figure in this operation was Guy Debord, and the cooperation between Debord and Constant would be a key factor in the initial development of Unitary Urbanism; a critique of the totality of capitalist society, modernity and its megalomaniac city plans.[1] The SI denounced the existing practices of urban development and how they served the ideological purpose of capitalism. They also denounced the linear capital time by their commitment to 'transience' through adopting concepts of the *dérive*[2] (to drift) and *détournement* (rerouting or hijacking).

'New Babylon' would be the most ambitious attempt to envisage the possible implications of Unitary Urbanism. The title was taken from the post-revolutionary Russian film made in the 1920s about the Paris Commune, which already invoked revolution, while projecting another of a spatial kind, where he imagined the space of justice as a space of no labour, designed for the nomad.[3] (Fig. 1)

In the context of the Biennale, 'New Babylon' was used as an anchor to read another radical time—the permanent temporariness. What becomes of building and dwelling, when living in refuge, exile and migration? What becomes of the temporary when it mutates into a permanent situation? Through analysis of three spatial moments, Constant's 'critique' of modernity is critiqued, and his title appropriated and negated. The first moment considers Nahr el-Bared, a Palestinian refugee camp in Northern Lebanon that was

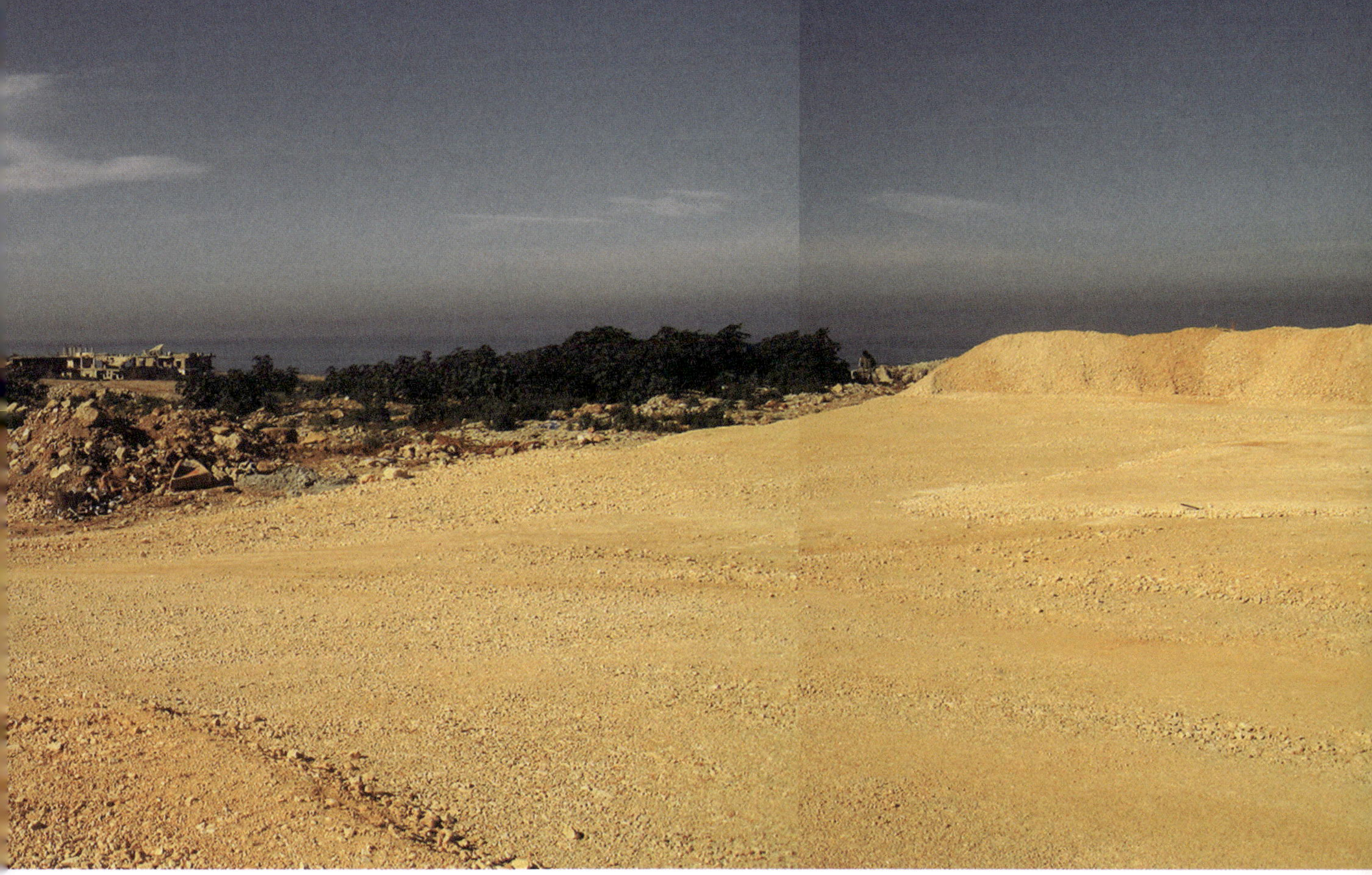

destroyed and reconstructed, an augmented oxymoron of the notion of suspended permanence. I worked here as an architect in the reconstruction. The second is Amman, the capital of Jordan, where I lived most of my adult life. This is a city that triggers subtle suspended temporalities in its relation to Palestine and its Palestinianness. The last is Kuwait, where I was born. This was the base for many Palestinian migrant workers, especially after the oil boom, and played an important role in Palestinian history up until the Gulf War.

Palestine as a Radical Site of Knowledge

How does the world look if we look at it from Palestine, epistemologically? With this question, Ismail Nashif anchors his book, *Al 'Ataba fi Fath al Epistem*, which literally translates into the 'Threshold to conquering Epistemology.'[4] The author reads modernity epistemologically from Palestine, for being an intensification of a colonial moment, and Palestine from modernity—that refuses or is unable to see the former and consequently generates its absence. To claim that we can only understand the epistemic Palestine through the Modern project is a highly problematic claim that carries contradictions of crucial dimensions on the act of dismantling the collective and individual Palestinian self. However, this attempt aims to reveal the Palestinian site as a possible bearer of an alternative knowledge that could dismantle the 'safety valve' of the modern epistemic structures.[5] The spatial implication in the title indicates the necessary measures; one must depart from absence as a portal to dismantle knowledge structures. This theoretical proposition will be used here as a framework from which another one is built, exploring the invisibilities within cognitive Palestine.

> Modernity, Octavio Paz says, is an exclusively Western concept that has no equivalent in other civilizations. The reason for this lies in the view of time that is peculiar to the West, by which time is regarded as being linear, irreversible, and progressive.[6]

A debatable thought—especially in the centrality of the West, but something is striking in the notion of linearity that Paz suggests, and not only in linearity of time, but of knowledge and space as well. In his book, Nashif explains this linearity of modernity and its knowledge through the metaphor of a Modernist building. The Modern building is a temporal and spatial configuration which arranges the pace of time and movement of the place; those who occupy this building are

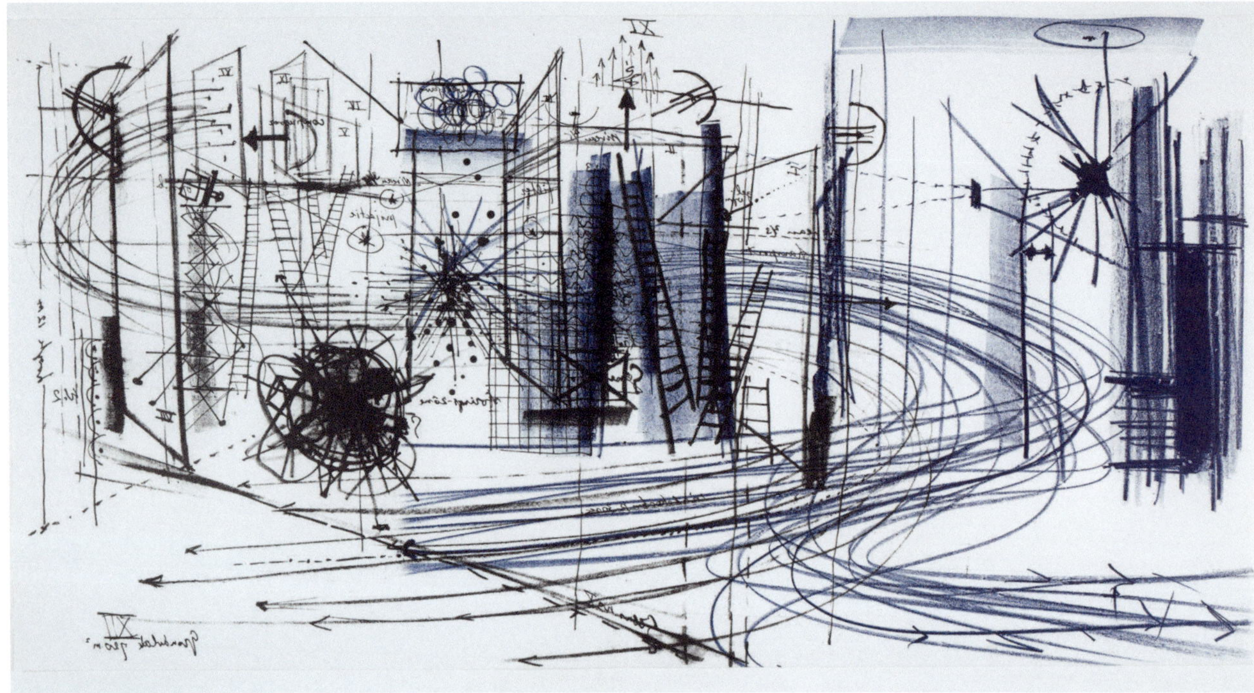

captive to its incremental linearity and clarity. From this, we understand that the 'unannounced' adversary of modernity is obscurity.

We must recognise the successive failures of modernity and the plight of dwelling it inscribed. Alienation and deterritorialisation were enhanced by the rationality of modernity and its different forms of architecture, later abused by notions of efficiency and profit under capitalism. Little by little, an unbridgeable gap grew between dwelling and architecture, and poetic dwelling is what remains.[7] Departing from the existential impossibility of dwelling, many tried to rethink 'building,' some in a romantic and some in a humanistic way. Still others in complete opposition, critical and extreme, believed that the only thing left for humanity was to start all over again.

Another level of deterritorialisation appears when we live in temporariness, in refuge, in exile, when even the poetic dwelling is lost.[8] What becomes of building and dwelling when living in suspension, in the temporary, and what becomes of the temporary when it is constantly mutating into permanence? What is permanent temporariness?[9] Understanding dwelling in temporariness, in this extended refuge and exile, is further complicated when juxtaposed with the processes of modernisation and modernities in its 'host' countries.[10] "While modernity gave rise to the notion of the nation-state, it was also the moment of refuge and exile in the Arab region. This can be seen as an inscription of a colonial effect onto space."[11]

From here, we must then shift the introductory question, by altering the position of our gaze, and depart from absences within epistemic Palestine. What are the invisibilities beyond what is being written as centres and as peripheries within the Palestinian context? What are the spaces produced in parallel to the main timeline, or the narrative of Palestinian exodus? What is beyond the clear spatial and economic centres (architectural icons, traditional knowledge, intersections with British mandate and missionary influence)? What is beyond the clear peripheries (camps, their extensions and marginal migration)?

Both centres and peripheries remain intellectually and spatially represented in knowledge coming from the centre, including that of intellectual elites or Palestinian bourgeoisie, and also from the periphery—although they cannot exist easily within the same knowledge production structures. In this extended refuge, exile and migration, is it possible to step

Fig 1 (Above): Constant Nieuwenhuys, New Babylon, 1963. N°9, book, lithography: 40 x 38 x 1.5 cm. inv. 999 01 15. Collection Frac Centre-Val de Loire. © Adagp, Paris, 2020.

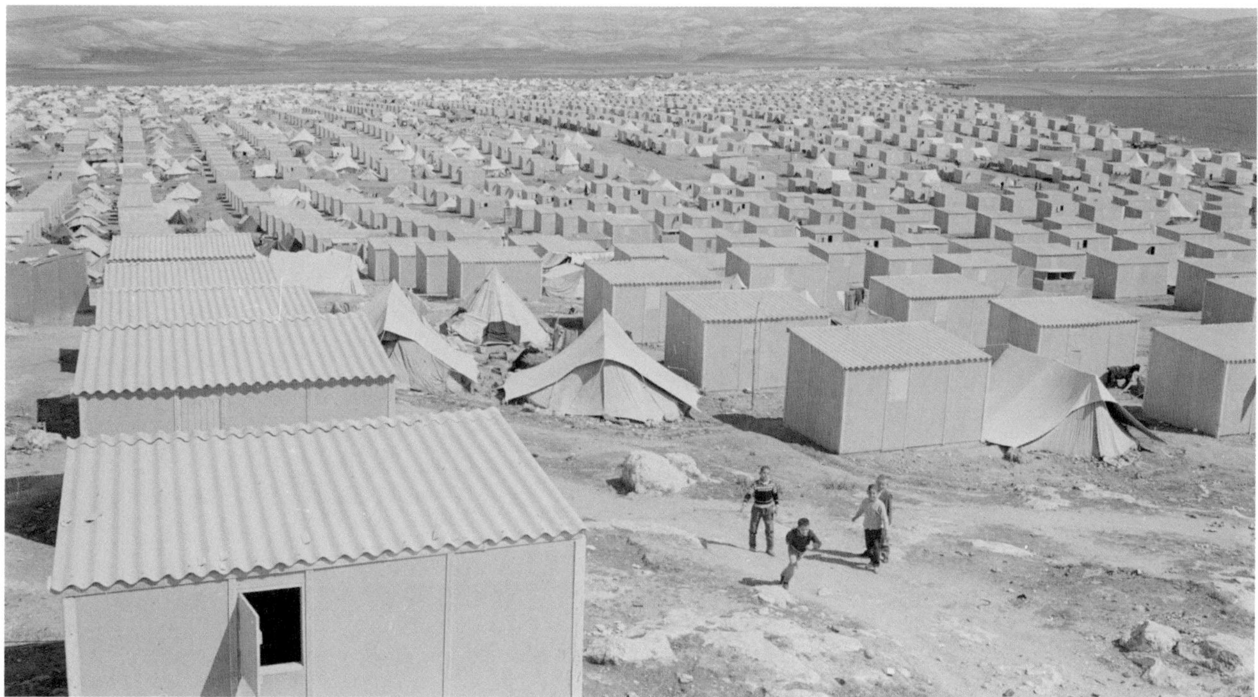

outside these defined centres and peripheries, into a more fluid topology? How do we capture the inscription of time onto space in representing the undefined? If architecture in the temporary is semiotically referencing Palestine, or more specifically, the return to Palestine, then its materiality is not necessarily ephemeral. Can architecture of the temporary be considered Palestinian architecture, particularly given that it is produced mainly outside of Palestine?

This is not an attempt to define vernacular Palestinian architecture, a debate about authenticity or an attempt to counter the myth of the 'land without people' with narratives of 'cities erected from nothingness,' legitimising Israeli settler colonial practices.[12] Rather, this is a questioning of the knowledge accumulated by building and dwelling in the 'material and immaterial' temporary. Can one trace an embedded knowledge within the material? Can we trace different dwellings that could have mutated from a 'central' typology? Then, to rephrase Nashif's question, what is modernity from the perspective of permanent temporariness? This can be unpacked through the construction of 'scenes' in a nonlinear temporal sequence.

Fig 2 (Above): Overview of Baqa'a Palestinian Refugee Camp, Jordan.
© 1969 UNRWA Archive Photo by George Nehmeh.

Scenes: 2007, 1969, 1980

In 2007, Nahr el-Bared, a Palestinian refugee camp in the north of Lebanon, was completely bombarded and demolished by the Lebanese army after an armed conflict with Fath al-Islam, a predominantly foreign Islamist fundamentalist group that had planted itself in the camp just six months earlier. Due to the demolition, 33,000 refugees were displaced to the Beddawi Camp (a Palestinian refugee camp located 5 km east of Tripoli) and adjacent areas (Fig 1).

The case of Nahr el-Bared (NBC) evoked the relationship of construction and land to time. The idea of reconstructing the destroyed camp held a revolutionary potential both politically and spatially. However, the Lebanese state and army gradually became involved in the process, imposing a vision of security and sovereignty through planning, and a possibility to create a 'model camp,' an idea enabling further destruction.[13] For me, an architect working on the reconstruction, the central question shifted from how to rebuild a camp, into how to dwell, live and die in a state of suspension; in waiting.

In Beddawi Camp, where most of NBC residents were taking refuge, a spontaneous grassroots initiative emerged, mobilised by a general conviction that el-Bared's destruction and the government's plans for it were politically motivated. The initiative was named Nahr el-Bared Reconstruction Commission for Civil Action and Studies (NBRC). NBC was

built incrementally by its residents since its establishment in 1949 (one year after Nakba in 1948). With no documentation of its built environment except for a few aerial photographs, the only way to restore the spatial history of the camp was to reconstruct it from residents' memory. Plans of social structure, urban fabric and individual households were drawn and validated by the community and NBRC. These documents were unprecedented in their nature and effect, and therefore forced the process of reconstruction to follow a set of principles set by the community in partnership with UNRWA (The United Nations Relief and Works Agency for Palestine Refugees in the Near East) and NBRC. These included demanding return to the original location, restoring its fabric and involving the community in planning and design.
The extraterritoriality of the camp had allowed for its mass destruction; invisibility from the law followed by absence from documentation. However, this invisibility also made the reclamation of the space possible. The process of mental mapping and recollection restated its right to space, and therefore the return to the camp.

The camp reconstruction processes depended on documents retrieved from residents' memories, which is always a subject of debate, disagreement and validation. A gap emerged between imagined or remembered space, reclaimed space and reconstructed space. One afternoon, after a long debate with one of the NBC resident regarding his 'memory' of his destroyed household, he decided to show me what he had recorded on his mobile phone from live TV coverage of the attacks on NBC. The video depicted a building in the middle of a semi-ruined context that, after a few seconds, collapsed. His daughter and wife could be heard screaming in the background. For the man, this video was evidence of his past. He said calmly: "Just count the columns." His memory required a mechanical procedure of analysing the violence in the video frame, its planes, pixels and other variables, just to extract the only reclaimable thing: the number of columns. The number of columns indicated the area of the common structural module used in the camp—around 3 metre structural span which is an essential aspect of local construction knowledge.[14] In the absence of the building in the image, the façade became increasingly visible.
In a picture from the UNRWA archives of the Al Baq'a Camp on the north-west outskirts of Amman, Jordan, taken in 1969—the transformation of tents into modular barracks is documented, which thereafter transformed into concrete block walls. [15] (Fig. 2)

Fig 3 (Opposite): Saba Innab, Drawing from Tomorrow, Poetry will (not) be the House of Life, 2017. Collection of FRAC Val de Loire.

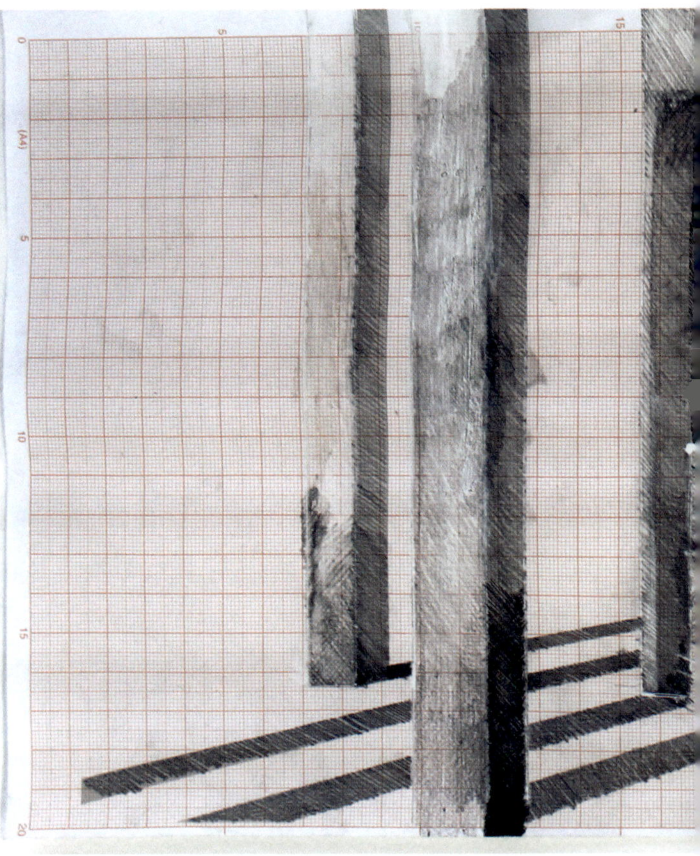

The moment of destruction portrayed in the video is projected in this archival image. The module was multiplied, expanded and proliferated, transforming the temporary into permanence. Can we see or follow this transformation beyond the boundaries of the camp, beyond the ephemerality and physicality of space? The moment of transformation of the tent to the wall is the same moment of transformation of the pilotis space in a Modernist apartment building in Kuwait in the 1970s and 1980s to accommodate migrant workers, many of whom were Palestinians.[16] This particular building is a reference to a pattern of transformation in the Modernist building's logic, the clarity and linearity of spatial organisation, circulation and pilotis, which in this pattern of transformation meant something else—additional accommodation and affordable housing for migrant workers. The transformation of the pilotis space is another inscription of time onto place, illustrating the schism between those who plan and desire, as opposed to those who dwell and inhabit. (Fig. 3)
Here, we consider two moments—the former is archival, the latter is imagined or reclaimed from memory. The first moment in the Al Baq'a photograph represents a module and

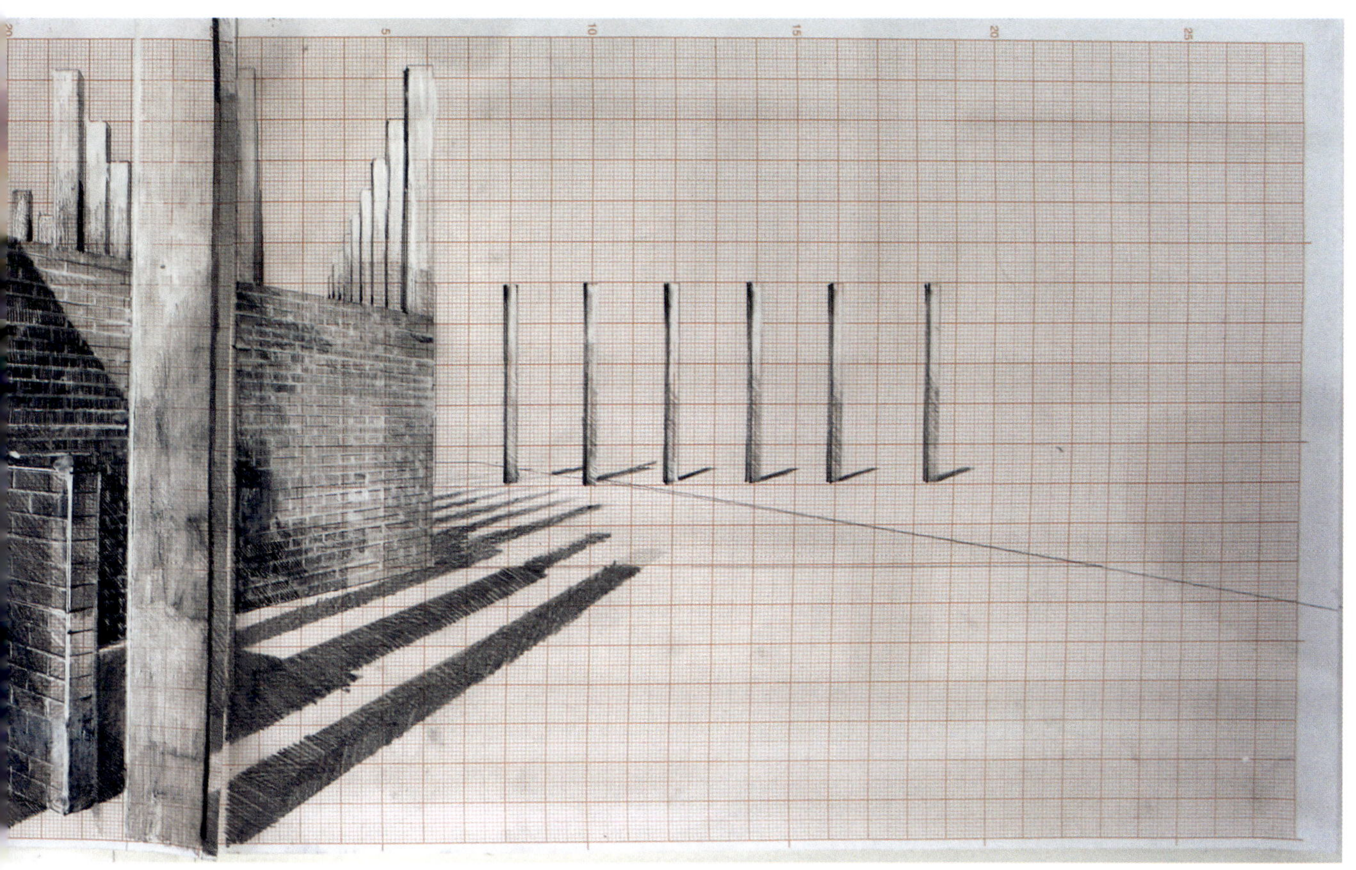

what it signifies of domination and subjugation. The other represents the prescribed vision of the architect, and the Modernist grid. Between these two moments lies a spectrum of permanent temporariness.

Kuwait was one of the first cities in the Arabian Gulf to experience the material effect of petroleum exploration. With this exploration, in 1946 it underwent massive infrastructure development in the name of modernisation, encouraging large scale labour importation from neighbouring Middle Eastern countries in the 1960s and 1970s to meet new skilled and unskilled labour demands, shifting the economic focus from port to oil.[17] The first step in this transformation was the State's commission of a master plan in 1951, intending to make Kuwait "the best planned and most socially progressive city in the Middle East."[18] By connecting urban planning and social progress, the Kuwaiti ruler echoed the city-planning discourse of the high Modernist avant-garde led by Le Corbusier and the *Congrès Internationaux d'Architecture Modern* (CIAM).[19]

Building the spectacle of national image and dwelling are two parallel lines that sometimes never meet. Reclaiming these spaces extends to become part of the deterritorialisation of migration, and the migration of labour. Like the schism between those who envision and those who dwell, the schism between architecture of need and architecture of desire is revealed in spaces of migration and refuge. By deconstructing a spatial moment into angles, materials and know-how, another layer unfolds; regional references, alienation and attempts to unravel the unknown emerge in the context of modernisation in host countries. These fragments of space are not only an extension of the Palestinian refuge and exile but become part of the deterritorialisation of the working class and migrant workers.

In this ongoing recollection of spaces, investigation moves from the material to the immaterial, and then to the behavioural, a record of architecture in permanent temporariness is built. (Fig. 4)

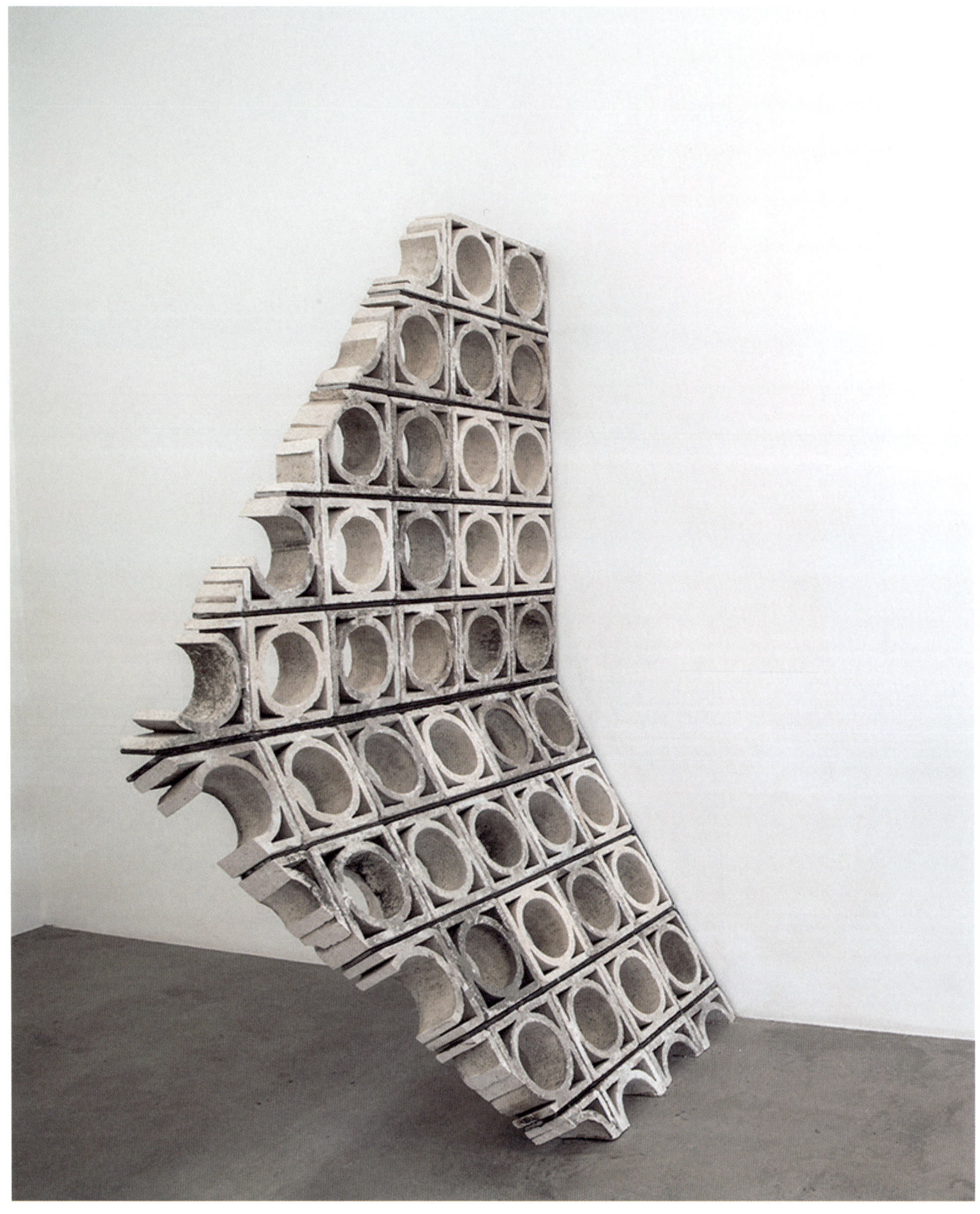

Can permanent temporariness be documented, archived and recognised as part of the architectural typologies and archetypes of theory and history, rather than simply a side effect? Can the process of unfolding embedded meaning challenge existing knowledge structures?

Towards Alternative Epistemic Structures

This process of collecting spaces and patterns of temporariness is an attempt to read beyond clear centres and peripheries and their representations. For example, in every map, we can read authority in what is visible and what is invisible. Mapping the marginal would be a product of the same power structure and logic of authority embedded within this particular tool. What is needed then, is a method of collecting what is not possible to represent in the existing knowledge production tools and processes, as an attempt to create alternative epistemic structures. This process of collecting spaces and patterns of temporariness is an attempt to read beyond the 'representable,' or the defined representations of centres and peripheries. While a total liberation from the existing tools of representation is unlikely, a destabilisation of writing and classification is attainable by considering the 'irrepresentable.'

Fluid spaces and hybrid typologies, including the transformation of the pilotis space, are one example of the extended Palestinian exile that becomes part of the deterritorialisation of migration, and the migration of labour. If we reclaim these spaces, document and analyse their typologies and knowledge structures, not only do we stand to collect what is irrepresentable. We also facilitate an architectural history of the temporary that intersects with the main history written by the centre. This parallel timeline is a bearer of alternative epistemic structures.

01 Hilda Heynan, *Architecture and Modernity* (Cambridge: MIT Press, 1999), 151.
02 The idea of urban wandering relates to the 19th century concept of the flâneur, theorised by the poet Charles Baudelaire.
03 Peter Wollen, "Architecture and the Situationist International" (lecture, The Architectural Association, London, May 15, 2015).
04 The translation is the author's interpretation of the title. 'Conquer' (fath) could be replaced by 'open' or 'unravel.'
05 Ismail Nashif, *Al 'Ataba fi Fath al Epistem* (Beirut: Dar al Farabi, 2014), 105.
06 Heynan, *Architecture and Modernity*, 9.
07 See Martin Heidegger, "Building Thinking Dwelling," in *Poetry, Language, Thought*, trans. Albert Hofstadter (New York: Harper Colophon Books, 1971).
08 Saba Innab, *How to Build Without a Land*, Universes in Universes (2014).
09 This term is used by Sandi Hilal and Alessandro Petti to indicate the transformation of the physical temporariness of the camp into concrete urban densification. I use the term to express a more complex state of Palestinian deterritorialisation, beyond and outside the physicality of the camp, to tackle the notion of dwelling in the temporariness.
10 This term references countries 'hosting' Palestinian refugees, used here critically.
11 We can look at this metaphorically and factually: in 1948, one year after its independence and establishment,the Hashemite kingdom of Jordan was redefined and doubled in population after receiving the first waves of Palestinian refugees. In 1950, the Jordanian parliament voted for political unity with the West Bank of Jordan River (demarcated by the Jordanian-Israeli armistice of 1949 after the first Israeli occupation of Palestine in 1948, Nakba). This unity redefined the boundary of Jordan. Saba Innab, Tomorrow, *Poetry Will (not) Be The House of Life*, 2017, mixed media, FRAC Centre, Orléans.
12 See Sharon Rotbard, *White City Black City: Architecture and War in Tel Aviv and Jaffa* (London: Pluto Press, 2015).
13 The Cairo Accord: in 1969, the Lebanese army commander General Emile Bustani and PLO represented by Yasser Arafat, reached an agreement that was moderated by Gamal Abdel Nasser. The agreement established principles under which the presence and activities of Palestinian guerrillas in south-east Lebanon would be tolerated and regulated by the Lebanese authorities. Under the agreement, the 14 official UNRWA camps in Lebanon were removed from the jurisdiction of the Lebanese army, and placed under the authority of the Palestinian Armed Struggle Command. This allowed Palestinians to participate in the armed struggle against Israel and self-governance in the camps, which continues today.
14 Farah Koubayssi, "Nahr el-Bared: Hekayat Lujou' w Damar w Hisar," *Al-Mansour Journal* 11 (2008): http://almanshour.org/node/1918.
15 Prefabricated shelter commonly called barracks.
16 In reference to the building I was born in, in Kuwait, 1980.
17 Al Issa, "Modernizing Kuwait: Nation-building and Unplanned Spatial Practices," *Berkeley Planning Journal* 22 (2009).
18 Farah Al-Nakib, *Kuwait Transformed: A History of Oil and Urban Life* (Stanford: Stanford University Press, 2016).
19 Ibid.

Fig 4 (Opposite): Saba Innab, Then We Realized, Time is Stone, from Al Rahhalah (The Traveller), 2016. Claustra and metal structure: 225 x 150 x 120cm. Image courtesy of Marfa Gallery and the artist.

BANGKOK BASTARDS

Chatpong Chuenrudeemol

Bangkok is Kuala Lumpur is Manila is Rangoon is Vientiane is Hanoi is Jakarta.

Bangkok is slowly becoming indistinguishable from its ASEAN counterparts, as more buildings become commercially privatised, air-condition-reliant and culturally insignificant. The locally insensitive and tropically negligent design approach in Bangkok can be attributed to two things: Western Modernist design principles and the global commercial development forces that have adopted the former as its signature style.

Bangkok Bastards are the antithesis to the developer-driven architecture and urbanism that have dominated our city.

Bangkok Bastards are homegrown architectural concoctions researched and documented by CHAT architects. They are nonhuman entities created by the city's forgotten citizens—illegal squatters, street vendors, migrant workers and other individuals of 'questionable origin.' From temporary construction worker houses to semi-legal shantytowns to underground sex-motels, these vernacular typologies are scattered thoughout the city. They are built with cheap, local, scavenged materials in simple yet ingenious ways. Recycled timber, corrugated zinc sheets, broken cement fibreboard and disposed vinyl Red Bull banners become the impromptu material palette of such ad-hoc hybrid architecture. There is no orthodox architectural theory behind their conception. They are crafted by everyday people simply trying to survive and thrive in an unforgiving Asian metropolis.

Due to their illegitimate origins, lack of historical pedigree and 'cheap' appearance, these Bastards are considered unrefined scars in the city, unworthy of investigation by most Bangkokians, including architects. However, due to their honest responses to the city's real-life conditions, it can be argued that Bangkok Bastards are the most authentic form of vernacular architecture in Thailand's urbanism.[1] At first glance, these Bastards may not directly resemble the most widely recognised Thai vernacular typology: the wooden house on stilts. However, the improvisational strategies utilised in their conception are borne of the same spirit that created their rural cousins. The wooden prototype our forebearers invented to withstand floods, droughts and other perils in the untamed natural environment has been hybridised to negotiate the challenges presented in tropical urban life.

Bangkok Bastards produce unique boundary conditions which reflect the complexities of life in the Thai capital. Since the inhabitants of these structures are individuals on the fringe of society, their shelters are frequently illegal or temporary. In most cases, however, they are forced to negotiate compact and constrictive sites. The interior spaces, frequently hot, poorly ventilated and dark, are used mainly for sleeping at night. Bangkok Bastards therefore deploy a strategy of 'colonising' the public domain to create additional usable space. Plastic stools and potted plants slowly creep onto public sidewalks or narrow alleyways, creating outdoor living rooms that are interstitial conditions between public and private.

Opposite: Makkasan Flood Reservoir Community-a vibrant shanty town located at a no-man's land intersection between a flood reservoir canal and two expressway overpasses. Photography by Chatpong Chuenrudeemol.

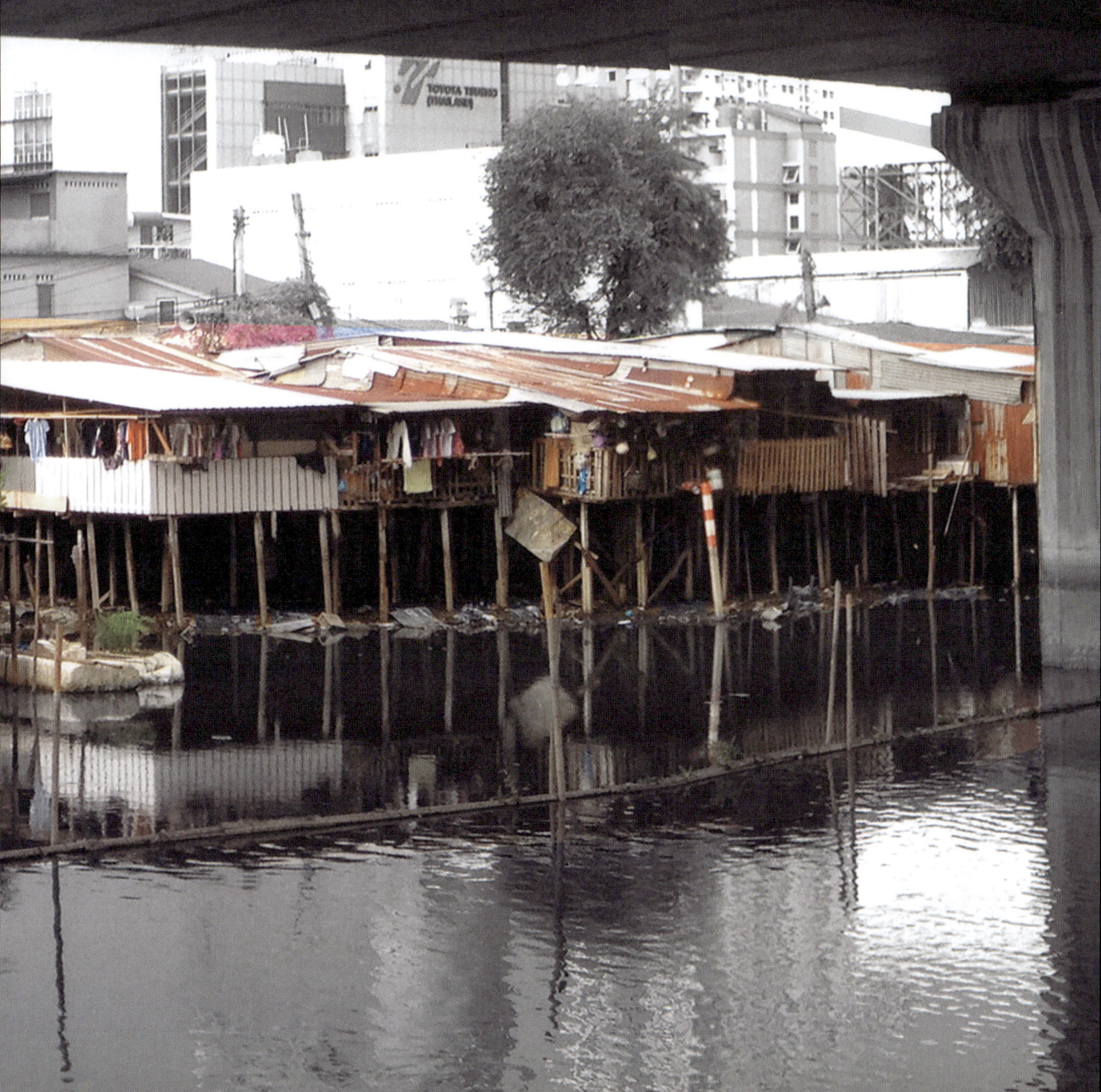
TOYOTA

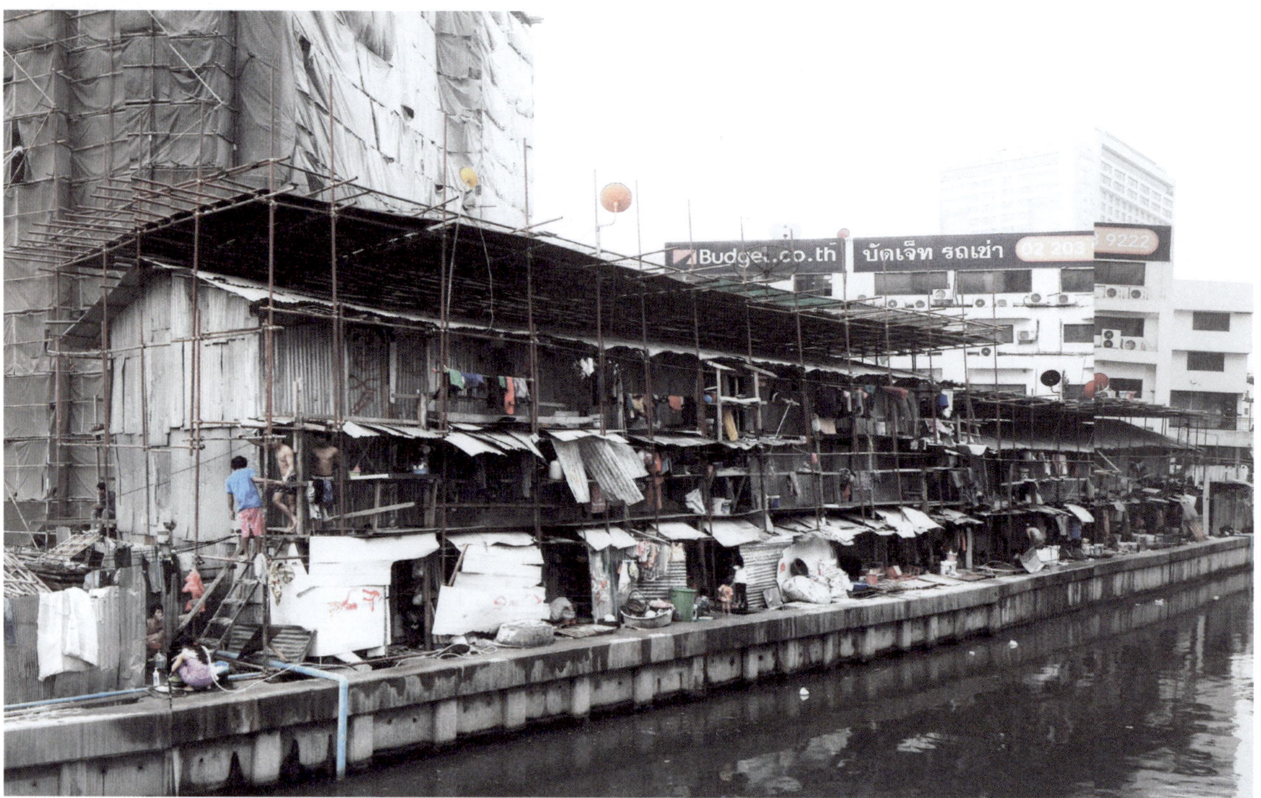

The Construction Worker House

In Thailand, construction workers live on the actual job site in which they are working. This allows developers to minimise time and expense required in transporting workers to and from off-site accommodations. In exchange for free living accommodation, the workers are tasked with building their own houses on the construction site. The results are incredibly ingenious examples of temporary tropical architecture that is cheap, flexible, messy and adaptive to indigenous lifestyles in urban tropical conditions.

The construction worker house typology consists of two main components: the core and the scaffolding. The core contains cellular living units, each bound on four sides with privacy walls constructed from scavenged corrugated sheets, plywood or cement fibreboard. They are frequently windowless, incredibly hot, stuffy and uncomfortable—used mainly for sleeping. During the day, workers prefer to spend their time outside of these cramped interior quarters. The scaffolding, a multi-purpose light framework that wraps the living units, allows for this desired outdoor living. The scaffolding becomes covered walkways and open staircases that link each unit, but also acts as multi-function living spaces that accommodate eating, cooking, drinking, napping, lounging, washing and hanging laundry. The scaffolding is always constructed as well ventilated semi-outdoor spaces, either in the form of a double-loaded corridor wind-tunnel or a single-loaded corridor that acts as outdoor verandah. The scaffolding provides necessary transition zones between indoors and out, allowing construction workers a third space—that blurry zone between indoor and outdoor, between work and play. Such transitional layers are sorely lacking in contemporary modern architectural imports to Bangkok from the West, which contain hard boundaries between inside and outside. Solid walls and fixed glass panes do work to keep polluted outdoor air out and conditioned air in. But this perimeter condition completely negates the porous thresholds and soft boundary conditions that allow Bangkok street culture and indoor-outdoor tropical living to flourish.

Above: Canal-side Construction Worker House at condominium high-rise construction site in Rama 9 District, Bangkok. Photography by Chatpong Chuenrudeemol).

Opposite: Exploded Isometric of Construction Worker House, Rama 9 District, Bangkok shows core living units and the scaffolding component that provides circulation, informal living terraces and plywood canopy for protection against falling high-rise construction debris. Image by CHAT Lab.

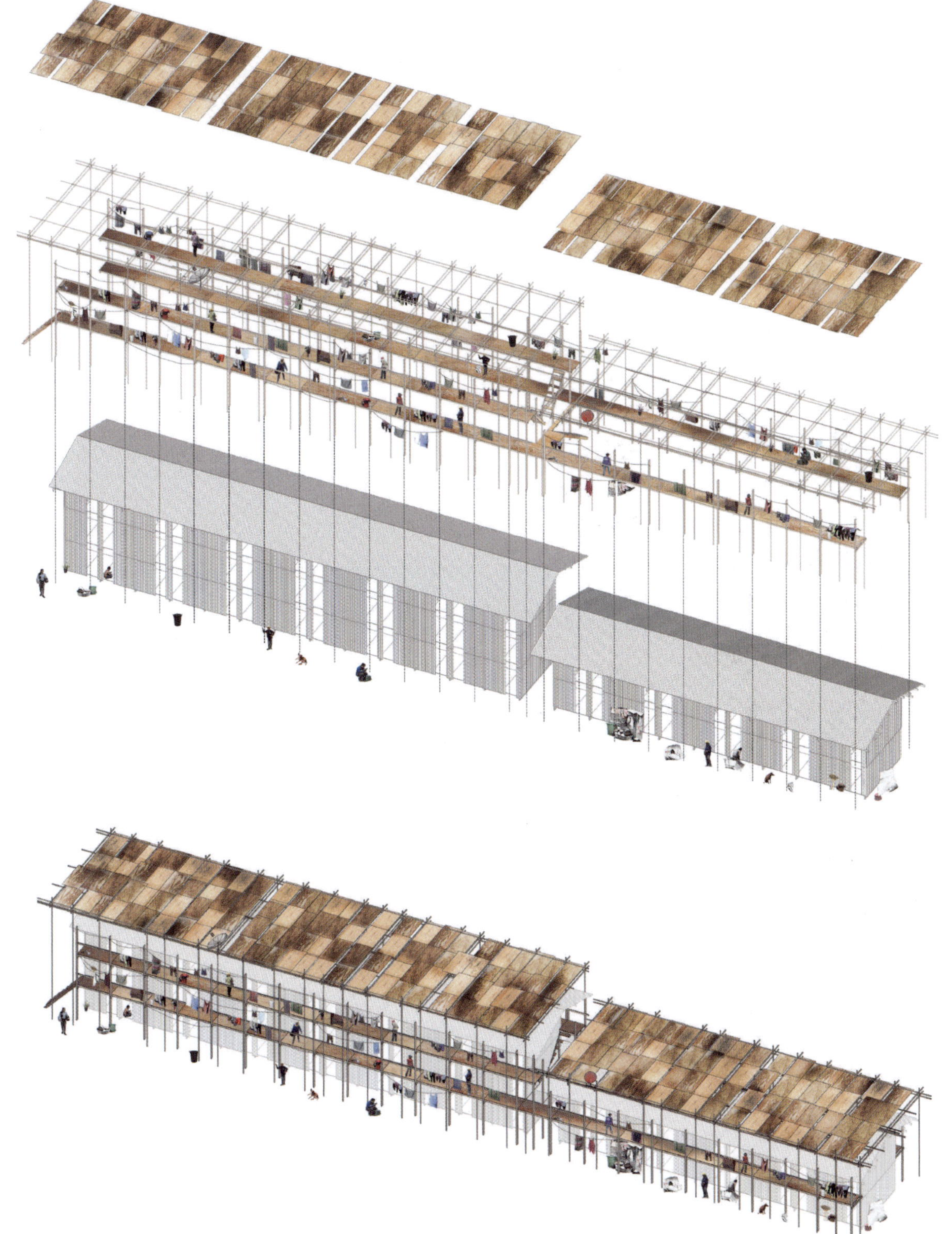

The Curtain Sex Motel

One of the most unique typologies of Bangkok Bastards, the curtain sex motel, was created to satisfy one of the city's underground naughty secrets; a motel whose design, with its cleverly orchestrated spatial sequence, protects the anonymity of clientele who wish to keep their romantic interludes under wraps. From the street, the structure appears like any other concrete frame infill building designed in the Late Modern era of the late 1960s and early 1970s. Its defining characteristic is a small void at street level that allows guests to inconspicuously penetrate the building perimeter in the safety of their cars. Emerging from the street tunnel, guests find themselves in an open-air auto courtyard, lined with brightly coloured curtained parking spots. A hotel attendant will quickly usher the car into an available parking spot, directly linked to a private 'love suite.' Once the car is securely parked, the curtain is pulled shut, giving the couple complete privacy to continue their romantic interlude. A secret exit allows the lovers to drive away unnoticed through a side alley.

Apart from exhibiting a spatial narrative for one of Bangkok society's shady secrets, the curtain sex motel also demonstrates a clever architectural response to the challenges of tropical city living. The courtyard void at the centre of the building is continuously ventilated as air from the street tunnel is pulled through the court opening above by the principle of stack effect. The minimal tunnel opening also allows just enough city-tainted air to enter the court to remove excess heat and humidity, but not too much that dust and street noise overpower the space. This careful negotiation of clean vs. polluted air in the Asian metropolis is rarely found in contemporary structures.

The Samsen STREET Hotel

Today, our cities are largely conceived by designers and developers as clean, diagrammatic exercises in Modernist form-making. We champion a globally-recognisable design language unencumbered by culture and climate. Slanted roofs, overhangs and verandahs have no place among clean glass, steel and concrete blocks with flat roofs. As such, the modern urban infill building is missing the critical interstitial perimeter zone, or transitional verandah condition, to filter the harsh sun, rain and thermal transfers inherent in Asian tropical climate zones.

In the Samsen STREET Hotel, the idea of the 'urban scaffolding' provides the required buffer zone that can become a space of informal, tropical indoor-outdoor habitation. This component is one of many strategies derived

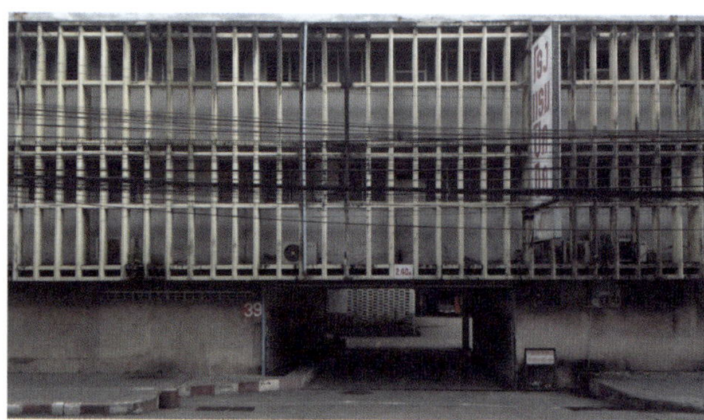

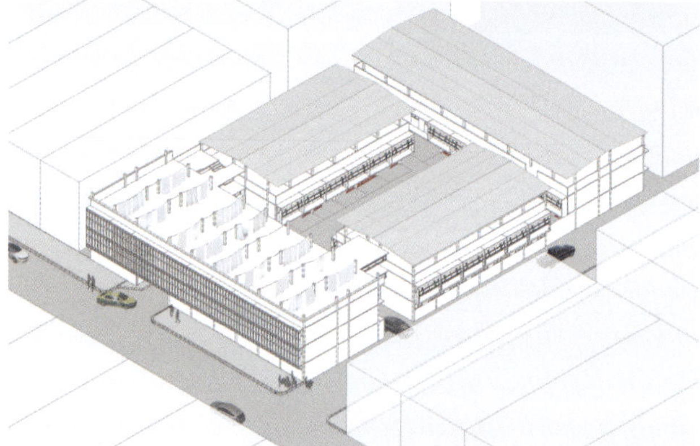

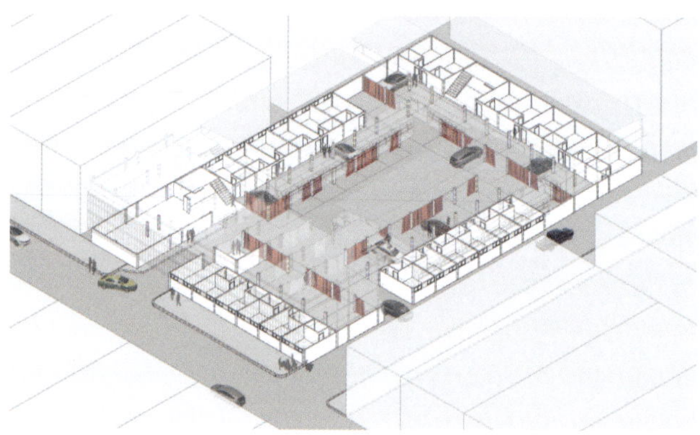

Above (top): View of Picnic Curtain Motel street façade with auto tunnel. Photography by Chatpong Chuenrudeemol.

Above (middle): Isometric of Picnic Curtain Motel" Image by CHAT Lab.

Above (bottom): X-ray Isometric of Picnic Curtain Motel, highlighting the spatial qualities of the auto-curtain court and 'love suites.' Image by CHAT Lab.

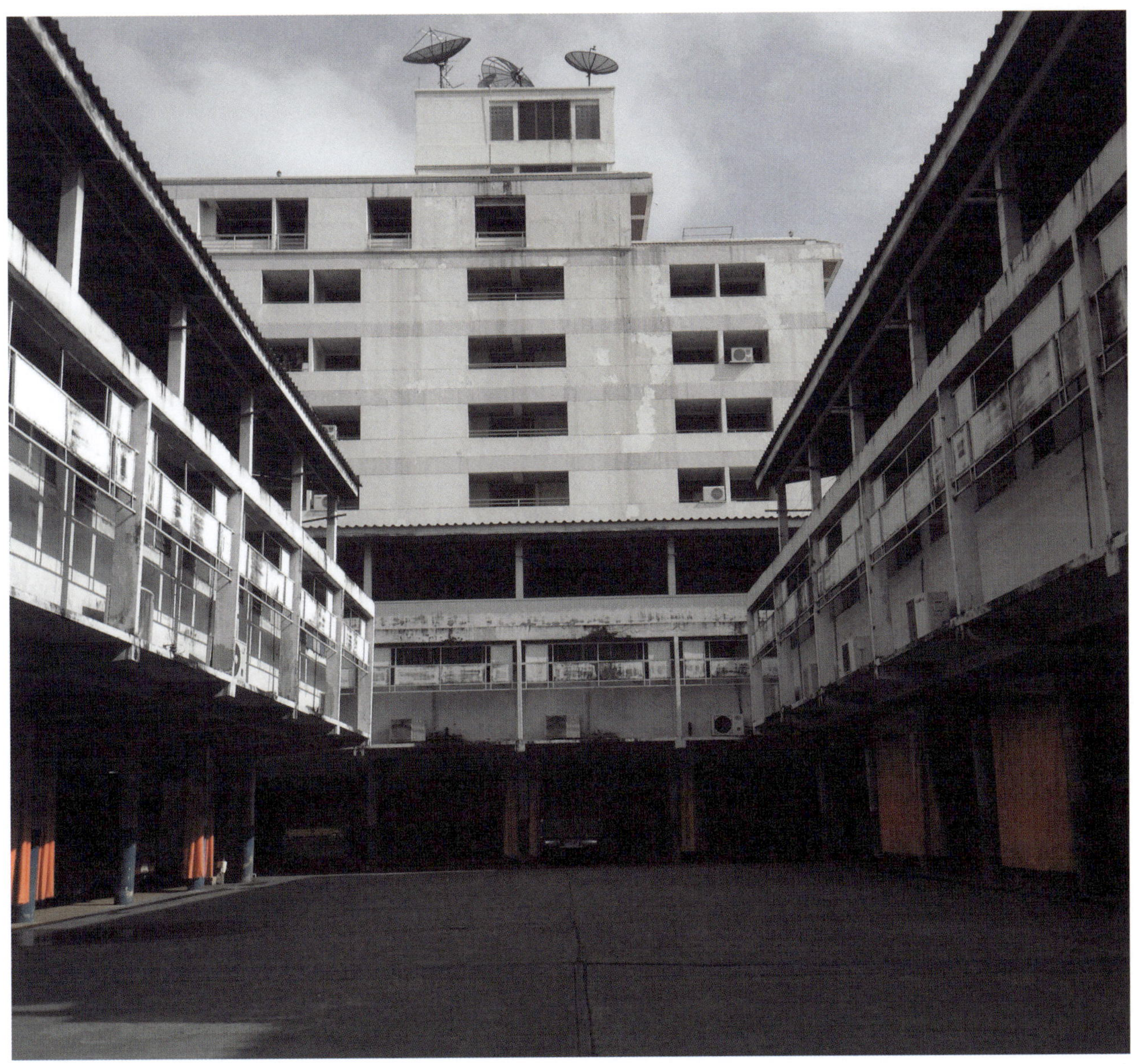

Above: View of internal courtyard lined with curtained parking spaces leading to 'love suites.' Photography by Chatpong Chuenrudeemol.

from CHAT Architects' Bangkok Bastards research. Through the critical examination of local curtain sex motel typologies, temporary construction worker housing and mobile street food architecture, we were able to mine these existing 'live' street typologies to propose new urban programs and derive an authentic hybrid architectural language to celebrate the cultural identity of the developing ASEAN city. Our Samsen STREET Hotel involves the renovation of a curtain sex motel which seeks to turn the existing curtain sex motel model 'inside out,' both formally and programmatically. New 'living' scaffolding components create a new public interface, transforming the once dark and introverted building with a legally questionable program, into a new 'street hotel' typology to re-activate public life in this former red-light district. The existing structure is finished with plain grey polished cement plaster, while the new interventions are inserted in the form of three muted green scaffolding components: the *soi* (alley), the *rabeang* (sidewalk terrace) and the *nahng glang plang* (outdoor movie theatre).

The *soi* (alley)

Existing guest units on the street façades are fitted with new 2.40 x 1.20 metre cantilevered daybed boxes, allowing the owner to sleep an extra third guest in each room. The negative space created between the daybed extrusions create continuous *sois*, or alleys, that house the building's MEP systems. Stairs, catwalks and platforms in this snaking façade scaffolding allow building maintenance to reach all mechanical, electrical and sanitary components without having to go through each room. On weekends, festivals and special occasions, the *soi* scaffolding is utilised as elevated performance stages for neighborhood street concerts.

The *rabeang* (sidewalk verandah)

A new canopy scaffolding with customised street furniture makes use of under-utilised set-back zones around the plot perimeter, allowing activity from the hotel to spill out onto the street and vice versa. Mobile tables and seating (hacked from everyday objects like local fruit delivery carts) can be rolled out to colonise the street during holidays and festivals when the street is blocked off from traffic. The *rabeang* scaffolding also becomes a 'plug-in' space for local street food vendors to escape the recent efforts of the Thai military government to 'clean up' the streets. The hotel aims to create a new business model where entrepreneurs and local vendors can collectively create value for each other. The hotel supports the local vendors by ordering authentic dishes, like Thai custard (*kanom krok*), to serve their guests for breakfast.

The *nahng glang plang* (outdoor theatre)

The secret auto-curtain court is transformed into an active outdoor movie theatre. The new swimming pool is not for swimming as it is a soaking cinema lounge. A new type of scaffolding, with 'leg-dangling' balconies, encourages guests to turn outward to watch the outdoor movie. In doing so, the guests turn to face each other across the theatre or down into the pool, allowing them to stimulate conversation in this new public domain.

The Samsen STREET Hotel utilises existing strategies derived from local Bangkok Bastards to create a new locally-derived design framework for Thailand and South-East Asia. The research of hybrid typologies not only provides us with effective local, ready-made solutions, but encourages us to embrace a spirit of flexibility, utilisation of immediate resources and real-time improvisation to create new solutions that go beyond conventional design theory. This will lead us towards a contextually responsive and culturally-rooted South-East Asian architecture. As a first requirement, however, architects—both professionals and students—must move away from the lazy habit of mining global design websites, magazines and blogs for aesthetic precedents. We must look at what is immediately around us with critical eyes and begin the process of identifying, analysing, recording and cataloguing these invaluable local street typologies. Bastards can be found on any street, alleyway or empty lot in every city, large or small, in South-East Asia. They can be easily overlooked because they blend into their contexts effortlessly, organically creating urbanism as a continuous flow, encouraging public life by blurring boundaries and thresholds. However, once identified, they can be an invaluable alternative for a commercially-driven, modern architectural agenda that contributes to the homogenisation of the ASEAN metropolis.

01 Chatpong Chuenrudeemol, "Bangkok Bastards," in *The Asian Everyday: Possibilities in the Shifting World*, ed. Erwin Viray (Tokyo, Japan: TOTO Publishing, 2015), 20-21.

02 Chatpong Chuenrudeemol, "Tropical Hybrids: An Adaptable Equatorial Architecture for Asia's Untamed Tropical Urbanism," *World Architecture Magazine (China)* 345 (March 2019): 16-23.

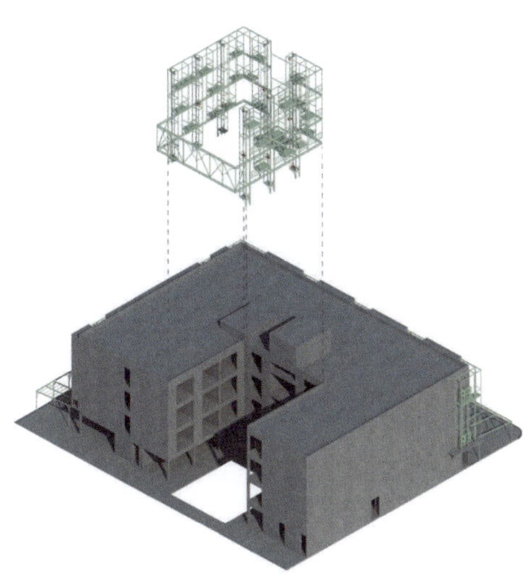

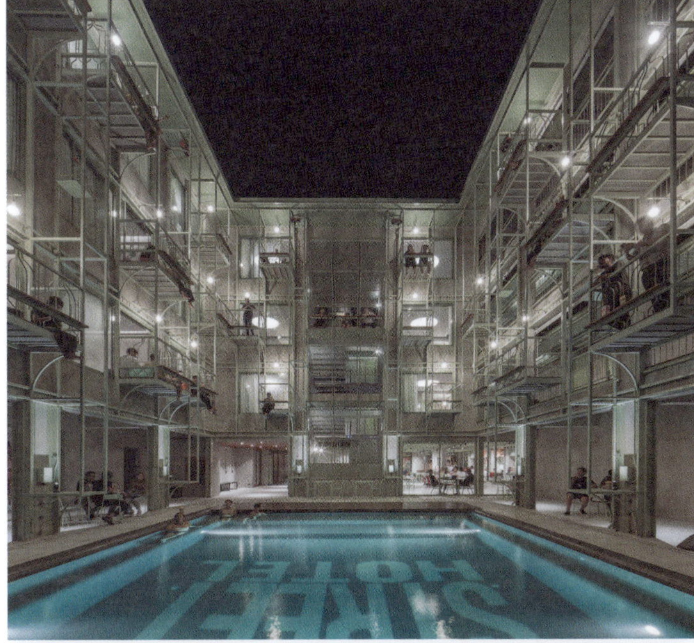

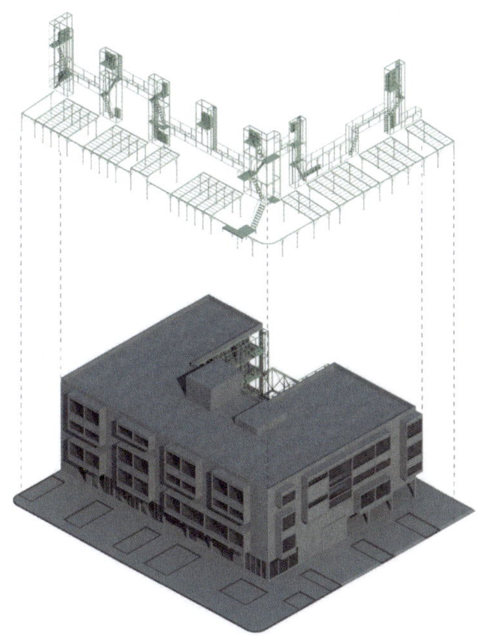

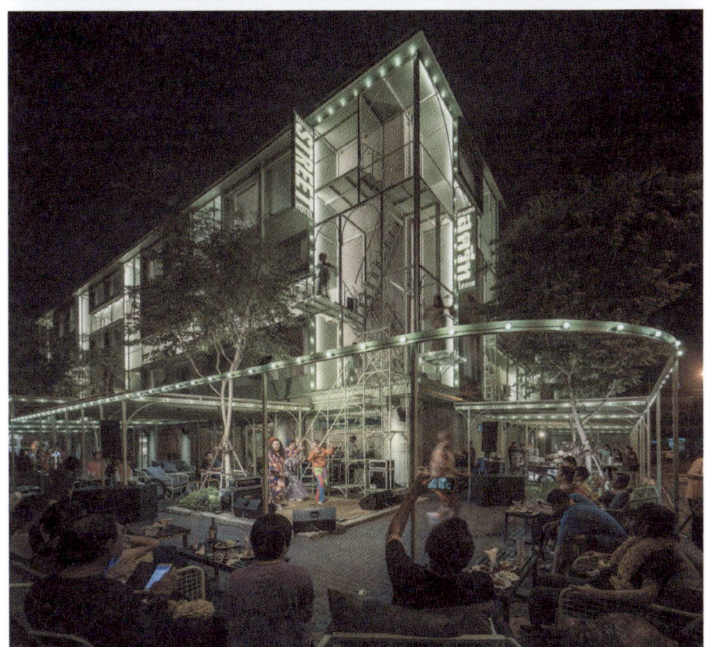

CHAT Architects, The Samsen STREET Hotel, Bangkok, 2019.

Top Left: Rear view of existing curtain sex motel structure with exploded 'outdoor theatre' scaffolding. Image by CHAT Lab.

Bottom Left: Street view of existing curtain sex motel structure with exploded 'vertical alley' and 'sidewalk terrace' scaffolding. Image by CHAT Lab.

Top Right: View of new hotel courtyard with outdoor theatre scaffolding and 'leg dangling' balconies. Photography by W Workspace.

Bottom Right: Street View showing how 'Vertical Alley' scaffolding is utilised as Vertical Stage for neighborhood concert performance. Photography by W Workspace.

GENTLE NEGOTIATIONS OF THE CIVIC PRACTITIONER

FIELDOFFICE ARCHITECTS IN TAIWAN

Kenneth Wu & Hsin Yeh

A small island country, Taiwan resists a number of impositions by larger political and economic forces external to their borders. The inertia of such powers to affect change upon Taiwan on the global stage, compounded by local consciousness to balance urbanisation with natural preservation, convey Taiwan's imperative of maintaining its unique identity. Undoubtedly, as a result of the country's recent investments in cultural production, Taiwan maintains a steadfast but freely creative output. Such output extends to encompass architecture and urban design, as both international and local architects work to enhance civic life within Taiwanese cities and regions. Fieldoffice Architects are one such local firm paving the way for urban redevelopment, utilising the unbounded opportunities of a self-sufficient Yilan County to establish a democratic approach to practice. In a closer reading of Fieldoffice Architects' strategic mediation with the immediate community, a potent sense of political and social agency emerges to reclaim what was once commonplace responsibilities of the civic practitioner.

Huang Sheng-Yuan founded Fieldoffice Architects not in one of Taiwan's economic urban nodes, but in the rural context of Yilan County, where they maintain a clear investment in the landscape they share with the community. For Huang, the practice arose from "an alliance of gathered will," a collective ambition to be empowered as democratic agents of their self-initiated urban regeneration.[1] Such socio-political spirit is fuelled via the positioning of Fieldoffice Architects in the slowness of Yilan, external to any circumscribed urban centre. Geographically, Yilan is essentially adjacent to Taiwan's capital city, Taipei, albeit separated by the Hsuehshan Mountain Range. Along with the Zhongyang Mountain Range to the south and the coastal edge to the east, the edges of the Yilan County triangular plain are clearly defined. These boundaries imbue the fertile agricultural land of Yilan with a sanctuary-like quality, protected from the environmental and urban consequences of the neighbouring metropolis. The demand for self-sufficiency within this geological sequestering forges a continuous respect for nature that is reflected in Yilan's open history of advocation for natural preservation and conscious land use.[2] Huang Sheng-Yuan's office is located at one such typical farmhouse plot in Yilan, where rice field precedes garden. His practice's ethos thus directly aligns with the community's untrammelled independence.

Fieldoffice Architects' commitment to the peri-urban condition of Yilan leads many to a reductive reading of their work as a form of architectural Regionalism. Indeed, the connotation of Frampton's rigid sense of critical regionalism is disingenuous to Huang Sheng-Yuan's ambitions of the practice to challenge the "inadvertent postcolonial self-exile" inherent in Taiwan's political history.[3] In fact, it is a conscious pursuit of creative freedom by Huang in direct response to the suppressive nature of martial control under the Nationalist Party, a regime that assumed control after Japanese colonial occupation.[4] The martial period lasted for forty years until 1987—only seven years before the formation of Fieldoffice Architects. One of the primary failings of critical regionalism is its masquerading of canonised Western thought as incontestable universalism, at the expense of the legitimacy of other non-canonical knowledges.[5] By focusing on Fieldoffice Architects' contribution to Taiwanese architectural expression, Taiwan's epistemological claim to architectural discourse is highlighted as distinct and agentic in the face of an otherwise Eurocentric understanding of the built environment. Instead, a contemporary re-evaluation of critical regionalism reclaims Frampton's original allusion towards "cultural, economic and political independence" departing from the normative that has since been neutralised in favour of topological concerns and an aestheticisation of the rural and peri-urban condition.[6] Through Fieldoffice Architects' community-oriented ambition, they are able to facilitate such independence via an astute prioritisation of the everyday citizen within the broader scale of civic projects.

Given their political agency, Huang and Fieldoffice Architects understand the great influence architects have on the everyday life of users in the civic domain. This sense of responsibility can be read as an extension of philosopher Hannah Arendt's notion—that political ability is the innate capacity to not only judge what is required but have the power to persuade the community into action.[7] Huang Sheng-Yuan evokes this responsibility most distinctly in his ability to embed the practice within Yilan's primary administrative decision-making. One of the main factors that led to the formation of Fieldoffice Architects within Yilan County was the influence of Huang's Tunghai University classmate, Chen Teng-Chin, who took a post-graduate position as a public servant for the Yilan County government centred on urban policies. Such a career path for an architectural graduate is not uncommon in Taiwan and results from an "active public-private exchange through which university experts are recruited to serve as leaders of city architecture and urban policy departments."[8] Consequently, local administrative teams often possess a high level of architectural and urban design proficiency, who in turn have the agency to invest public spending into the various cultural centres of Taiwan. However, where the approach of Fieldoffice Architects has differed from other international firms, such as Shigeru Ban Architects in Tainan, Mecanoo in Kaohsiung or Toyo Ito Architects in Taichung, is in the negotiation of hierarchies between public and private space. Certainly, public space has not been neglected in any of these major projects, but the unquantifiable nature of truly unprogrammed space has positioned it as an afterthought to architectural form. In the case of Fieldoffice Architects, a foundation of open negotiations and empathetic discussions towards an active goal of "positive emptiness and undefinedness" comes from an affirmative collaboration between the practice and the local government.[9] The transparency and equity of Yilan's administrative power structure is integral to the goals of equality and respect which Fieldoffice Architects aim to achieve for the community in Yilan.[10] In a project like the Luodong Cultural Working House, the clear prioritisation of public space can be seen in their decision to push the built form to one side of the large site, elevated from the active public plane. Such a gesture suggests Fieldoffice Architects' successful advocacy and an establishment of a mutual understanding for public space with their client: the Luodong local government. The simple but expansive canopy that formalises the cultural and social activities of the people clearly reflects the architects' drive to "break institutions so that they [are] immersed in their surroundings," culminating in "a platform that is always open to the public."[11] The importance of the programmed architecture recedes behind the many informal activities that occur under the canopy. Simple in expression, the horizontal roof structure provides ample shelter for typical gatherings like youth dance groups, picnics and Taichi practice while also providing the necessary structural housing for the audio-visual equipment used to facilitate municipal events. Here, the architecture exists as a backdrop that frames the "spontaneous and imaginative attitude" of users.[12]

Viewed in contrast with Luodong Cultural Working House, the public space provided by recent major works by international firms across Taiwan act more like compositional devices to frame the monumental status of the architecture beyond. In this sense, emptiness employed as a framing device departs from Fieldoffice Architects' use of positive emptiness. Regarding the sweeping plazas that surround Mecanoo's National Kaohsiung Centre for the Arts or Toyo Ito's Taichung Metropolitan Opera House, emptiness has a subtractive effect—to remain relatively empty, and in doing so serve as a pedestal for the perfectly framed building. This proliferation of global architecture firms in the country suggests a lack of confidence by key decision-makers that Taiwan can contribute to an international discourse on the built environment.

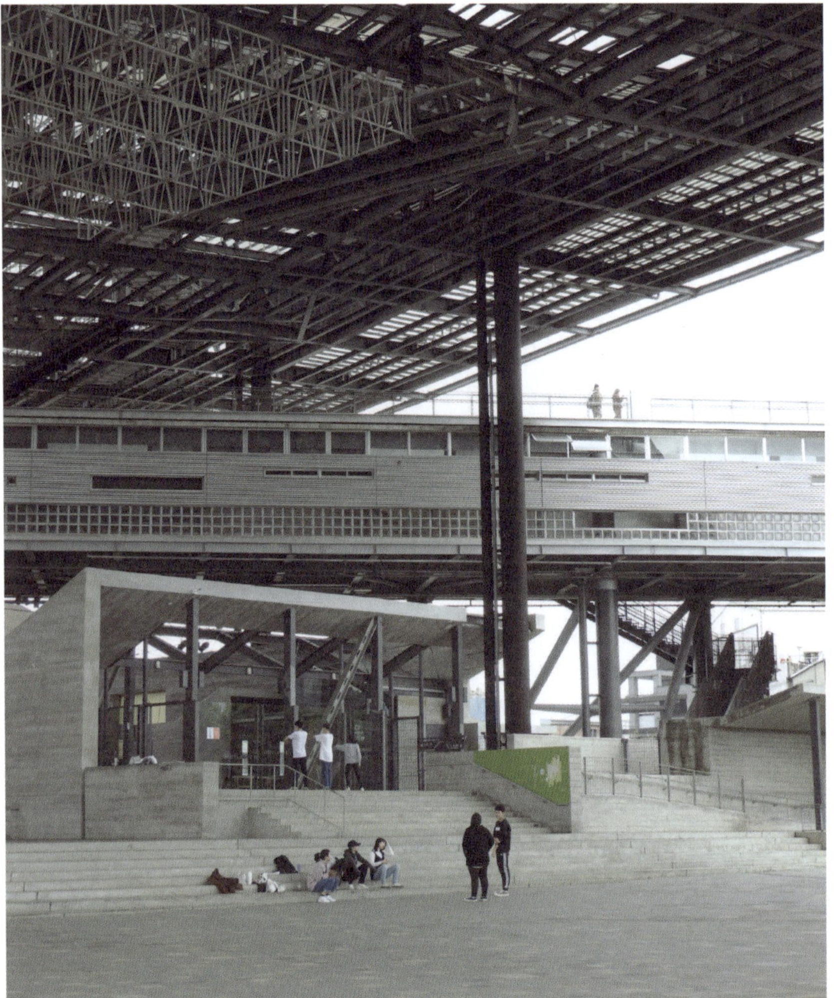

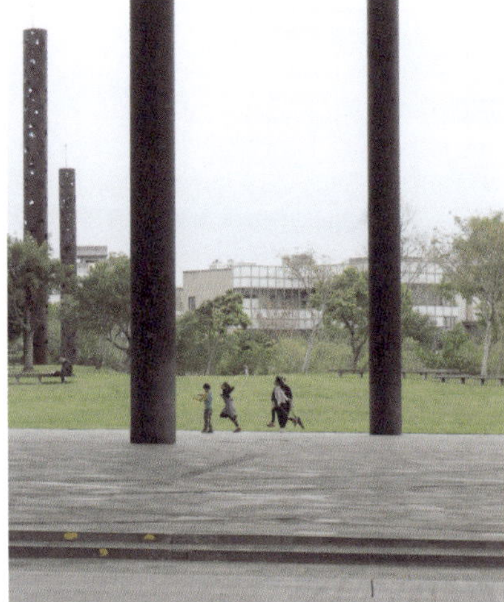

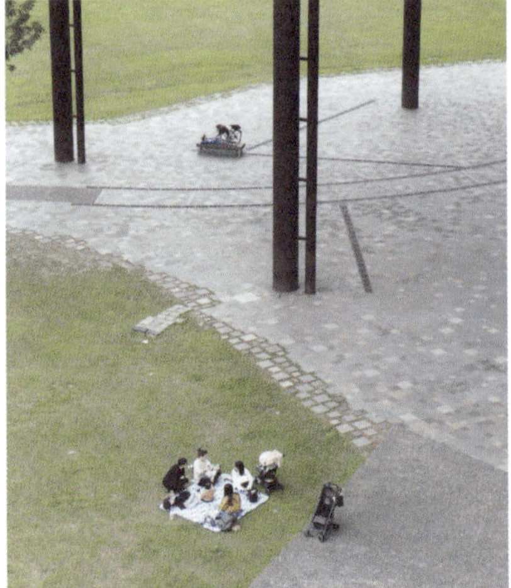

Fieldoffice Architects, Luodong Cultural Working House, 1999–2014. All images by Kenneth Wu.

By contrast, Huang Sheng-Yuan's approach aims to shift Taiwan's appetite for global architecture, and validate the efforts of Fieldoffice Architects for a cultural and social response that adds—rather than subtracts—from their immediate socio-spatial surroundings.

Whilst on an urban scale Fieldoffice Architects actively engage with the broader community to negotiate a collective output, they are equally invested in the internal social structure of their office to ensure authentic collaboration. The unique office structure of Fieldoffice Architects indicates a clear intent to break down the social and professional boundaries of architectural practice. The designers not only work together, but live together as well, spread across three houses surrounded by farmland—including one household which the workers share with Huang's mother.[13] While this arrangement might appear as a perversion of the professional model, it emerged naturally as a result of the early circumstances of the practice. Nevertheless, the blurring between personal and professional relationships has become a unique and organic solution to maintain an informal and democratic coexistence. Unsurprisingly, the practice certainly feels more like a "self-sustaining architectural school" than an office, and the team more like an intimate group of friends.[14] Their eagerness to experiment is a result of the trust placed in one another, regardless of experience. The disparate aesthetic output that emerges from this polyphonic decision-making process is what Huang is most proud of. The office is a collision of people from many different cities, with designers coming from Tainan, Changhua, Kaohsiung and Taitung alike to bring with them their own intrinsic interests; everybody "does what they like."[15] In the same way that Fieldoffice Architects found Yilan as a haven for self-sufficiency free from the power of urban structures, Huang has established a sense of self-sufficiency in the form of democratic collaboration. The success of this democratic approach means that Huang is at peace with the practice functioning in the future without him.[16] This philosophy has been ever-present since the practice's inception, with their name (田中央) literally translating to the unglorified banality of their circumstance: 'to be in the middle of the field.' It is not the place that is reflected in the aesthetic and formal output of work by Fieldoffice Architects, but rather a physical manifestation of the social network that the practice has established in order to produce what is seen as a collective Taiwanese voice.

To engage in architecture for Fieldoffice Architects is to enact in "a gentle process of a socio-political movement."[17] With this in mind, Fieldoffice Architects' sense of agency arguably finds its most sound manifestation at the Cloud Gate Theatre project in Tamsui. Following a seven year period of negotiations between both client and local authorities, Fieldoffice Architects have conceived the Cloud Gate Theatre as a performing arts centre which overlaps interests of the dance group, local government, and public. At ground level, the existing factory building is retained and repurposed as communal living quarters for the Cloud Gate Dance Theatre—Taiwan's leading dance company. Perched above is the newly constructed performance space, crowning the top of the hill. Crucially, beyond architectural intervention, the most apparent communal asset to the site is the 'emptiness' that Fieldoffice Architects strive for; an absence of a mono-specific architectural program. Whilst the architecture serves as the main protagonist, just as much planning and design went into the surrounding landscape to encourage a freedom of use by the local community. In addition, several assurances were set in motion to ensure the public intent of the project. Over the seven-year project period, a constant dialogue between Cloud Gate Dance Theatre and the New Taipei City government led to the signing of a Build-Operate-Transfer (BOT) contract for a forty-year operating right to use the public hillscape.[18] Undoubtedly, the formal expression of the theatre has become emblematic for the community, but it is equally the role of Fieldoffice Architects as intervening mediator to improve the qualitative outcome of the project both as a successful private organisation and an active public space. In the forty-year history of Cloud Gate Dance Theatre, before the completion of the new theatre complex, "there was never one day where all departments worked under the same roof."[19] Perhaps using their own practice as a proof of concept, Fieldoffice Architects' proposal for a gathering of vocation and living extends their belief of "creating a newly-found local life through professional integration."[20]

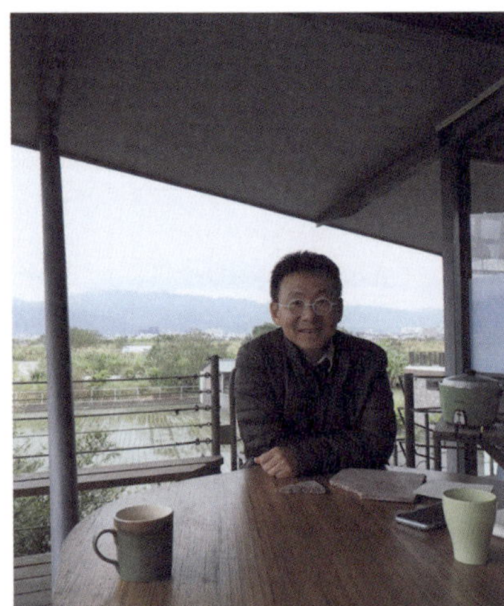

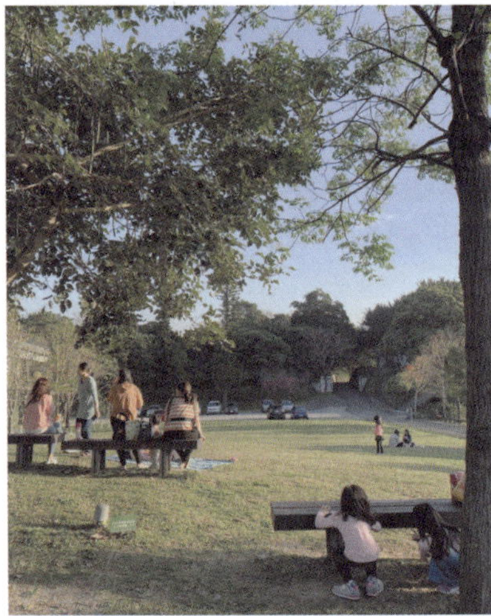

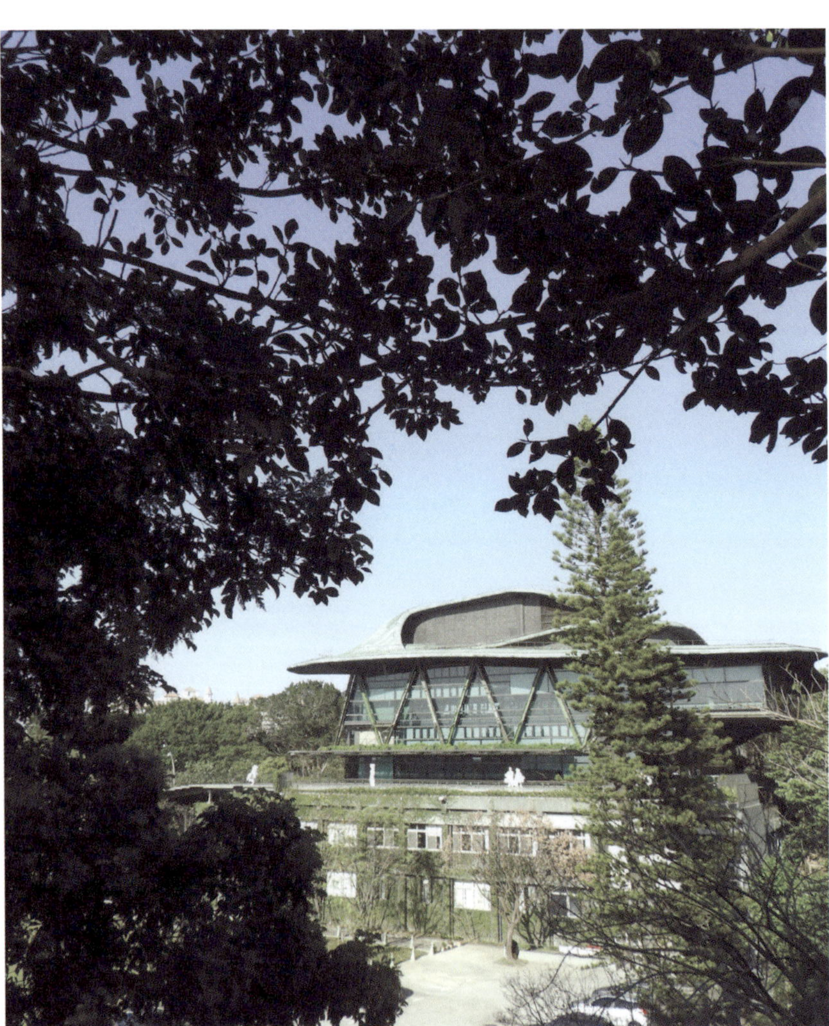

Top Left: Huang Sheng-Yuan at the Office terrace overlooking the surrounding farmscape, Yilan, 2020.

Bottom Left and Main: Fieldoffice Architects, Cloud Gate Theatre, 2008-2015.

The Cloud Gate Theatre project exemplifies the fertile creative spirit that exists within Taiwan; where architect, client and government can have an equal creative license to ensure a democratic process of mutual investment.

The introduction of the work of Fieldoffice Architects is a gentle assurance that Taiwan can continue to express their creative freedom in the face of political uncertainty. Topological place is just one factor that drives Taiwan's unique creative output and remaining within this classification of regionalism ignores the subtleties and differing realities of practices such as Fieldoffice Architects. Opening architectural discourse to a more pluralistic outlook will allow non-canonical knowledges to find their own epistemological validity within a global discourse. A greater focus can be placed on Taiwan's positive social context that enables the willingness to collaborate between authorities, professionals and the public. This may offer a new perspective on how architects can re-evaluate their immediate tools to shape the city and engage in greater connection with civic responsibility.

01 Fieldoffice Architects and Huang Sheng-Yuan, *Living in Place* (Tokyo: TOTO Publishing, 2015), 11.

02 Yilan's rich history of environmental consciousness stems from the farmers' and local government's successful protest against the construction of the Sixth Naphtha Cracking Plant from 1987 to 1991, utilising the new wave of liberalisation carried by the 1987 lifting of martial law. This political success later led to the formalisation of Yilan's branch of the Taiwan Environmental Protection Union NGO. For a detailed account of the Sixth Naphtha Cracking Project and other environmental resistance movements around Taiwan, see Ming-Sho Ho, "Resisting Naphtha Crackers: A historical survey of environmental politics in Taiwan," *China Perspectives Special Feature: The Rise of Environmentalism* 3 (2014).

03 Ibid., 10.

04 Huang Sheng-Yuan, interviewed by Hsin Yeh and Kenneth Wu, Yilan, February 20, 2020.

05 Duanfang Lu, "Entangled Histories of Modern Architecture," in *Non-West Modernist Past: On Architecture and Modernities*, ed. Jiat-Hwee Chang and William S. W. Lim (Singapore: World Scientific Publishing Co. Pte. Ltd., 2012).

06 Tom Avermaete et al., "Revisiting Critical Regionalism," *OASE #103 Critical Regionalism Revisited* (2019): 10.

07 Arendt specifically outlines political ability as "the ability to see things not only from one's own point of view but in the perspective of all those who happen to be present." Hannah Arendt, "The Crisis in Culture: Its Social and Political Significance," in *Between Past and Present* (New York: The Viking Press, 1961), 221-23.

08 Yasuaki Onoda, "The Architectural Culture of Taiwan, a Special Island," *A+U Feature: Making Friends with the Land, People and Time - Architecture in Taiwan* 18:10, 577 (2018): 92.

09 Juhani Pallasmaa, "Architecture for Healing - the Urban Surgery of Sheng-Yuan Huang," in *Living with Sky, Water & Mountain*, ed. Chun-Hsiung Wang and Wen-Jui Chang, 16th International Architecture Exhibition, Venice Biennale (Taiwan: Alliance for Architectural Modernity, 2018), 16.

10 Huang, interview.

11 Fieldoffice Architects and Huang Sheng-Yuan, *Living in Place*, 227.

12 Pallasmaa, "Architecture for Healing - the Urban Surgery of Sheng-Yuan Huang," 17.

13 Huang, interview.

14 Fieldoffice Architects and Huang Sheng-Yuan, *Living in Place*, 275.

15 Huang, interview.

16 葉連廣 [Yeh Lien-Kuang], "漸漸沒有「黃聲遠」的田中央？ [a Fieldoffice Architects Gradually without Huang Sheng-Yuan?]," in *在田中央, Mark* (Taipei: Locus Publishing, 2017), 60.; author's translation.

17 Chiu Chen-Yu, "Kaksi Arkkitehtia Taiwanista [Two Architects from Taiwan]," [Two Architects from Taiwan.] *Ark: Arkkitehti arkitekten* 112, no.6 (2015).

18 David Mead, "More Than Just a Theater," *Taiwan Review* 66, no. 6 (2016), https://taiwantoday.tw/news.php?unit=20&post=102545.

19 Fieldoffice Architects and Huang Sheng-Yuan, "以打造一個家的心情來接生 [Giving Birth in the Mindset of Building a Home]," in *在田中央, Mark* (Taipei: Locus Publishing, 2017), 42.; author's translation.

20 Fieldoffice Architects and Huang Sheng-Yuan, *Living in Place*, 11.

SURFACE TENSION

BLUEPRINTS FOR OBSERVING CONTAMINATION IN THE SYDNEY HARBOUR ESTUARY

Victoria King

King is a recent architectural graduate from the University of Melbourne. In 2019 King was awarded the RIBA Silver Medal for her graduating design thesis project 'Surface Tension.' The RIBA Silver Medal is awarded annually by the Royal Institute of British Architects and is considered the most prestiguous award for architectural students at Masters level.

Sydney Harbour is regarded as one of Australia's most significant biodiverse estuaries, yet, it is also one of its most contaminated. Walking along the folded edges of its tributaries and embayments one encounters a hybrid shoreline, where remnant bushland makes way for modified landscapes that have constructed a new littoral zone.[1] Growing up in close proximity to the city's prized waterway, relics of Sydney's industrial era are inconspicuous, yet ever-present.

A 'blind spot' is an obscuration of the visual field, an imperceptible territory that lies outside the limits of our awareness. The boundaries that define these limits of perception are often indiscernible, framed by a valuing of progress and modernisation that perpetually tells us what (and who) to overlook within the landscape. With the passing of time, processes of material instability in the built environment, namely contamination and decay, continue unobserved.

Indeed, 'blind spots' manifest outside of human timescales. For example, they may accumulate within the shifting sediments of the benthic seafloor, or at the infinitesimal crumbling of a seawall.[2] Conservationist Rachel Carson poignantly described these processes as acts of "slow violence" on the landscape "that patiently dispense their devastation outside of our flickering attention."[3]

Countering this, Ignasi de Solà-Morales' seminal text *Terrain Vague* provides an alternative evaluation of 'blind spots' within post-industrial contexts as productive sites for experimentation. Amidst debates in mid-1990's Western Europe over the future of large decommissioned and degraded industrial complexes, Solà-Morales theorised the *terrain vague* to find an alternative signification for the city's unincorporated margins. According to Solà-Morales, territories that were "un-inhabited, un-safe, un-productive" possessed an evocative potential established by the passing of time and the "loss of limits."[4] A paradigm shift in the era of the Anthropocene now prompts design practitioners to reconsider the spatial and temporal scales at which they work, opening new possibilities for the city's *terrains vagues*. By engaging with the complex reciprocity of human and non-human systems in the built environment, we can no longer overlook the impacts of contamination and decay on our fragile natural ecologies.

Opposite: Map of Sydney Harbour Estuary.
All images by author.

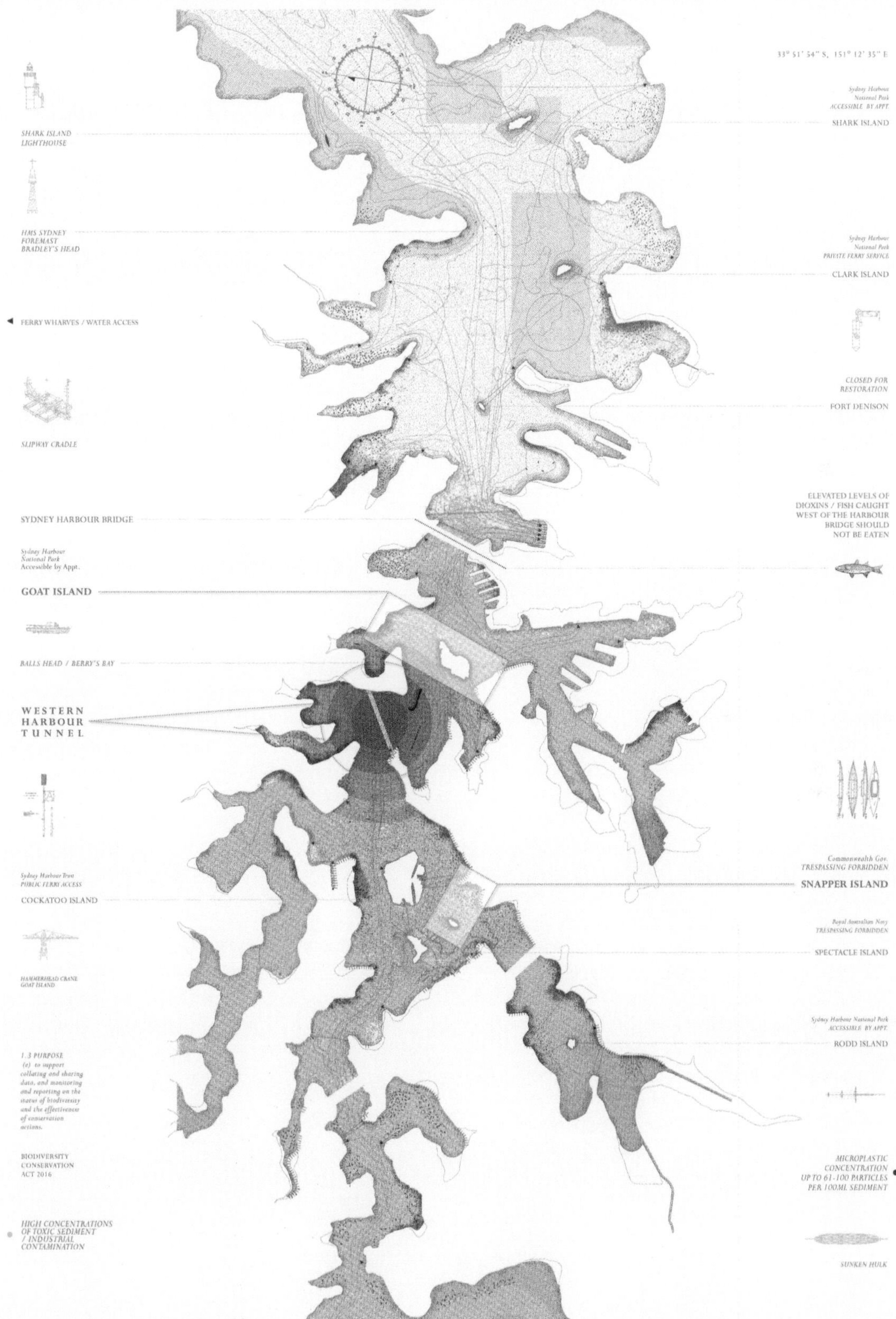

SYDNEY HARBOUR ESTUARY

This design thesis, completed under the guidance of Gini Lee and Alan Pert at the Melbourne School of Design, draws attention to several 'blind spots' that are perpetuating environmental degradation within the Sydney Harbour Estuary. Over two centuries of colonial occupation, wharves, shipyards and industrial relics now define a highly modified and dilapidating shoreline. Extensive land reclamation has resulted in the depletion of 80 percent of rocky intertidal habitats, whilst microplastic debris is accumulating to unprecedented levels.[5] Most disconcerting is the revelation that the Estuary bears a toxic underlay of heavy metals and dioxins so dispersed along the benthic sea floor it is impractical to remediate. Startlingly, this unstable condition remains largely outside of public perception, and as Gavin Birch, a geoscientist from the University of Sydney suggests, its effect on ecosystem functioning remains largely unknown and unmonitored.[6]

The continuing legacy of anthropogenic stress within the Estuary prompted a process of design research that surveyed its pre-industrial past, present and future state of degradation. This entailed a gathering of material from a wide variety of sources, incorporating data from multiple knowledge sets. A sample of this included footage fragments from immersive field trips in the Harbour (via dinghy, ferry and water taxi), measured site drawings of the Goat Island Shipyard, archival maps and photographs, collected scientific reports and literary descriptions, among others. From this, analytical drawing served as a critical method for synthesizing and making visible imperceptible connections across the Harbour. Nigel Bertram describes the potential of this process to construct new types of drawings that help to reveal the unseeable, "the act of drawing aids [the] analytical processes by allowing a coalescing of knowledge sets . . . a type of communication that explores and exposes ideas simultaneously."[7]

Emerging from and in tandem with the methods described above, five drawing sets speculate on the proposal of three marine observation facilities at the following sites: the proposed Western Harbour Tunnel, the working shipyard at Goat Island and the former naval training depot at Snapper Island. Each of these sites were revealed to exist "between the organic and the inorganic, between nature and artifice" and thus embody the rich potential of Solà-Morales' *terrain vague*.[8] Accordingly, they serve as fertile sites by which to imagine the way in which the archive of history may be brought into the cultural currency of the Anthropocene era. Within each drawing, the 'blueprint' was utilised as both a visual cue and conceptual framework to assign new responsibilities to relic, existing and proposed infrastructure within the Estuary.

The collective assemblage of drawings with complementary material—including film footage, archival imagery and physical models—combines to form a subjective yet holistic representation of Sydney Harbour as a complex cultural landscape. This method was similarly evident in Momoyo Kajima's curation of *Architectural Ethnography*, an exhibition for the Japanese Pavilion at the 2018 Venice Biennale.[9] By assembling diverse drawings of disparate scales and styles, Kajima expresses the potential of architectural drawing to exist as both instructive document and narrative device.

Drawing Set—Three Productive Artefacts

The selected drawing set examines three maritime relics: the Cardinal Mark, the Slipway and the Vessel, as prompts in the reinvention of harbour infrastructure to observe several anthropogenic stressors.

Opposite: Artefact One–The Cardinal Mark.

BALLS HEAD / *YURULBIN* / AQUATIC DISPOSAL

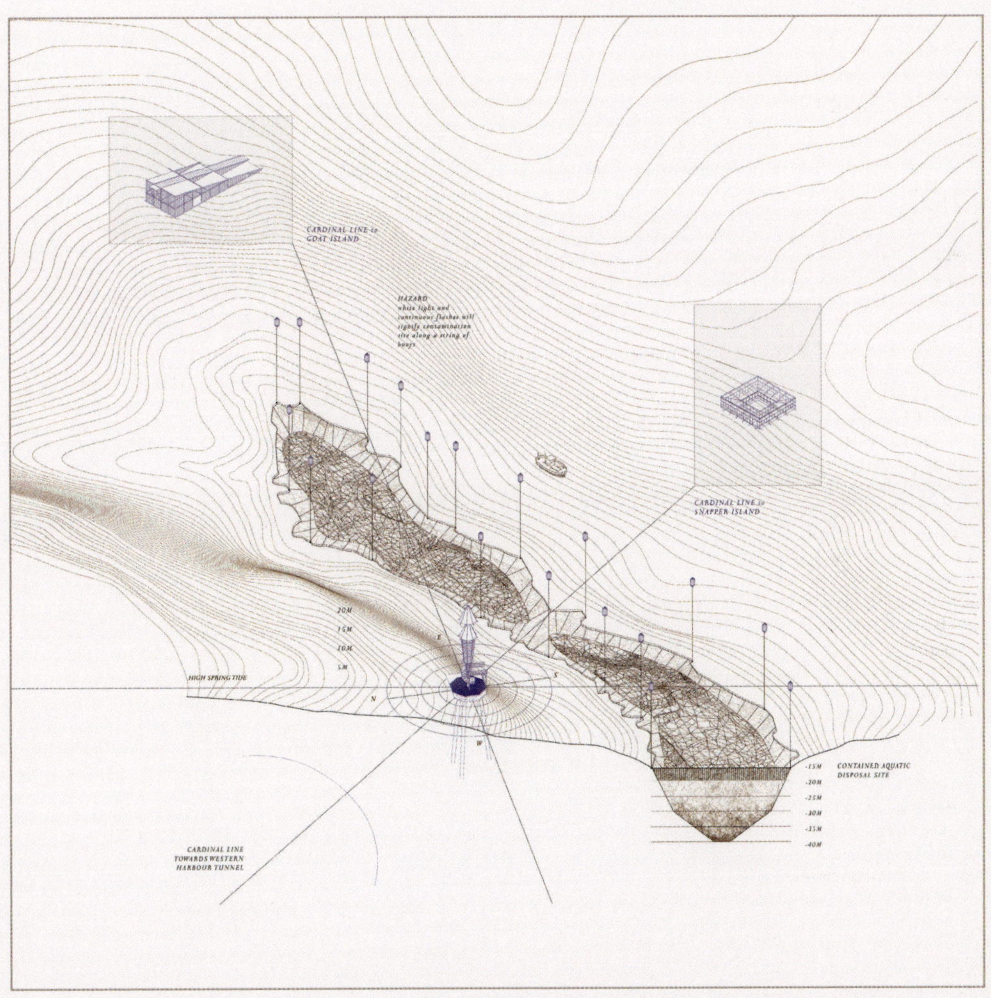

The cardinal mark indicates that safe water lies in a compass direction away from a site of underwater danger. Here, a cardinal mark is constructed upon the edge of the Balls Head 'sink hole', a monitoring beacon at the proposed dump site for half a million tonnes of contaminated sediment, dredged excess from the construction of the *Western Harbour Tunnel*. Continuous data collection will measure physical and biogeochemical variables, testing for traces of seepage within the water column.

GOAT ISLAND / *ME-MEL* / SHIPYARD

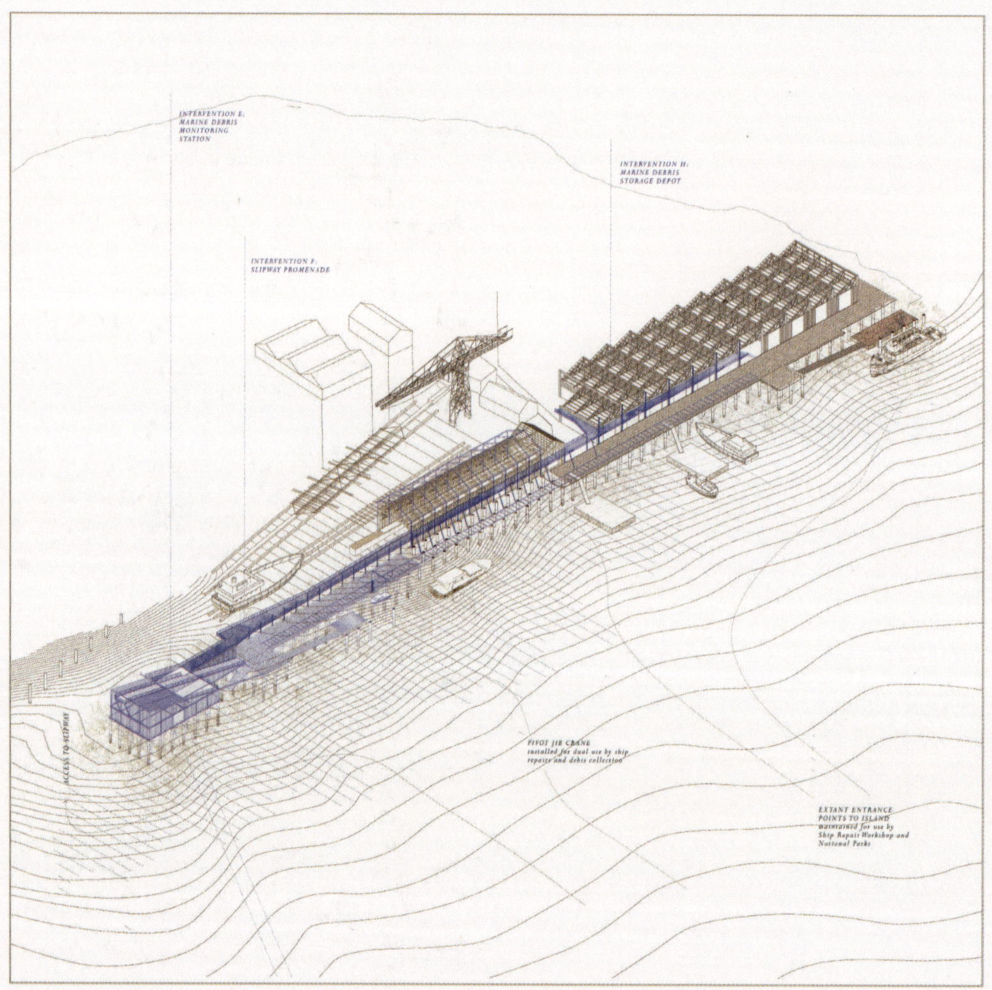

A slipway affords the transition of a vessel from land to sea. The reconstruction of the former broadside wharf establishes a collection and storage repository for marine debris, affording the transition of abiotic matter from sea to land. Debris is collected, analysed and observed along the promenade, aided by cranes, cradles and winches. The reconstruction of the wharf will form a datum of programs that reflect the new use of the island : a place of renewal for boats, the monitoring of middle estuary conditions and repository for collected marine debris.

Artefact One—The Cardinal Mark

Hundreds of buoys and cardinal markers assist safe navigation throughout Sydney Harbour. Using a combination of top marks, the Cardinal Mark indicates safe passage away from a site of underwater danger.

Plans for the imminent construction of the Western Harbour Tunnel, at the heart of the Harbour, threaten to dislodge 500,000 tonnes of contaminated sediment, stirring a toxic plume in its wake. Bioaccumulation of contaminated sediments increasingly threaten marine biota, observed in the strict ban on eating fish caught west of the Sydney Harbour Bridge.[10] In response, a fixed-point observation tower is proposed to signify the 40-metre depression in the harbour seafloor earmarked as the dump site for contained aquatic disposal. Here, the tapered silhouette of the Cardinal Mark has been flipped on its head, drawing attention to the concealment of contaminated material that lies below the water's surface. Serving as both anchor and mast, the Cardinal Mark encapsulates a field of buoyant devices monitoring contaminants in the water column.

Artefact Two—The Slipway

A slipway affords the transition of a vessel from sea to land, supported by a system of cradles and winches.

Goat Island bears the last industrial-era shipyard in Sydney Harbour that is still in functional use. In 1901, the island was claimed as headquarters of the Maritime Services Board, and for over 80 years was exploited as a shipyard for the maintenance of its fleet of working vessels. In 1994, the incorporation of the island into the Sydney Harbour National Park saw the working existence of its wharf workshop facilities significantly decline.

At this site, a proposal for the reconstruction of the collapsed broadside wharf provides new amenity as repository for the collection and storage of microplastic debris in the Estuary. Here, the functional qualities of a slipway are reconsidered for the retrieval of plastic debris, where a tapered docking station with sloping channels allows debris nets to be slipped (hauled) from the water for observation. The reconstructed wharf stitches together a datum of new structures—a trawling depot, elevated promenade and storage repository—amongst existing shipyard facilities.

Opposite: Artefact Two–The Slipway.

Artefact Three—The Vessel

A vessel is defined by a strict arrangement of decks and passageways, ordered from bow to stern. The seaworthiness of a vessel relies on the material stability of its hull, requiring continual repair and maintenance.

Snapper Island is the smallest island in Sydney Harbour, yet the most radically transformed. For millennia, the site was a rocky intertidal outcrop, colonised by oysters. In 1930, Snapper Island was reconstituted by naval officer Leonard Forsythe, who leased the Island to create a voluntary sea training establishment. Forsythe exerted his influence in a violent process of land reclamation, constructing a new island edge with stone seawalls formed to represent the bow and stern of a ship. Yet, since 1980 the site has been inconspicuously degrading, alongside transferal of ownership to the Commonwealth. A composite of foreign materials, corrugated iron, timber, lead paint and asbestos fragments sit atop deposits of reclaimed fill. The stone seawalls that Forsythe constructed 90 years ago are beginning to break down and are threatening to expose contaminated surface soils to the Harbour.

Speculating on the renewal of the former training depot, Snapper Island is re-conceived as a vessel and observation facility to stimulate the regeneration of depleted intertidal habitats. A collection of observation structures reconstructs lost fragments of the former training depot, including a fly deck and observation tower, while the foundations for a new biogenic rocky reef are prepared to stabilise the Island's eroding shoreline. Over time, recycled oyster shells meld with new oyster larvae to stimulate the accretionary growth of a larger rocky reef ecology. In doing so, non-human actants return as resident occupants of the island.

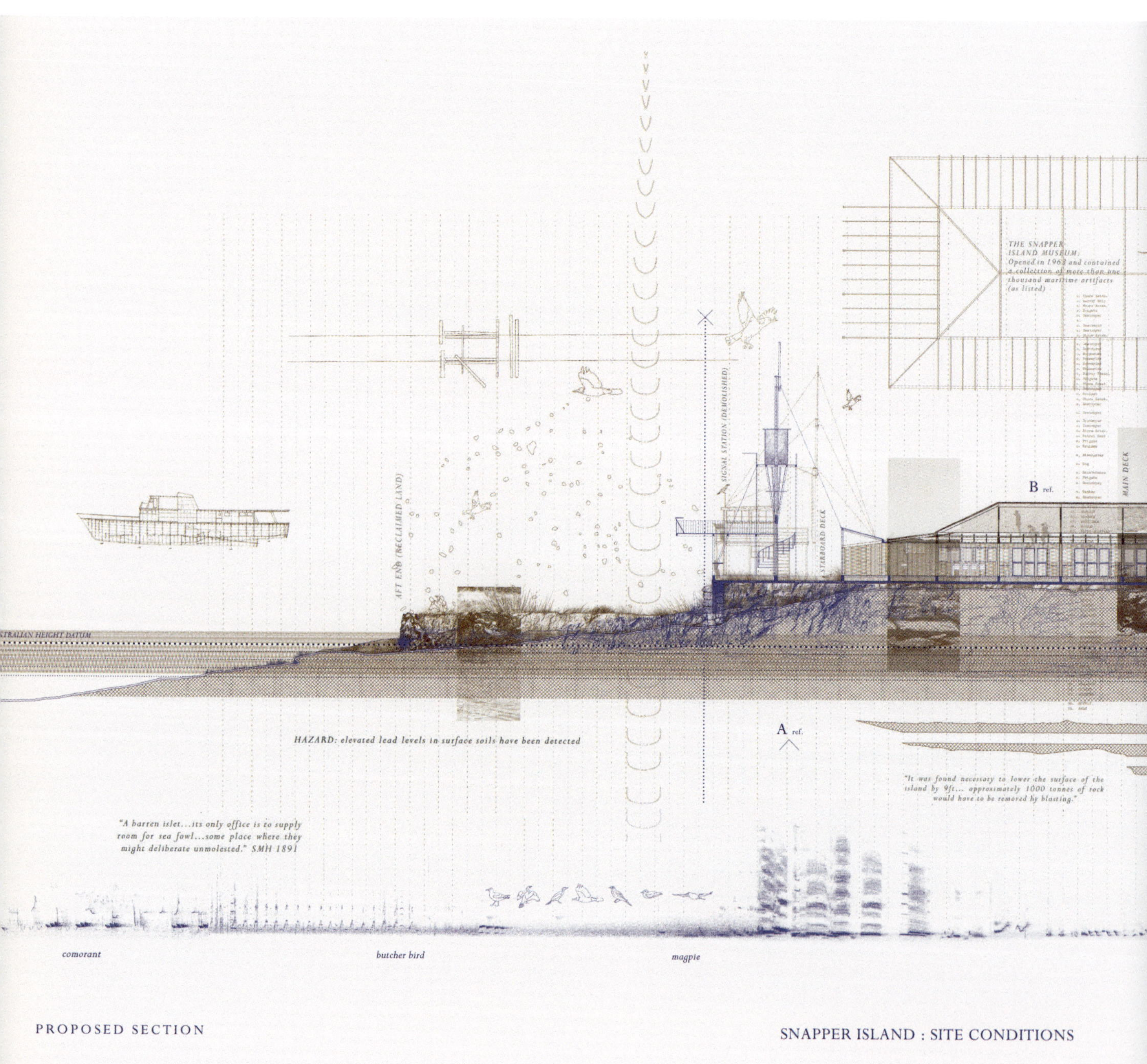

Artefact Three–The Vessel.

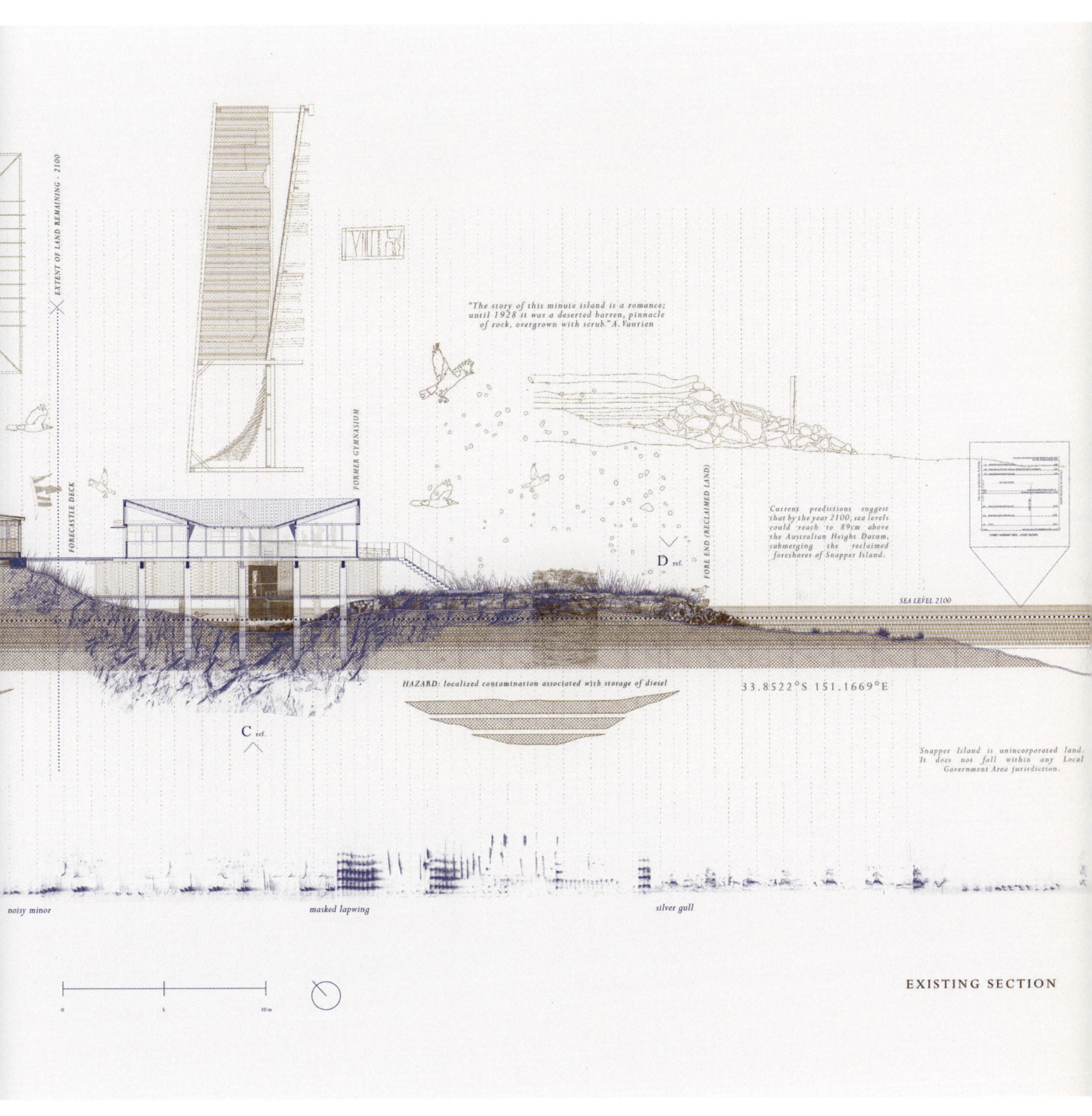
EXTENT OF LAND REMAINING - 2100
FORECASTLE DECK
FORMER GYMNASIUM
"The story of this minute island is a romance; until 1928 it was a deserted barren, pinnacle of rock, overgrown with scrub." A. Vaurien
D ref.
FORE END (RECLAIMED LAND)
Current predictions suggest that by the year 2100, sea levels could reach to 89cm above the Australian Height Datum, submerging the reclaimed foreshores of Snapper Island.
SEA LEVEL 2100
HAZARD: localized contamination associated with storage of diesel
33.8522°S 151.1669°E
C ref.
Snapper Island is unincorporated land. It does not fall within any Local Government Area jurisdiction.
noisy minor
masked lapwing
silver gull
0
5
10m
EXISTING SECTION

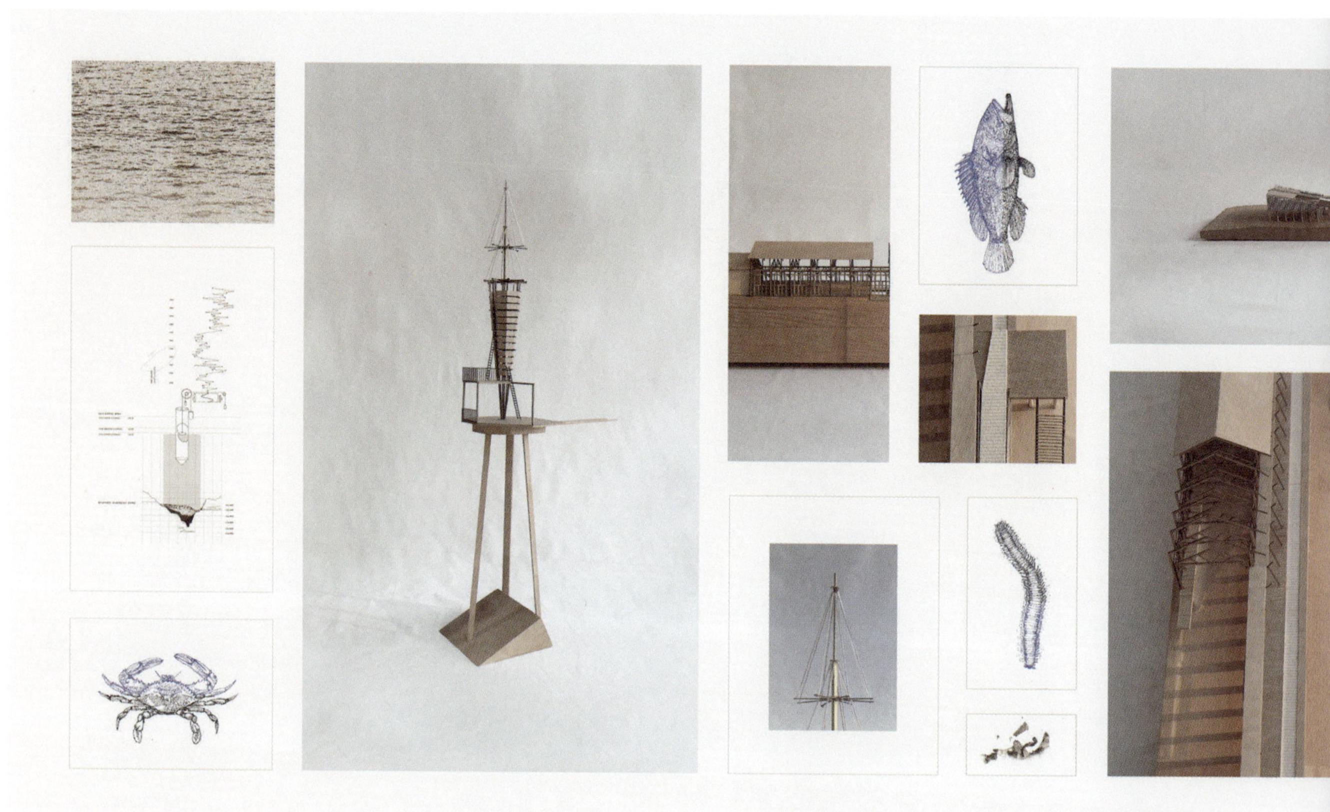

Breaking the Surface

By re-examining Solà-Morales' *terrain vague* within the context of the Anthropocene, we may work towards dissolving the perceptual boundaries that cast a blind eye to the effects of degradation within post-industrial landscapes such as the Sydney Harbour Estuary. Embracing such contexts as containers of a shared, yet sometimes imperceptible history, requires an engagement with new spatial and temporal scales and thus new methods of representation.[11] Accordingly, design practitioners are uniquely equipped to catalyse this process, by surveying the concealed past in order to speculate upon the imagined future.

The methods undertaken in this design thesis afforded a novel engagement with a familiar context, one that is simultaneously an evolving cultural landscape and vulnerable estuarine environment. This process could be applied to hundreds of sites across the Sydney Harbour Estuary, and indeed many more post-industrial contexts worldwide. Together, these territories offer rich potential to speculate on new ways to sensitively and transparently integrate our built and natural environments.

Material Survey-Three Martime Artefacts.

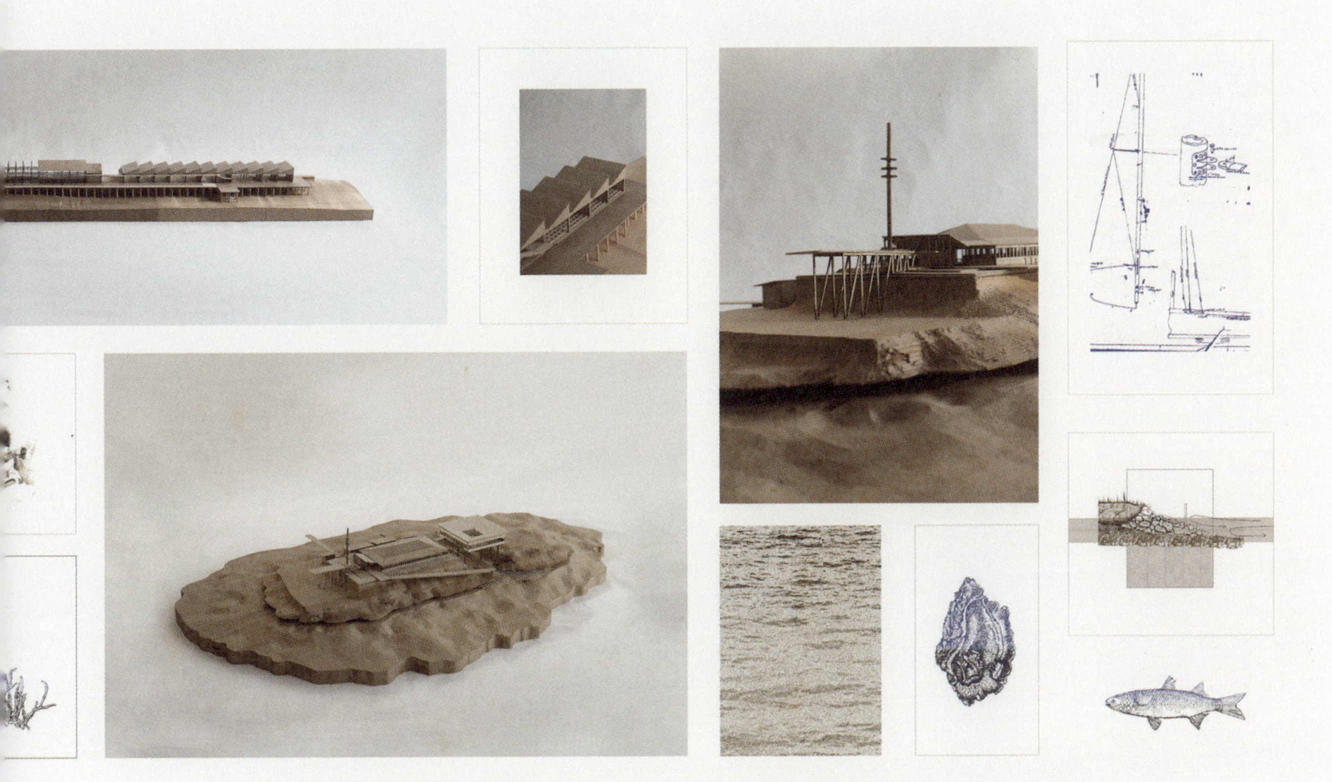

01 Littoral Zone: A term used in ecology that denotes the zone of the seashore between high- and low-water marks.
02 Benthic Zone: A term used in ecology that refers to the lowest level of a body of water, including the sediment layer.
03 Rachel Carson, *The Sea Around Us*, (Oxford: Oxford University Press, 1951), 6.
04 Ignasi de Solà-Morales, "Terrain Vague" in *Anyplace*, ed. Cynthia Davidson (Cambridge: MIT Press, 1995), 118-23.
05 Gavin Birch et al. "Sydney Harbour: A review of anthropogenic impacts on the biodiversity and ecosystem functioning of one of the world's largest natural harbours," *Marine and Freshwater Research* 66 (2015): 1088-1105.
06 Birch et al., "Sydney Harbour," 1088.
07 Nigel Bertram et al. *In Time with Water: Design Studies of 3 Australian Cities*, ed. Nigel Bertram and Catherine Murphy, (Crawley: UWA Publishing, 2019), 26.
08 Patrick Barron and Manuela Mariani, *Terrain Vague: Interstices at the Edge of the Pale*, (New York: Routledge, 2014), 2.
09 Momoyo Kajima, Laurent Stadler and Yu Iseki, *Architectural Ethnography*, Japan Pavilion at the 16th Venice Architecture Biennale,curators: Yvonne Farrell and Shelly McNamara, May 26-November 25, 2018.
10 Biota: A term used in ecology to refer to the animal and plant life of a particular habitat or region.
11 Barron and Mariani, *Terrain Vague*, 1.

CONTEMPLATING THE VOID

IN CONVERSATION WITH EDITION OFFICE

Aaron Roberts and Kim Bridgland are the directors of Edition Office, an architecture studio based in Melbourne. Edition Office crafts highly contextual, site-specific responses that advocate the profession's capacity to challenge accepted truths and desensitise us to dominant histories and narratives. Rather than specified readings, Edition Office's residential and museological works favour ambiguity and open-ended inquiry, across the oft bounded territories of architectural thought and practise. These seek to evoke a "taxonomy of perspectives," as well as less tangible, phenomenological qualities evoking the site and its custodians.[1]

With our curiosity piqued by their recent National Gallery of Victoria commission 'In Absence,' completed with Yhonnie Scarce, Inflection Vol. 07 editors initiated a dialogue with Aaron Roberts and Kim Bridgland, to interrogate their philosophical frameworks and architectural process. A concurrent resurgence in public debate around Reconciliation between Indigenous and non-Indigenous Australians added weight to a discussion centring on the scars of imposed and erased narratives. The highly tangible and spatial genesis of Edition Office's work through models, diagrams and exhibitions, informed a parallel lens bridging the conceptual and physical, inanimate and personal.

Edition Office & Yhonnie Scarce, In Absence, National Gallery of Victoria, 2019. Photography by Ben Hosking.

Thousands of black glass murnongs (yams) line the seemingly charred interior of the project's two central chambers. Together, these reference eels caught in Indigenous aquaculture systems and the interior of smoking trees used to preserve them.

Inflection: You have described your approach to practice and research as akin to an act of uncovering. Throughout your work, latent histories and narratives seem to be brought forth from the landscape to create cultural enquiry and dialogue. How important are the ideas of dissonance and historical narratives within architecture?

Edition Office: There is an immense range of cultural and historical narratives embedded within the built environment and within the sites that we seek to build upon as architects. These narratives, however, are not carried evenly within the general population of this country, as those storylines that represent the dominant cultural perspective (of white European descent) are privileged over those of minority voices, especially those of Aboriginal and Torres Strait Islander heritage. Dissonance occurs when an opportunity is created to see historical narratives outside of one's own cultural gaze, which may clash with the stories of place that we currently hold. As our towns and cities are often the backdrop to where we have lived and grown up, we generally accept these stories without questioning who or what they represent, and importantly what has been forgotten or ignored.

Architecture has an extremely important role not only in sensitively responding to the needs of the communities that it serves, but in giving presence to marginalised voices and their lived experience within our collective story. With that presence comes greater authority to have a stronger level of political self-determination.

Your recent NGV Commission, 'In Absence,' seeks to interrogate the false narrative of Terra Nullius. What inspired you to uncover these false narratives and how are they manifested in your project?

This nation was formed on the premise of great deceit and trauma to its Indigenous inhabitants. To allow this to happen a narrative had to be constructed within the collective mind of the Colonial project—that the original occupants of this land were not sufficiently worthy and that they had no rights to the lands that they had been caretakers of for over 60,000 years. The underlying premise of this false narrative still exists today and continues to devalue the lives of our First Nations people. Given the high level of public and media exposure the NGV architecture commission enables, we sought to utilise the opportunity to provide a platform to give a tangible presence to this narrative in a way that could not be ignored or turned away from.

This 'presence' is one half of how the work operates, as an affective physical entity of resonant scale within the NGV gardens, the split at its centre representing both the false absence of a people and the enormity of loss over 230 years of dispossession of Indigenous lands and lives. The other half of how this work operates is experienced linguistically—here in this piece of writing, and within the two symmetrical inner chambers of the work. Both provide a space for dialogue through which Indigenous and non-Indigenous communities can see one other as equals, providing an opportunity for knowledge sharing and truth telling.

In this project, you worked in collaboration with Indigenous artist Yhonnie Scarce. Can you expand on the significance of this collaboration, and the narratives that this work refers to?

We had admired Yhonnie's work for many years and saw the commission as an opportunity to reach out to her and start a conversation which we hoped might turn into a collaboration and friendship. That conversation formed a shared desire to bring exposure to Indigenous history and ingenuity that has been suppressed from our national story. With this exposure, we also hoped to highlight the erasure of First Nations perspectives from within our colonial history. The marginalisation of Indigenous voices has a long and painful history in this country that continues to this day. The more we give space for these voices to be heard, the more we open the doors to the truth telling process that we must go through if we are to provide any meaningful pathways towards reconciliation in this country.

The specific narratives that this work refers to are those of Indigenous architecture and infrastructure in the form of ancient stone fish and eel traps, and managed agriculture, which according to the law of the British Empire, were all requirements of a sufficiently evolved society, a society which therefore had rights to its own lands.

In your experience working with Indigenous Australians, what forms of knowledge have they been eager to share and what do you think the role of non-Indigenous Australians is in this process going forward?

There is so much knowledge and information out there, it is not locked behind closed doors, all we have to do is choose to see it and choose to engage. For the same reason that men should read books written by women so they can enjoy, support and better understand the lived experience of half the global population who are provided a different level of privilege, so too should non-Indigenous people engage with First Nation literature, music culture and politics. In doing this, there is no loss, there is no erosion of our own cultural heritage, or a giving up of who we are. Instead we are embracing the opportunity to push against the edges of our own personal understandings of the world, and to come to know its depth and complexity.

Opposite: Edition Office & Yhonnie Scarce, In Absence, National Gallery of Victoria, 2019. Photography by Ben Hosking.

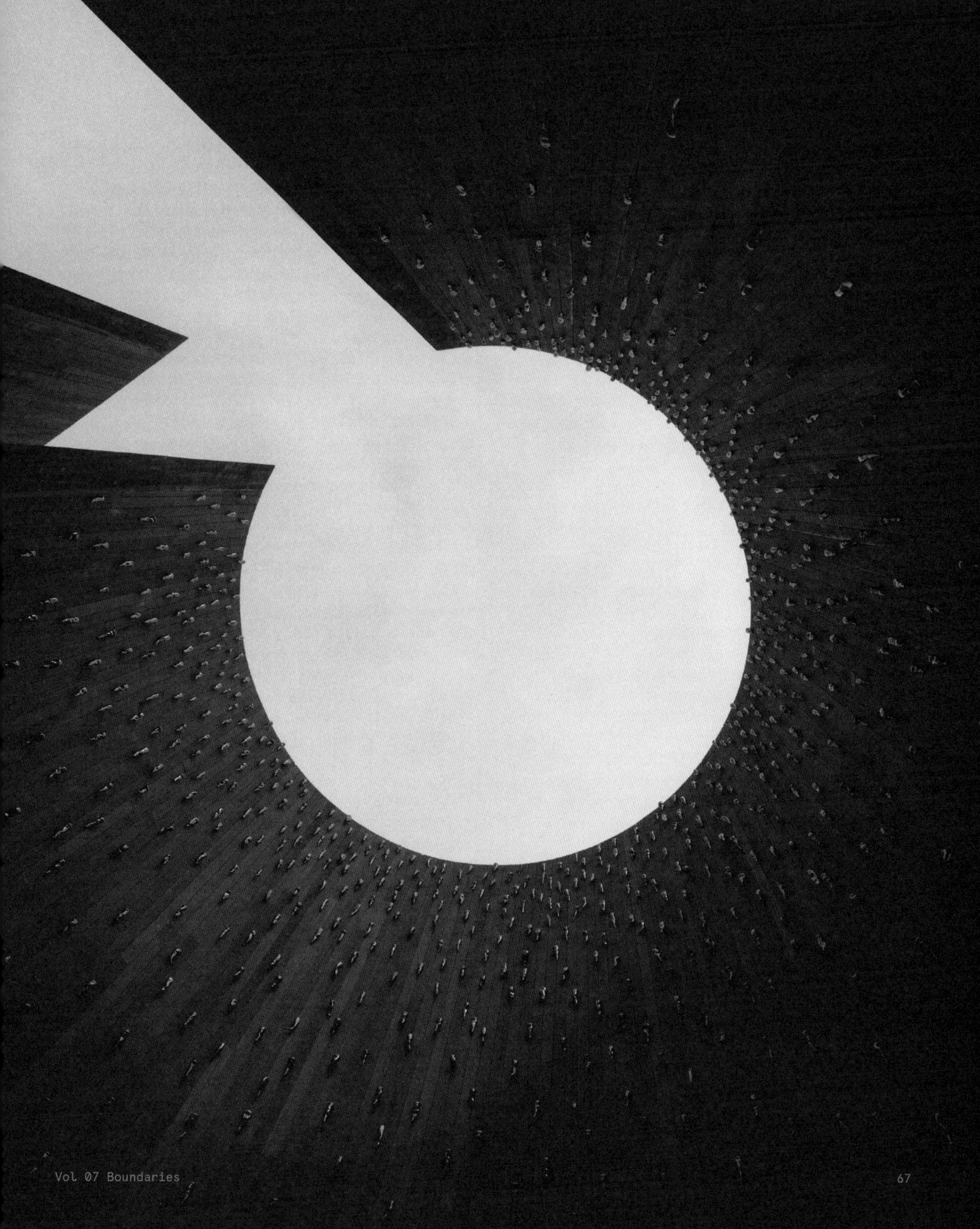

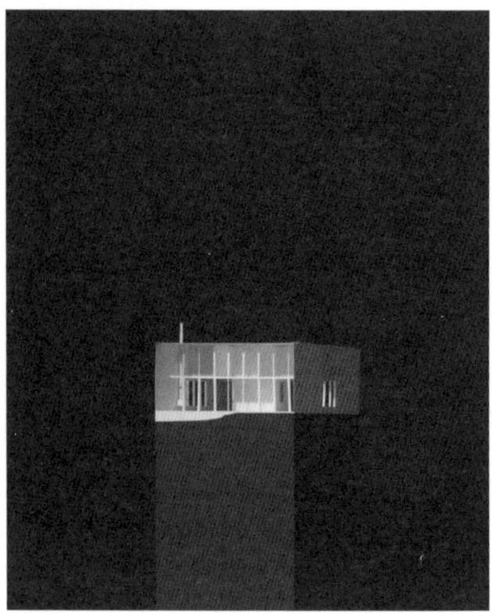

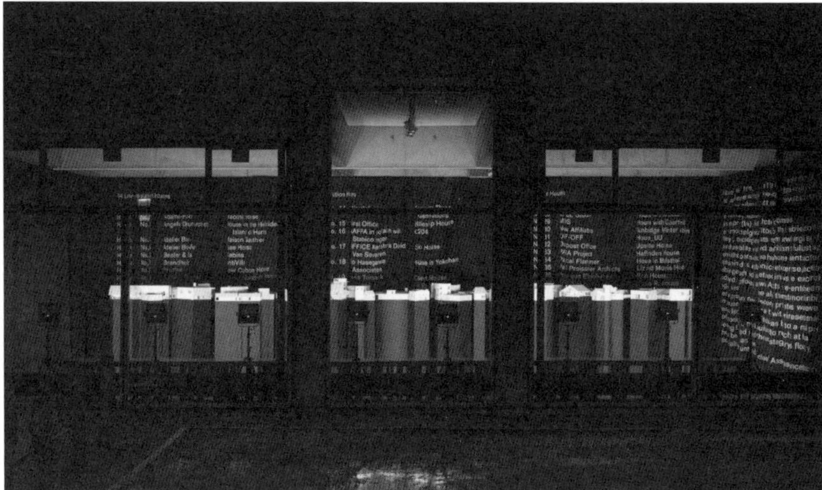

Do the scales of the gallery and the urban mutually inform each other in your work? Do you ever think of your architectural projects being experienced in a manner akin to your exhibited projects in galleries?

There is significant overlap and feedback between the work we present within a gallery setting, which we see as a form of discourse, and the architectural work that is built in urban or remote contexts. These parallel streams continue in the same trajectory and inform one another. We understand contemporary art to be a form of civic dialogue that uses the medium of the work to carry the ideas that we want to communicate. Architecture must be able to perform and engage simply for what it is, a physical mediator of space and time. Beyond this fundamental level of performance, we are incredibly interested in creating buildings that are able to trigger a response derived from our collective understanding of the world, aggregating and questioning these experiences through the lens of architecture. The late Caribbean poet and philosopher Édouard Glissant describes this collected socialised self as the "imaginary." For Glissant "the imaginary is all the ways a culture has of perceiving and conceiving of the world. Hence every human culture will have its own particular imaginary [sic]."[2] It is then the active discourse that we each bring to the encounter of architecture, and through it the world, that is of interest. We observe how this relational dialogue is influenced by our culturally conditioned concept of the world, our gaze, which is further conditioned or modified by the discourse, associations and provocations that take place within the gallery setting.

You recently featured in the exhibition '44 Low-Resolution Houses,' which examined the influence of technology and the virtual upon the contemporary experience of architecture. How do you see this museological work in the context of your other projects, which are often highly contextual and spatially resonant? Could it be framed as an antithesis which brings into focus your interest in site and culture?

This exhibition gathered together a number of architects and projects that seek to use basic geometric primitives as their primary formal or spatial generator. Rather than as an antithesis, we see this approach as being central to our work. Although they are each sited within, and are responsive to their location, our projects are not telling the story of that place, but act as a reference point or mediator for how that location may be experienced. We find that a considered use of acute restraint within a project provides a very useful tool for facilitating this type of redirection of focus. For example, the highly clarified plans of both the 'For Our Country' memorial and 'In Absence,' allow for them to be encountered quite authentically. As they are absent of recognisable or familiar aesthetic languages, these projects require you to experience them on your own terms. It is your active encounter of these works that brings into focus your own relationship to the context (site, culture, self) that they are situated within.

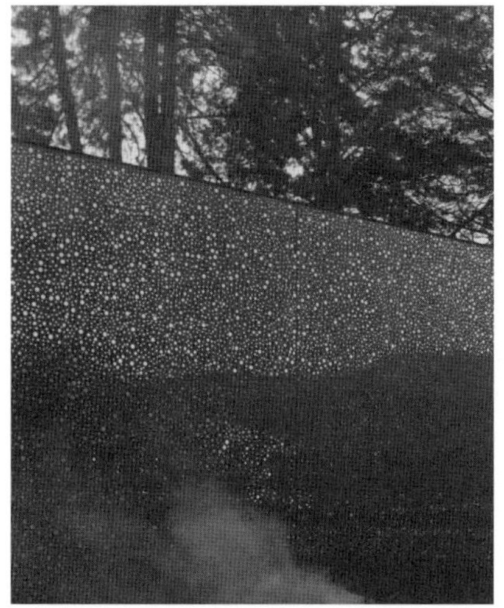

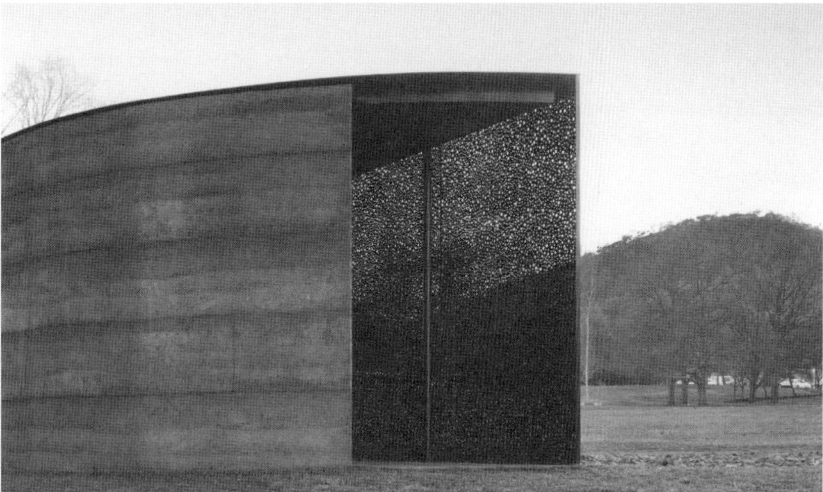

Both your NGV Commission 'In Absence' and Aboriginal and Torres Strait Islander War Memorial 'For Our Country' articulate the void and acknowledge loss. Could you expand upon how you believe architects and Australians more generally today should be engaging with this absence and rebuilding our appreciation and safeguarding of Indigenous knowledge?

Both of these projects provide an opportunity to contemplate Indigenous loss at the same as their strength and resilience, in a way that seeks to privilege the Indigenous gaze and to normalise exposure to it. We see that it is the responsibility of non-Indigenous Australians to personally seek out and to become informed about Aboriginal and Torres Strait Islander knowledge and history in order to overcome the inadequate education we have received and to overcome the bias and gaps in empathy we inherit when we fail to understand those who are different from us. The architectural community has significant power in deciding what narratives we choose to give credibility and authority to when embedded within the fabric of our towns and cities. For this reason, architecture is inherently a cultural and political act, however if we fail to see this relationship, if we fail to see that so many minority voices are typically missing from the table, we'll continue to disenfranchise them, even if it is our intention to do the opposite. This is why education is only a step along the path to supporting self-determined, Indigenous-led expression and autonomy within the built environment.

A reflective, sober tone seems to permeate the formal gestures and materiality of your work. Does this relate to a postcolonial Australian consciousness you are hoping to evoke?

We seek to create a distilled, elemental quality in our work so that it may achieve a level of singularity. We aim for the work to become an entity in and of itself, a medium, and from that point exist in relationship to the context that it is situated within. 'In Absence,' perhaps our most clarified work, sets up a relationship to its context and acts as a medium to carry cultural narratives through the essential spatial and material qualities of the project. We understand context to be environmental, topological, climatic, social, cultural and historical, which is driven by the encounter we each bring to our interaction with it. In this way the works are ambiguous. They are not themselves carriers of knowledge, but are devices through which we can see the narrative lines we each bring to the work.

01 Dan Rule, "The Volume of Place," 2016, accessed June 1, 2020. http://edition-office.com/archive/the-volume-of-place/

02 Édouard Glissant, *Poetics of Relation*, ed. Betsy Wing (The University of Michigan Press, 1997).

Opposite: Edition Office with Michael Meredith & MOS, 44 Low-Resolution Houses, Princeton University, 2018. Photography by Michael Vahrenwald/ Esto.

Above: Edition Office & Daniel Boyd, For Our Country, 2019. Photography by Ben Hosking.

THE TERRITORIES OF BIM

Peggy Deamer

Architecture's potential role in our spatial, economic, and social reality depends on breaking the spell of architectural autonomy—the idea that our discipline has its own independent history, concerns, and language; and that it has its own dedicated disciples who preserve these conditions. One could say that this spell was created to justify all the things that architects could not know or control: budget, procurement, construction methods, carbon-footprint, post-occupancy, etc. But technology today allows us to know many of these things early on and now claiming ignorance and/or disinterest is not acceptable, wise, or helpful. At the same time, while 'architecture' gains from technological innovation, not all advantages are distributed equally. Tools that make architecture a strong player in the economy, which is so important, can also leave behind those that actually produce the project—the architectural worker.

Building Information Modelling (BIM) becomes a lightning rod in this evaluation. As a digital, collaborative, 3-D approach to design and hailed as the managerial system that pulls architecture into the 21st century, it takes both the heat and the kudos for what 'technology' has wrought on our profession. While not the be-all-and-end-all of programs, apps, or softwares that coordinate the interaction of AEC actors, it is a reasonable stand-in for the issue this article wants to explore: the role of information technology on architectural work.

As I have written elsewhere, BIM is singularly responsible for deflecting the traditional idea of the architect as the special, singular holder of design, sitting at the top of a pyramid as his/her designs trickle down to increasingly distant and passive office workers, constructors, trades, and fabricators.[1] The sharing of the BIM model with the owners, the staff, the contractors, the engineers, and the fabricators has multiple positive consequences for the architect. It ensures that a design does not go too far down the pipeline before it is determined to be too expensive, unbuildable in the manner conceived, or hideously carbon producing. It assumes that everyone involved in the process is a contributor to the design outcome, making all 'designers' in the true definition of the term—figuring out a positive and elegant outcome. In conceiving and developing the project three-dimensionally, it forces designers to think more spatially and experientially. And in making us smarter about the things that matter to the owner, it makes us more trustworthy.

The technological displacement of the hierarchical pyramid model of designer-to-builder with a horizontal one based on collaboration is powerful in itself. SHoP Architects, innovators in BIM and other (then) 'new technologies,' has from the start taken advantage of various software technologies in different projects. Their BIM-powered on-time and on-budget delivery of the West Side Highway crossing bridge post-9/11 (2002) rested on their ability to work in 4-D, where critical path scheduling or sequencing and assembly of construction determined design from the start. For their Mitchell Park project for Greenport, NY (2002-5), they used CAC-CAM technology to produce the first project—at least for them, and probably at this scale for others—to design and build without one printed, 2-D drawing; design parametrics/codes went directly to production parametrics/codes. Their Meatpacking District housing, Porter House (2003) for which they were architect and developer, was noteworthy for integrating the parameters of zoning, air rights, costs, scheduling, and structural limitations. SHoP's 290 Mulberry Street condominium project (2008) was the first office-wide implementation of BIM, where staff working on the complex brick-panelled facade could negotiate the various parameters with live links to the owner's consultants (financial and legal), the contractor (phasing, quantity and quality verification), and the architect's own systems consultants. Their ability to document existing conditions and project the procurement of the innovative design for the new 'thick' and occupiable facade for the Fashion Institute of Technology (FIT) (unbuilt, 2003-2006)—complex programmatically, structurally, and materially—led to their getting the larger commission of construction administration for all of FIT's campus-wide upgrade because they could produce better, faster, and more complete documentation of the as-built conditions and quickly identify structural and mechanical clashes in all the renovation work.

But much of BIM's magic rests on its implications as much as on its technology. One is the entrée into other areas of expertise through the holistic picture that BIM offers to extend reach, power, and reward. SHoP is as proud of the fact that contractors and subs are involved and empowered from the start as they are about the efficiencies BIM brings to the projects.[2] It was clear that traditional architectural firms consistently failed to grasp the full potential for BIM to facilitate in-depth and financially consequential decision-making while WeWork did. And the building information technology consultancy group, CASE Inc., whose mission it was to train firms in the use of BIM, became the design/development arm of their client, WeWork.[3] Researchers at Kieran Timberlake (one being my former student) are leaders in BIM-integrated environmental impact assessment; while advancing the shifts to a low- or zero-carbon economy, the firm has captured a whole new area of architectural expertise.

Another area of expertise is the new kind of contracts that follow logically from the shared, collaborative design process offered by BIM. Clearly, if the contractor is participating early on in the project's design, s/he has been chosen before the competitive bidding process, itself an important break with standard proceedings that prevent the inclusion of the builder in design decisions and instigate animosity between the architect, owner, and contractor. But in further redefining the contractual relationship between these three main players, Integrated Project Delivery (IPD) contracts have them share risk, reward, and responsibility. SHoP was one of the first firms to use this type of contract, taking full advantage of the control and reward that comes with it. In IPD, the owner, architect, and relevant contractors together decide upon, validate the project's targets, confer and agree on resolutions affecting cost and scheduling unanimously. The owner puts aside the agreed upon project budget—the sum of the direct costs plus the profit that will be divided by all parties—and when the project comes in on time and on budget, all share the profit. All, in other words, are incentivised to be transparent and honest throughout the process. Direct costs of materials and labour are paid throughout, so no one is stiffed in the process. No money is put aside for potential lawsuits, since they are prohibited in this type of trust-based contract. It is almost magical in changing animosity into mutual support, in replacing defensiveness with openness, and in allowing architects to be rewarded from the success of a project.[4]

In addition, the implicit advantage of BIM is the reconception of the staff worker. Because design is 'real' from the start (materials identified and their thicknesses established; etc.), those working in BIM must know something about the physical making of space. Younger staff, all using BIM, are therefore no longer mere draftspeople, but actual design implementers. Indeed, in this generation of design firms, many principals do not know BIM and are particularly reliant on young staff to explore meaningful design solutions. In the firms that really embrace BIM, the old hierarchy of office power is shaken. Larger social implications follow. Within the office, the 'designer/employer' and 'staff/employee' distinction begins to disintegrate. External to the office context, architectural workers identify with construction workers, whose future tasks the designer needs to imagine, and the divide between white-collar and blue-collar workers could break down.

In other words, what starts out as technical advantages for the BIM worker becomes identity advantages as well, and as such, bring changes in how we identify with others and from there, society.

But for the most part, this is not how BIM is experienced, nor has it brought these social adjustments. Staff do not generally feel empowered and resent their role as 'Revit-monkey.' Where the former draughtsperson role at least offered the satisfaction of making beautiful drawings, Revit/BIM seems to limit choices from a prescribed library with virtually no aesthetic appeal and encourages endless iterations and wheel-spinning exasperation. Firm owners resent the fact that Autodesk and other software producers have an economic incentive to make a firm dependent on their software, even as people in the firm know more and quickly move beyond the software's limitations.

I have always thought that the failure of BIM to fully realise its capacity to reconceive the value, relevance, and rewards of architectural work lay with the conservative nature of our discipline, both in the academy and in practice. In the academy, we still teach in a Beaux-Art system of charrettes, individualism, competition, design and representational virtuosity, heroic programs, and the honoring of past masters; in this context, BIM is marginalised. And in the profession, despite the logical displacement of the designer/draftsperson wrought by BIM, firms use BIM not as a new system of reorganising the design process but merely as a system of production efficiency and better coordination with contractors; many, if not most, firm owners have little interest in displacing the traditional hierarchy of designers over production staff, partners over employees.[5] I still believe that these conceptual limits to real boundary breakthroughs are pointless and self-imposed. But something else, I have come to see, limits BIM's realisation and a democratic redefinition of architectural work.

Implicit in the BIM construct—and information technology that it is standing in for—is a techno-centrism that foregrounds technology as an end and not a means. Techno-centrism, driven by a capitalist economy that supports companies motivated by shareholder short-term profits, does not have either the empowered worker or a just spatial society in its ideology.

Specific aspects of its ideology can be examined. First, the owner of the software, as hinted above, is motivated to capture and control the technical apparati used in an office. Its goal is defensive, not expansive, and a company like Autodesk, which sells not just the software but the in-house technical support that comes with it, wants to secure its territory. Parallel to this support, however, the designers in the office, more agile and inventive than the big corporation, have already recoded and remixed their various apps according to their needs. Software companies have little incentive to have its users learn coding and develop their own unpaying modes to explore design more thoroughly, communally, and intuitively.[6]

Second, architecture is an extremely small market, and any company wanting to survive in the techno-driven economy will quickly move outside the architectural market. Autodesk for example, came into being with AutoCAD (the main supplier of BIM through Revit,) grew with its Sketchbook purchase and Revit development, and now has moved into digital prototyping for all forms of manufacturing and into visual effects, color grading, animation, game development, and design visualisation for media and entertainment.[7] Expansion into these areas is natural for survival in capitalism and Autodesk is not a particular culprit. While this cross-fertilisation of technologies and techniques can offer architecture extra-disciplinary skills, it is just the case that the prize for them is not a better architectural profession. It is selling its product by ensuring that offices depend on their goods.

Third, BIM operates in a discourse of efficiency that does not question who gains or loses when things are made more efficiently, nor whether the efficient outcomes are themselves desirable. Architecture firms buy into this discourse when they adapt BIM for production streamlining in lieu of rethinking the design work apparatus. As Phil Bernstein has analogised, focusing exclusively on productivity, efficiency, and cost/schedule conformance "is to miss the real opportunity for change, like measuring the success of surgery not by whether the patient is cured but by how fast the procedure was completed."[8] At the same time, it ignores the actual people who perform the productive function. BIM should emphasise the ability of participants to contribute ideas and solutions, not push digital items from one side of the computer to the other. Indeed, the collaborative design process is anything but efficient; it is messy, rhizomatic, creative, and often time consuming. If we want to 'cure the patient,' we need to embrace the fact that collective creativity is not a linear process. Again, efficiency is the call capitalism makes to those who own the means of production, not those supplying the labour.

Fourth, techno-centrism participates in the particularly hyped-up techno-utopianism that is central to the neoliberal economy. Information technology currently drives the American economy, and while the government turns a blind eye to its labour abuses and impingement on privacy and civil liberties, the IT industry wants us consumers to believe that we need to constantly update our knowledge and appliances to avoid being left behind; we are not supposed to stop and contemplate where this leads. BIMers merely follow this trend when it announces proudly that 'Next generation BIM' is shaping the construction industry's digital future with advancements in generative design (software algorithms, data analytics, wearables, augmented/virtual/mixed reality, 3D printing, robotic construction, manufacturing of buildings, reality capture, digital twins, IOTs, and artificial intelligence). Do we really want to see 3-D printed buildings? Does that work for either architects or architecture? Does anyone other than the developer want robots doing construction in lieu of people, or artificial intelligence designing our built environment in lieu of architects?

And finally, as these last questions imply, techno-centrism is intrinsically entwined with automation. As sociologists of technology have suggested, automation can be divided into two categories: the sort that replaces labour with machines; and that which creates new, more complex tasks for humans. The first pushes down wages and employment; the second can restore workers' fortunes. Historically, it is suggested, these two drives have stayed in balance by market forces—where automation led to a labour glut, more productive ways were found to put people to work (this is why previous predictions of technology-induced joblessness have proved to be mostly wrong.) But today, with tax codes that expose governmental biases towards capital, labour loses out and unemployment becomes permanent. As Daron Acemoglu and Pascual Restrepo write, "an 'almost singular focus' on artificial intelligence, might be tilting firms towards automation, and away from thinking up new tasks for people."[9] We can maybe get behind the idea of a universal basic income that will support the unemployed construction workers (robots) and architects (artificial intelligence), but I suspect we would all rather be working, and consider now why we are going down this road.

Thoughts

Architectural information technology has been examined here in light of its capacity to break down architectural boundaries that are neither rewarding nor socially productive. BIM serves as an example of a technology that offers great possibilities for this breakdown but also seems to keep other labour-unfriendly boundaries intact. It hopefully is clear that this article does not argue against technological advances in our profession. If we want to change the circumstances of architectural workers, be they employees or employers, we need to grab on to a new future; there is nothing to be gained by nostalgia for the past. But upholding technology for technology's sake, without an understanding of how it is deployed and for whom, misses the fact that it is not the technology that can save us; it is, rather, how it is managed, shared, and put to use. All of us who work in our discipline, either in the academy or the profession, must be alert to undemocratic boundaries that come in the name of 'innovation.' The real boundaries that need to be cracked are those that prevent all of us very smart and very well educated architects from making our fullest contribution to spatial and communal justice.

01 See the introductions to both *Building (in) the Future: Recasting Architectural Labor*, co-editor with Phil Bernstein (New Haven: Yale School of Architecture, 2010) and *BIM in Academia*, co-editor with Phil Bernstein (New York: Princeton Architectural Press, 2011), as well as "Marx, BIM, and Contemporary Labor" in *BIM Futures 2013 - Thought Leaders* Kensek, Noble eds. (New York: Routledge, 2014).

02 At FIT, SHoP set up a site office in a trailer - an I-Room equipped with SMART Boards, where architect, consultants, contractor, and key trades could meet physically and virtually and review up-to-date progress models. This came with immediate buy-in and collaboration with all actors.

03 See Wanda Lau, "WeWork Acquires Case, Inc," *Architect*, August 05, 2015, https://www.architectmagazine.com/practice/wework-acquires-case-inc_o.
As we now know, WeWork has been dethroned as the premier new approach to both work and real estate. But at the time, 2015, the move to WeWork by CASE founders David Fano, Federico Negro, and Steve Sanderson, catapulted them into a much more powerful and lucrative arena. Many of my former students chose to work at WeWork instead of a traditional architectural office, knowing they would make about three times as much money, but also lured by the utopian message of WeWork's founder regarding a networked office environment.

04 For more on this unusual kind of contract and how it came to be, see my "Contracts of Relation" *e-flux: Representation*, Nick Axel, ed. 2017. The origin of IPD is not a development of traditional architectural contracts but the result of legal theorists who proposed "relational contracts" that incentivised mutual and lasting trust in a contract rather than punishment for not adhering to rigid forms of required behaviour and deliverables.

05 In 2015, I spent a summer interviewing 'BIM managers,' those people assigned to help a firm transition to BIM and work with all the people in the office to coordinate efforts. Almost all indicated that the firms that experienced the most satisfaction from BIM were offices where the partners were fully on board for the hierarchical changes that came with it. But all indicated that these partners were rare, and prevented real organisational change.

06 In 2014 and 2015, I followed SHoP's use of and struggle with BIM/Revit. They were delighted that BIM had opened up doors but were frustrated that they had quickly moved beyond Revit's capacity.

07 Much of *Avatar*'s visual effects were created with Autodesk media and entertainment software. Autodesk software also played a role in the visual effects of *Alice in Wonderland, The Curious Case of Benjamin Button, Harry Potter and the Deathly Hallows, Iron Man 2,* and many others.

08 Phil Bernstein, "Why the Field of Architecture Needs A New Business Model," *Architectural Record*, June 1, 2018. https://www.architecturalrecord.com/articles/13462-why-the-field-of-architecture-needs-a-new-business-model.

09 See Daron Acemoglu and Pascual Restrepo, "Robots and Jobs: Evidence from US Labor Markets," https://www-journals-uchicago-edu.eu1.proxy.openathens.net/doi/pdfplus/10.1086%2F705716. The authors also say that there is no guarantee that the workforce can up-skill to complete the new-economy tasks that innovators might dream up.

MISTAKEN IDENTITY

ARCHITECTS AS WORKERS AND THE POLARISING PANDEMIC

Frank Burridge

M-A-N-I-F-E-S-T-O

1
Enforce labor laws that prohibit unpaid internships, unpaid overtime; refuse unpaid competitions.

2
Reject fees based on percentage of construction or hourly fees and instead calculate value based on the money we save our clients or gain them.

3
Stop peddling a product – buildings – and focus on the unique value architects help realize through spatial services.

4
Enforce wage transparency across the discipline.

5
Establish a union for architects, designers, academics and interns in architecture and design.

6
Demystify the architect as solo creative genius; no honors for architects who don't acknowledge their staff.

7
Licensure upon completion of degree.

8
Change professional architecture organizations to advocate for the living conditions of architects.

9
Support research about labor rights in architecture.

10
Implement democratic alternatives to the free market system of development.

T-H-E
A-R-C-H-I-T-E-C-T-U-R-E
L-O-B-B-Y

Fig 1: Manifesto of The Architecture Lobby.
All images by The Architecture Lobby.

The Architecture Lobby is an international not-for-profit organisation that is dedicated to scrutinising the borders that structure our profession and changing them where they are unfair or unjust. Importantly, the Lobby is not only about achieving a set of outcomes that seek to improve the industry and the lot of architects. It also involves a shift in the way we see ourselves and our work, from which flows a shift in the way we relate to others and operate in the world. While The Architecture Lobby has a clear set of goals (Fig. 1), of equal importance is the process of architectural workers coming together, communicating and relating our experiences as workers, producing and sharing knowledge by working on political or social projects together, building up a way of seeing and acting in the world through productive disagreement and debate as equals, and providing the kind of mutual support, empathy and care that accompany solidarity and cooperation.

One of the insistent demands of the Lobby is that architects recognise themselves as *workers*. What might seem at first a trivially true statement—that we work—is given weight when we understand that our self-conception entails a certain way of relating to others. There are other self-conceptions that are tempting to take on—we could see ourselves as artists, geniuses, martyrs, service providers, social engineers, entrepreneurs, and each of these self-conceptions also gives us a different way of relating to others. The most common and deceptive misconception held by architects who care about social change is the idea that the primary way we create change is through our designs alone. This is usually the result of a misplaced or too narrow self-conception on the part of the architect. A few common misconceptions about the 'politics' of architecture and the way we recognise ourselves can be cleared up by looking at architecture through Jacques Rancière's notion of three 'regimes of art.'[1]

Mistaken Identity

Proponents of the 'ethical regime of art' believe works of art ought to tell people what is right, and indeed that educating the ignorant is the responsibility of art. Historical examples explain this most clearly. The works of playwright Bertolt Brecht used unexpected theatrical breaks to jolt people into an awareness of the artificiality of the show they were watching, ultimately telling them not to be passive consumers but active participants in judging the show; in assessing a portrayed moral dilemma or solving a mystery. Brecht's 'political' art rested on the assumption that audience members are not already thinking about what they are seeing, and that he was in a position to tell them how they should behave. Thus, it turns out to be a politics of social control through dictating the behavior of others.[2] For all one respects Brecht's politics and his plays, his is a position of hubris, which reminds us of architects who also see their work as 'telling,' 'dictating' or 'revealing' something to a user who is presumed to be passive and ignorant. At the beginning of the last century at AEG, Peter Behrens, along with his assistants Charles-Édouard Jeanneret, Ludwig Mies van der Rohe, Adolf Meyer and Walter Gropius, mass produced functional household objects designed to educate the masses on the modern way of life. They sought to place in citizens' homes objects that were functional but were also symbols of a new way of inhabiting the world, a new social order. As much as architects love to love this stuff, it is born of a desire to control, in this case to control the new German citizen.[3] The 'ethical regime of art' is premised on the idea that art has an ethical function to uphold social order, which would require us (architects) to see ourselves as separate from and more superior than the people we educate, such that we could tell others how they 'should' behave and how they 'should' live. It is a righteous position. This is at odds with the self-conception the Lobby demands, which is about seeing oneself as a worker equal to other kinds of workers and as fundamentally equal to those who use our designs.

Proponents of the 'representative regime of art' typically see themselves as artists by virtue of adhering to the established set of conventions of an art form. The conventions of modernity tell us two things: that each art form is defined by its material, whether paint, stone, words, space, and so on; and that artists use these materials to explore their art form in and for itself, which makes them autonomous from other kinds of making—e.g. those who make stone sculptures are doing something different from those who lay the stone in sidewalk curbs, or those who program digital artworks are different to those who program customer databases. Based on these conventions, it is tempting to see ourselves (architects) as artists who are (or, should be) autonomous from the mundane conditions of the industry that would sully our art (developers cutting costs, builders swapping out materials for cheaper products, planners telling us to change material finishes and so on). This would let us see developers, planners, builders and consultants as philistines who erode our art by trying to squeeze every dollar out of our architecture. This way of seeing would let us blame others for getting in the way of our making beautiful architecture. It would also lead us to believe that reaching the level of fine art, of beauty, in our works of architecture, despite these philistines, is a 'political' act because it involves a struggle against the prevailing economic and social conditions (in which we are not rightfully recognised as autonomous artists). The resulting architecture looks to us like a symbol of this struggle. We might then be tempted to call this architecture 'political' in as much as we are 'saving' our disciplinary ground. But in reality, this struggle is based on our own misconception that our work is separate from and above other kinds of work, and therefore that we ourselves are above other kinds of workers (both those we work with, and those who use our buildings). What the resulting architecture *represents* under the 'representative regime of art,' then, is our idea of disciplinary superiority. Like the 'ethical regime of art,' we can only believe in it if we place ourselves outside of and above other kinds of workers.

In the 'aesthetic regime of art,' art is not political because it serves to uphold the 'correct' social order, nor because it defends a set of disciplinary conventions and their sanctimonious place in society. Art is political because it models certain behaviours and experiences that foreground freedom and equality. Art lets you take the stuff out of which we construct our societies (words, stone, buildings, speech, anything really) and have complete freedom to rearrange that stuff into any configuration whatsoever. Anyone can do it—we often find the most unexpected people making art. This freedom is not for artists alone. Those viewing art enter a mode of looking in which they interpret and translate what they see, hear and touch into something that is meaningful for them. This private act of translation is an *aesthetic* act insofar as the viewer arrests the stuff that appears before them and constructs something new from it for themselves. It matches the artist's own aesthetic act of seizing some sort of material, seeing it otherwise to its typical uses and deploying it to their creative ends. In their aesthetic mode of looking, there is a kind of equality between those who make and those who view, which is opposed to the idea that those who view are merely passive à la Brecht. This aesthetic mode of looking can be applied to anything whatsoever, and therein lies another equality.

While in no way exhausting Rancière's notion of the 'aesthetic regime of art,' these cursory examples show there is a certain set of liberties and equalities in art which are of the aesthetic sort. It is not yet political liberty or equality, but art can provide a taste for freedom and a taste for equality, and thus open the way to the dream of creating these in society, as well as a sense that this is, indeed, possible.[4] Art in the aesthetic regime also provides a model for political action insofar as making and viewing art shows us that freedom and equality are not only states-of-affairs to be achieved in the future (what atrocities have been committed under a promise for these two things in the future), but are behaviours that we implement in the present—they are the very ways of making, seeing and doing that we take on in order to create equality and liberty for real.[5]

A consequence of Rancière's diagnosis of these 'regimes of art' is that an architect's design cannot stand in for activism. While Rancière's framework is useful to clarify some misconceptions about the way we recognise ourselves and the politics of design, Rancière has less to say about political activism itself.[6] Here we take leave from his theory. Architects do not become political through their designs, but because they participate in a network of activism—whether that be protesting, campaigning, organising, arguing, petitioning, researching, lobbying, teaching, learning and all the other ways you get your hands dirty while doing real politics and creating real social change. Designing can become one political act among many for an agent who is thoroughly involved in activism, but it never stands in for political action. Design becomes political when it is made by and for people who are struggling to have their voices heard as political voices, and who are operating in solidarity with other people who are more marginalised and whose voices are less heard.

Architects as Workers

Identifying ourselves as and with workers is the ground for The Architecture Lobby's activism. We do not shy away from the fact that we are workers, that we labour under the same conditions of economic production as other workers. We are therefore compelled to take the social and economic conditions of our work very seriously. We must ask: who is paying for our labour? Who is benefiting from it? Do we think this is right? And if we cannot do anything about it, why not and how can we change that?[7] We also have a responsibility to listen to and participate in the discourses of other kinds of workers and those who are excluded from the sphere of work, because our struggles are bound up together. It involves taking seriously the material conditions of our labour and the social problems these conditions pose—the intersections between the power dynamics of labour with gender, race, citizenship status, class and so on. We have to ask ourselves: why is it that *I* am able to do this kind of work, to get this kind of education, pass the necessary exams, to access working visas in other countries—and inversely, why is it that others struggle to or cannot? Because they cannot afford to 'gain experience' via unpaid internships? Because their voices are disregarded due to where they are from? Because they took time off work or study to raise children? Because they are worried that if they lose their job they will be considered too close to retirement age to find a new one? And so on. (Fig. 2)

In short, a consequence of seeing ourselves as workers is sensitivity to the material, social and political conditions that let us work. We are therefore compelled to do what we can to protect and enhance those conditions—namely, to protect freedoms and equalities that exist. Seeing ourselves as workers also means identifying with other kinds of workers, and we are therefore compelled to do what we can to go about creating freedom and equality where they do not exist. These are concerns that flow naturally from seeing ourselves as workers.

One of the unsavory aspects of a labour-oriented group of architect-activists, so I have been told by some architects and academics in Victoria, is the emphasis on architects as workers and the distinction this emphasis rests on: worker 'versus' owner. On the one hand I am told it is too antagonistic to describe the collaborative nature of architectural workplaces: owners working side by side with workers, and workers having agency to decide and manage important aspects of projects. This might be true of some architecture practices, but one only needs to look to @archishame on Instagram or the recent spate of COVID-19 firings in architecture firms to see that exploitation, unpaid overtime and antagonistic managerial practices are widespread. On the other hand, I am told emphasising the worker/owner distinction spoils architects' artistic autonomy with the mud of real material conditions of architectural labour by focusing on *working* rather than *works* (of architecture). This argument implies that we should ignore the realities of exploitation in our industry. It brings to mind the Ishigami apologists, who said: sure it was bad that Ishigami used unpaid labour for his Serpentine Pavilion, but look at how beautiful the architecture is—as though the ends justify the means. This is merely an excuse to continue the entrenched exploitation of vulnerable and precarious workers. The same can be said of apologists for Gehry's Guggenheim Museum in Abu Dhabi, which was built with indentured labour.[8] If anything, the fact that some architects and academics are worried about us identifying as and with workers is a good sign: they intuit the structural changes to our profession which flow from it.

The Polarising Pandemic

The worker/owner distinction has been proven salient by some architects' responses to the COVID-19 pandemic. The fact that many firms knee-jerked to firing workers in order to protect their bottom line proves that the distinction accurately describes an important power dynamic in architecture practice. The owners who lay off staff may think the way through the financial uncertainty of the pandemic is to fire their workers, sit tight on whatever profits they can protect, and 'dip into the labour pool' when things pick up again. The Architecture Lobby has been collecting testimonies from workers during this period, locally and internationally. Some of them are truly astounding. At the time of writing this article, our local survey has collected several reports of firms firing multiple staff due to COVID-19. We have had many informal testimonies of staff being 'asked' to take unpaid leave or be let go without notice—especially students of architecture and international workers, who are disproportionately affected—and the Lobby's international survey has gathered dozens of stunningly negative reports.[9] These actions are evidence that the antagonism of wage-workers by owners is still real in architecture, even in Australia where we 'have it pretty good.' The worker/owner division is one of the primary fault lines of inequality in our discipline. Without recognising these boundaries, we have no hope of making the industry fairer.

A glimmer of what could exist beyond the worker/owner power dynamic can be seen in the fact that many architectural firms in Australia are having ongoing, transparent dialogues with their workers about the developing pandemic and taking all measures to avoid firing (of which there are many on offer from state and federal governments—tax breaks, business loans, JobKeeper etc.). They see their workers as uniquely valuable, not as fungible labour; they see firing workers as taking away their livelihoods, not as protecting profits; they see the 'labour pool' as unemployed and struggling people, not as an economic convenience for their business. In short, these firms are declaring through their actions that we, as architects, are in this together, and that cooperation is the way through. The glimmer I see here is of a future where cooperation is the primary labour dynamic, not the worker/owner division. Much as these businesses should be commended for their actions during the pandemic, they are like 'benevolent dictatorships': even though things are good, the power ultimately rests at the top. They operate under hierarchical business structures with conventional employer/employee contracts. When it comes to choosing between protecting people or protecting profits, the workers' voice is only proportional to the owner's ear.

The difference between these two responses to COVID-19—the knee-jerk firers and the benevolent dictators—is not just a different way of running a business. It is a different way of seeing the world: one in which other people are resources to extract profits from, the other in which benefit is mutually derived by people with common goals working together. The latter reaches its ideal in the form of cooperatives, because in cooperatives not only is benefit mutually derived from cooperation, but the cooperating parties are freely associating with one another. Workers are not forced to relinquish power to an employer and sell their labour at a wage.

Members of The Architecture Lobby are engaged in projects in Victoria and around the globe to promote, educate and raise consciousness about cooperation as a viable replacement for conventional modes of practice. The international project involves developing a network of cooperative businesses that can share expertise and mutually benefit one another. Locally, we have been staging public events with speakers who run or are involved in cooperatives and are building our shared resources on how to start and run a cooperative architecture practice in Australia.

In other parts of the world, Lobby members are guiding small firm owners to cooperativise their practices. These projects are particularly relevant during the COVID-19 fallout. Historically, the number of cooperatives increases during recessions (ArchiTeam started during the early 1990s recession in Australia) and members of cooperatives report being less adversely affected by economic downturns than other kinds of workers.[10] It is our belief that enfranchising workers by structuring offices democratically will lead to the elimination of the pay gap, an increase in architecture firms designing zero carbon footprint buildings and leading our industry towards carbon neutrality, a distribution of profit that more accurately reflects the value of architectural labour, increases in business efficiency and increases in worker's empowerment and general job satisfaction.[11]

As workers, we should band together and create that future for ourselves. Firm owners and directors are, for the most part, not interested in doing it for us.

T-H-E—A-R-C-H-I-T-E-C-T-U-R-E—L-O-B-B-Y

I-N-D-U-S-T-R-I-A-L—R-E-L-A-T-I-O-N-S—I-N—V-I-C-

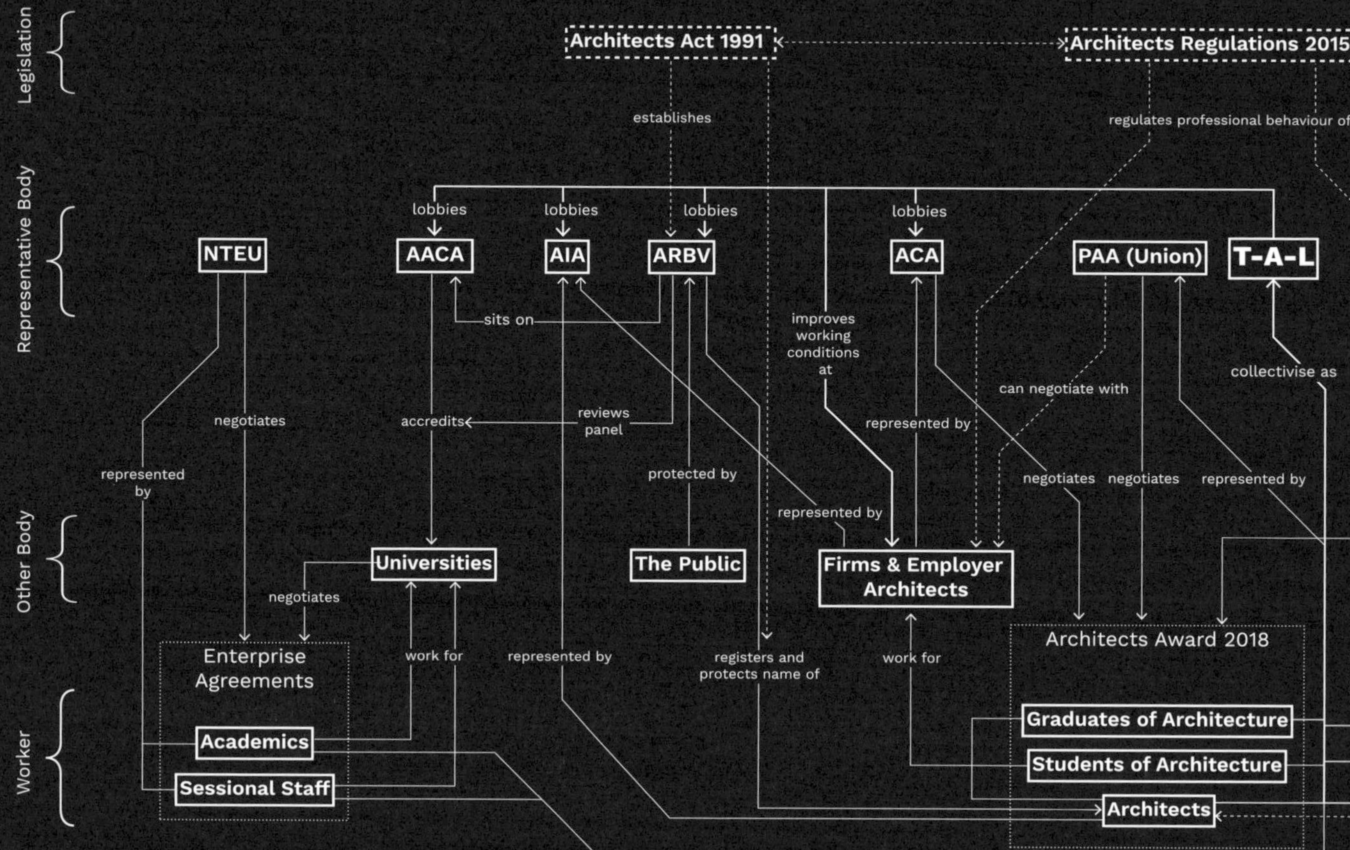

AACA = Architects Accreditation Council of Australia. The AACA is made up of the Registration Board of each state.

ARBV = Architect's Registration Board of Victoria. Each state has one.

AIA = Australian Institute of Architects. A professional institute of architects, graduates, students and affiliates in Australia.

ACA = Association of Consulting Architects. Represents employers in industrial matters (e.g. negotiating award wages). ACA is a registered organisation under the Fair Work Registered Organisation Act.

Fig 2: Industrial Conditions of Architectural Labour in Victoria.

PAA = Professional Architects Austalia. This is our union, which represents architectural works in industrial matters. Members can join to negotiate Bargaining Agreements with their employers. It is a chapter of Professionals Australia, a union for professionals in many industries. Professionals Australia is a registered business name of the Association of Professional Engineers, Scientists and Managers, Australia (APESMA), which is a registered organisation under the Fair Work Registered Organisation Act.

NTEU = National Tertiary Education Union. This is a union for people working at unversities. It is a registered organisation under the Fair Work Organisations Act.

-R-I-A

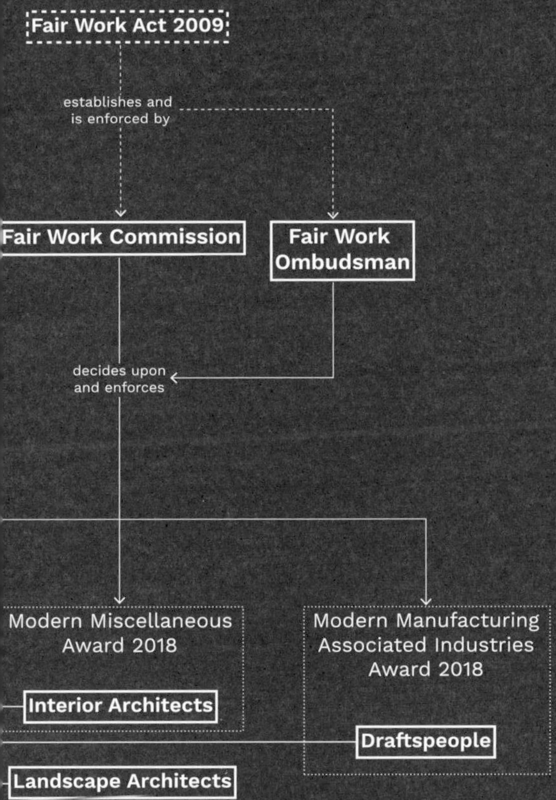

T-A-L = The Architecture Lobby. An international non-profit with a chapter in Victoria, made up of architectural workers advocating for fair and equitable labour practices in Victoria.

Fair Work Commission = Government organisation. The commission is the independent national workplace relations tribunal. It is responsible for maintaining a safety net of minimum wages and employment conditions, as well as a range of other workplace functions and regulations.

Fair Work Ombudsman = Government organisation. Enforces compliance with the Fair Work Act 2009, related legislation, awards and registered agreements. Helps employers and employees by providing advice and education on pay rates and workplace conditions.

01 Every nuanced aspect of Rancière's idea cannot be captured in such a short article. The reader will have to forgive me for selecting certain aspects and omitting others to illustrate a point. In using Rancière's framework of 'regimes of *art*,' I will have to assume that architecture is an art, and the reader might think I am undermining my own case that we should see ourselves as workers and not as artists. It would be obfuscation to deny that we are artists on some level. Our work is taken by most people to be part of the cultural fabric to which paintings, poetry, sculpture and the other arts belong. My aim is simply to clarify some of the consequences of emphasising that we are workers, not to wholesale deny that we are on some level artists, even if only in the eyes of others.

02 Jacques Rancière, *The Emancipated Spectator* (London: Verso, 2011), 1-9.

03 Jacques Rancière, *Aisthesis: Scenes from the Aesthetic Regime of Art* (London: Verso. 2013), 147-8.

04 Christopher H. Johnson and Jacques Rancière, *The Nights of Labor: The Worker's Dream in Nineteenth-Century France*, trans. John Drury (Philadelphia: Temple University Press, 1989).

05 Kirsten Ross, "Rancière and the Practice of Equality," *Social Text* 29 (Duke University Press, 1991): 57-71.

06 Ben Davis, "Rancière for Dummies," *Artnet Magazine*, August 11, 2006, http://www.artnet.com/magazineus/books/davis/davis8-17-06.asp.

07 Peggy Deamer's article in this edition of *Inflection* is precisely the kind of academic work that takes these questions seriously.

08 Michelle Chen, "The Guggenheim Doesn't Want Labor Activists Interfering With Its Luxurious Abu Dhabi Outpost," *The Nation*, April 25, 2016. https://www.thenation.com/article/archive/the-guggenheim-doesnt-want-labor-activists-interfering-with-its-luxurious-abu-dhabi-outpost/.

09 Malaysian Progressives in Australia's Facebook page, "International Students Here to Stay! #NoWorkerLeftBehind," April 08, 2020, accessed May 01, 2020, https://www.facebook.com/notes/malaysian-progressives-in-australia-mpoz/international-students-here-to-stay-noworkerleftbehind/2581584068785425/.

10 Virginie Pérotin, "The Performance of Workers' Cooperatives," in *The Cooperative Business Movement, 1950 to the Present (Comparative Perspectives in Business History)*, eds. Patrizia Battilani and Harm G. Schröter, (Cambridge: Cambridge University Press, 2012), 195-221, doi:10.1017/CBO9781139237208.011.

11 Kazuhiko Mikami, "Are cooperative firms a less competitive form of business? Production efficiency and financial viability of cooperative firms with tradable membership shares," *Economic Systems* 42(3) (2018): 487-502, https://doi.org/10.1016/j.ecosys.2017.11.005; Carla Dickstein, "The Promise and Problems of Worker Cooperatives," *Journal of Planning Literature* 6(1) (1991): 16-33, https://doi.org/10.1177/088541229100600102.

STRENGTH THROUGH GEOMETRY

IN CONVERSATION WITH PHILIPPE BLOCK

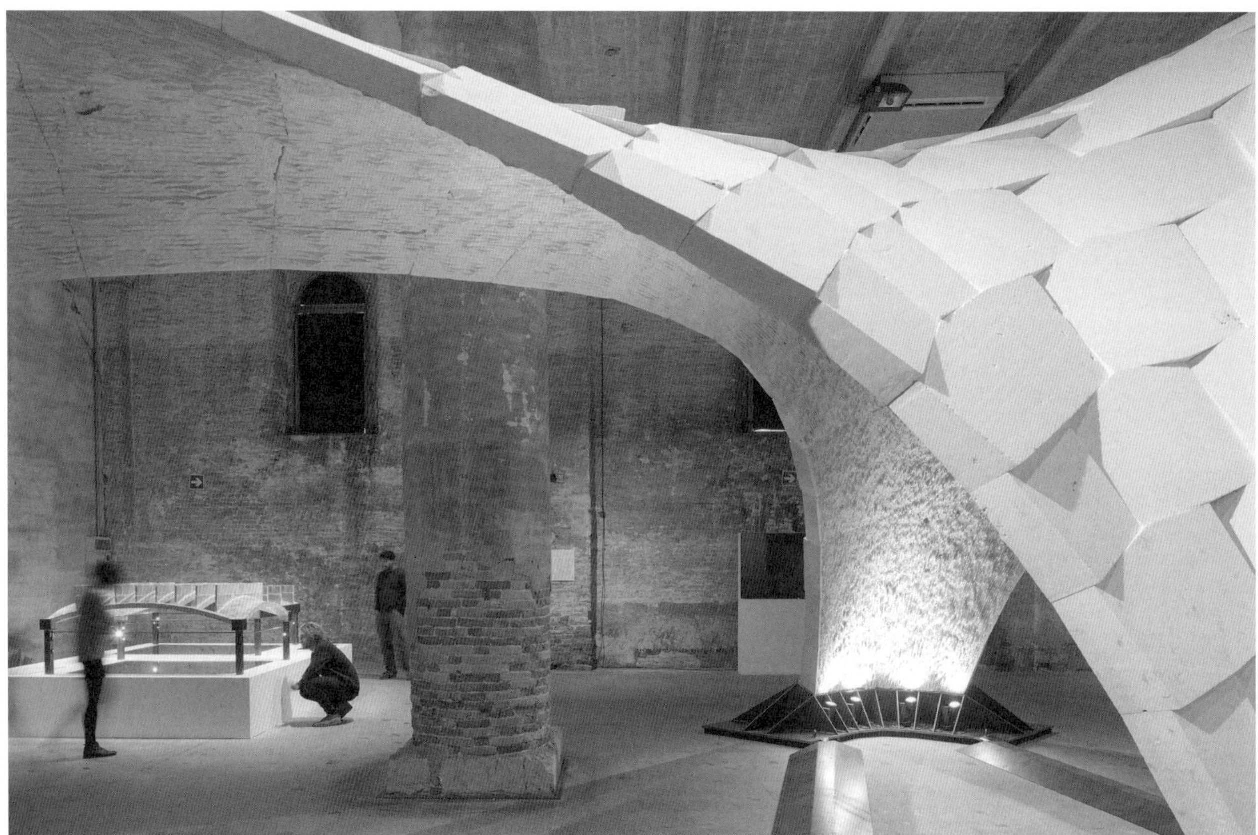

Dr. Philippe Block is a Professor at ETH Zurich, where he directs the Block Research group with Dr Tom Van Mele. In 2020, Professor Block visited the Melbourne School of Design to present his Treseder Fellowship Lecture, 'Strength Through Geometry.' The Block Research Group applies this same motto to their research on the design and engineering of novel shell structures. Professor Block develops computational structural design strategies utilising digital fabrication to push construction innovation and address the grand challenges posed by climate change.

Inflection **Vol. 7 editors interviewed Dr. Philippe Block in March 2020 after his lecture at the Melbourne School of Design. His most recent project, KnitCandela, developed with Zaha Hadid Architects in 2018, formed the basis of our discussion. Throughout the interview, Professor Block explained the complexities of developing global relationships, detailed his approach to reducing construction inefficiencies and outlined the need for environmental limitations for the profession.**

In your lecture, 'Strength through Geometry,' conducted at the Melbourne School of Design, you framed your work in relation to sustainable design principles: better materials, fewer materials and less waste. How do you see the processes of globalisation, increased urbanisation and population growth changing the nature of the profession in the coming decades?

The fact that there is a rapid explosion of urbanisation comes directly from population growth. We do not want to urbanise the entire planet and deplete our natural resources, but increasing populations go where there are opportunities and work, so we need to densify. In many developing contexts, low-cost or affordable housing solutions barely go higher than the ground floor, so that is a big challenge to provide solutions for multi-storey construction.

I like your theme because I think boundaries—in the sense of constraints—need to be given to architects in finding affordable, dignified housing solutions for people in developing contexts. If you as an architect/designer do not understand what the constraints are, then you cannot provide meaningful solutions within a reasonable budget. In my opinion, the profession will have to react to the pressures of climate change and the extraordinary quantity of housing that needs to be provided. The calculation by Bill and Melinda Gates that we need to build the equivalent of one New York City every month for the next 40 years in order to provide dwelling and infrastructure for the expected increase by 20% in world population by 2050 (which translates to over 2.1 billion more people on this planet), gives us an insight into the huge challenge of practically doubling the current building stock.[1]

We, as designers, architects and engineers must also find ways to justify our profession. There is pressure from industry partners who do not understand why our profession is lagging when it comes to efficiency in construction—efficiencies through automation that, for example, the car industry and other sectors have been able to achieve. Most of the world is not particularly interested in what we teach students in architecture school about spectacular spaces. It feels to me that a lot of emphasis in schools is on trying to educate the next Pritzker Prize winner, while we actually should spend much more time on providing quality solutions for the masses.

You have spoken about 'knowledge sharing' being an essential part of your work. How important is the consideration of local skills and 'capacity building' in your design process?

Extremely important. This is something that I underestimated in the early days of my career, when I had opportunities to do a few projects in Ethiopia and South Africa. Sustainable knowledge transfer through capacity building is the biggest challenge: how can you assist, help or innovate, without imposing. Immediately, I noticed that you need to inform and educate the architects and engineers—which is not specific to a developing context, by the way—to help find ways to work with the local building codes and regulations, and also to follow up with the workers. This is what constitutes the term 'capacity building.' It is not about giving a quick, one-off workshop. It takes years of follow-up if you want to do it seriously.

Opposite: Beyond Bending: Armadillo Vault, Venice Architecture Biennale, 2016. Photography by Iwan Baan. All images courtesy of ETH Zurich/Block Research Group.

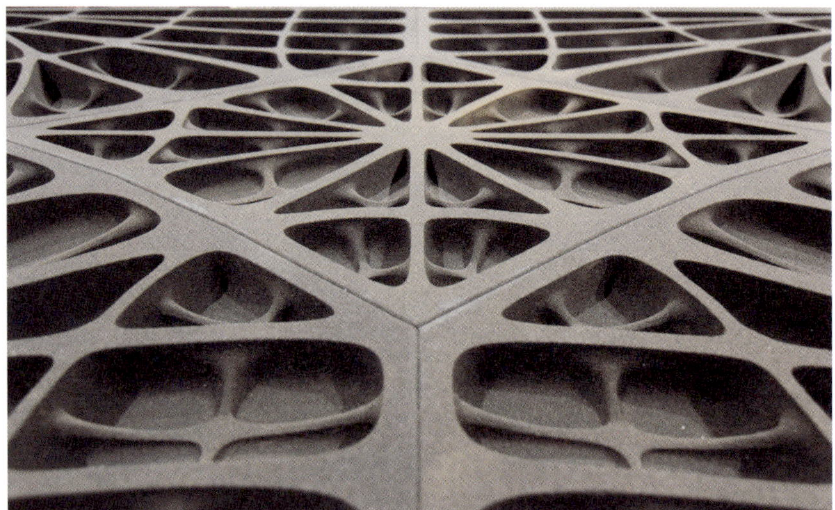

Beyond Bending: funicular floor slab system, Venice Architecture Biennale, 2016. Photography by Marc Duerr.

How do the inefficiencies of floor slabs contribute to the issues we face as a profession?

Oh, they are certainly relevant. Even Austria, for example, which is a developed country, has built 5 million square metres of floor area this year. Much faster urbanisation is happening in developing countries in Africa, in India, but also still in China—there are so many floors to be built.

What I find most interesting about all of this is that historically people did things significantly better. I think there were many reasons for this. There were not all these engineered materials that allowed one to build whatever one wants. In the past, the shapes they developed were more in line with what materials they wanted to use. For example, the vaulted ceilings and basements of older houses made sense because they were very cheap. These solutions grew out of fashion, partly because the language of modernism prized flatness, but also because labour was very cheap and material expensive—now it is the other way around. However, this discussion always needs to consider what is appropriate in which context. What I see happening now is that public pressure is starting to influence governments to impose regulation that makes clients pay the real cost of materials, thus taking into account the true cost of environmental consequences.

On that note, what is your view on sand? It is one of the most precious materials in our industry, yet it also comes from countries that are facing war and is transported to other parts of the world to build artificial land. Do your frameworks and technologies consider these issues?

Great that you bring it up because there have been many shocking publications about the scarcity of sand. Beyond the environmental pressure of running out of a natural resource, there are social issues brought about by illegal trading and mob-like behaviour associated with it. Actually, there is plenty of sand on the planet, but the sand used in concrete needs to be riverbed or coastal sand because these have sharp edges, which create a good bond. Desert sand, for example, is too round because of long-term erosion, which means that it does not have the correct structural properties. We are directly addressing this because if you get the geometry of a structural element correct, then you are not only reducing its volume, but you can also use extremely weak materials. As a result, all of these sands, but also alternative aggregates, can suddenly become structural, and you can start to use these low-pollution materials that have previously been discarded as solutions. But we have a lot of catching up to do—a lot of engineering testing has already been done to help us better understand these materials. Understanding the

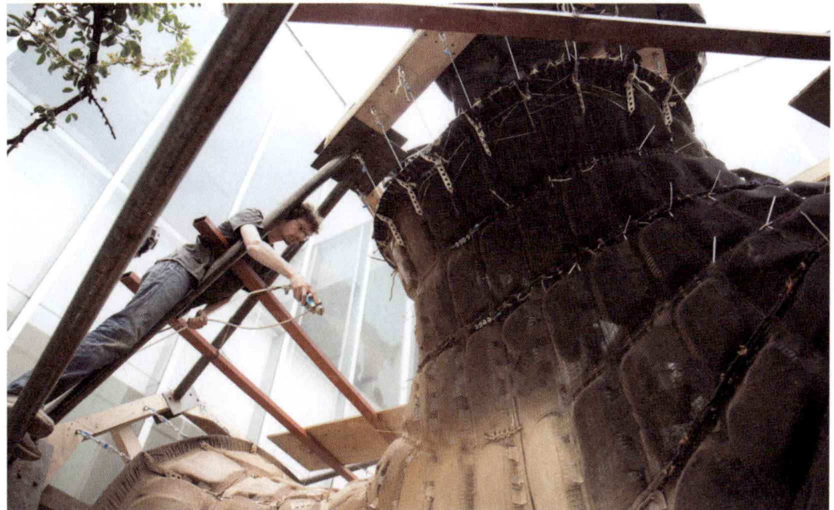

Application of the initial stiffening coating, an essential part of the KnitCrete system, KnitCandela, 2018. Photography by Mariana Popescu.

long-term behaviour of these alternative materials is a big challenge, since we do not have decades of testing data available. An additional challenge, or opportunity, is to figure out ways to use these materials in digital fabrication. For example, 3D printing of concrete-like materials seems very promising because it does not need formwork, but in the currently available solutions, it requires much higher cement ratios and all kinds of binders and chemicals. Thus, to make concrete 3D printing possible, you are essentially not improving much. So, how can we develop 3D printing materials that do not need to meet these higher cement ratios? Some recent research by my colleagues at ETH shows very promising results in this direction.

Do you think that the climate crisis requires architects to return to the mould of the master builder?

Yes, the master builder understood the rules and the constraints required to design appropriately with certain materials. They built all these structures centuries before the current theory of structures that focuses on stresses and equilibrium of forces. In the past, they used the right measures for these systems because compression and equilibrium are fundamentally questions of geometry. While modern engineering always looks at stresses, one cannot discover these beautiful equilibrium shapes if you focus solely on stresses. The master builders concentrated on local crafts and tectonics because they wanted to achieve structures with humble, simple materials. They did not have the overly engineered materials that we have today.

Do you think geometry is a link to connect different professions, such as material scientists, construction and those in the field of economics?

Another way to ask this question is: 'what glues all of this together?' I do believe that to bring different performances for different expert fields together you need common ground, a common language. I talk about the need for a 'glue' because, unlike the master builders of the past, the challenges and requirements of modern buildings are much more complex than they used to be. We can no longer have a master builder in the historical sense, not even a digital master builder—instead, we need a team that brings all the relevant expertise together. Indeed, that is where I see geometry fitting in—as a kind of common ground, a language that many people can understand.

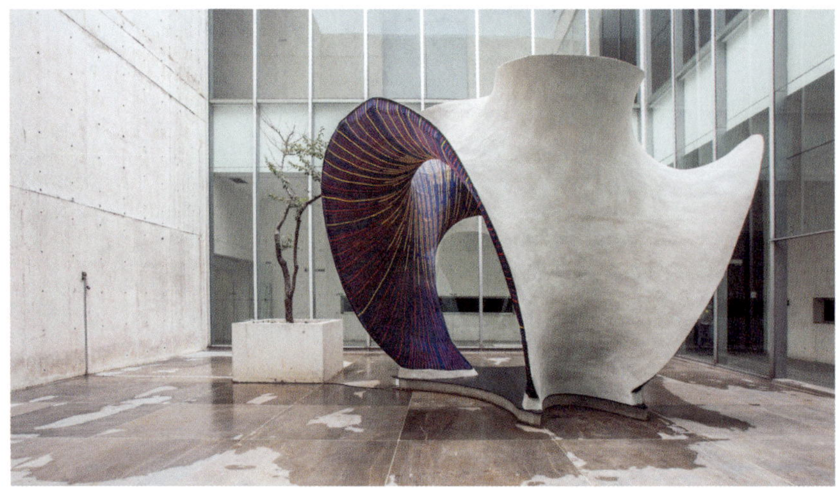

Finished structure, KnitCandela. Photography by Juan Pablo Allegre.

One of the criticisms levied at global architectural firms is a perceived lack of consideration for the contexts in which they build. How have you negotiated that sort of ethical problem, particularly in your project KnitCandela completed with Zaha Hadid Architects?

For that project, we worked together with a particular design team within Zaha Hadid Architects, called ZHCODE. I found it exciting to work with them; it clarifies that someone very vocal about sustainability can work with a firm that does not necessarily have that kind of image. Within ZHA, there is quite a lot of freedom given to ZHCODE to think about how we can couple our two design languages through computation, form-finding and structural considerations. They believe their forms offer all kinds of opportunities and benefits. Still, by collaborating with people like our group, they are trying to challenge themselves to find a balance between an aesthetic and structural efficiency. I like this tension because I think that it is important to convince offices like that to do things better (from a sustainability point of view) through long-term exchange and collaboration. Regarding local consideration and design aesthetics, Dr. Alicia Nahmad Vazquez, the founder of Architecture Extrapolated (R-Ex), who is from Mexico, organised the local contracting. That office's target is to up-scale local crafts through digital innovation and work with local contractors to stimulate knowledge transfer. As a side note, the shape of KnitCandela references the traditional dress in Mexico. The workers endearingly called this structure 'the scarf' because it resembled their traditional garment. The museum also marketed a special-edition scarf made by local artisans that was inspired by the pavilion. So, we hope we were appropriate and responded to a local context. Such feedback from the local workers validates that.

Does the term 'capacity building' then rely on developing a diverse set of relationships too?

In fact, I want to go even further. Because I had worked with Mexican artisans previously, I knew that they were exceptionally good at hand-rendered concrete works, and I trusted that we would be able to manage the tight time frame. In this case, understanding the local capacity was essential. I am happy to see that outcome, but I also see a danger. You do one pavilion or structure as a bit of a tease, and then you disappear, and the relationship goes away. To build those relationships, you also need to build up a long-term commitment, and it is not always obvious how that works. We still have a lot of work to do here.

Opposite: Interior of the finished structure, KnitCandela. Photography by Philippe Block.

01 Bill Gates, "Buildings are bad for the climate," October 28, 2019, https://www.gatesnotes.com/Energy/Buildings-are-good-for-people-and-bad-for-the-climate.

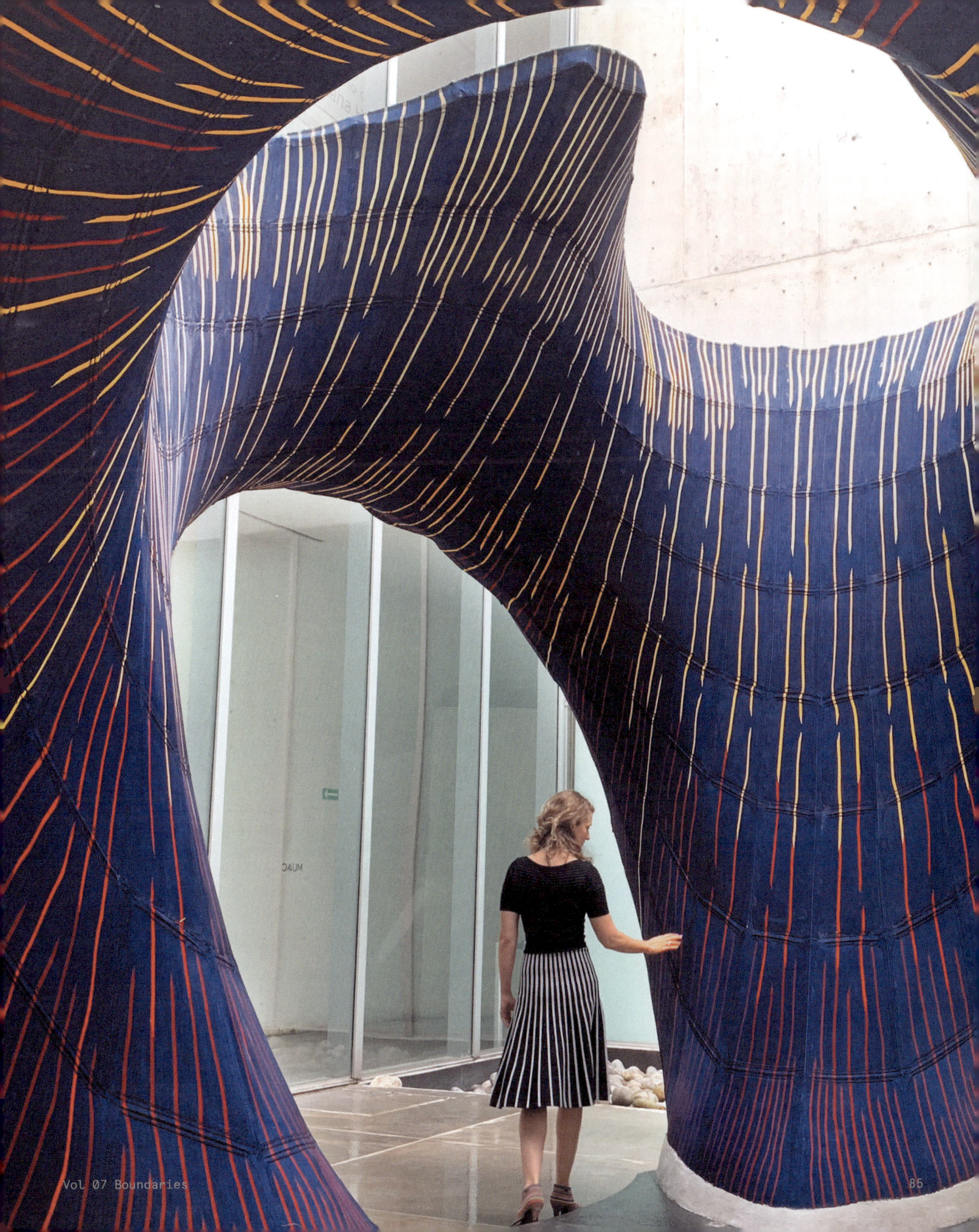

ONEH

RECIPROCITY AND REVIVING SOCIAL CONDUCTS

Shatha Safi

Since its foundation in 1991, RIWAQ—a Ramallah based not-for-profit organisation—has been preserving cultural heritage in rural Palestine. RIWAQ's work includes a Registry of Historic Buildings which catalogues some 50,320 historic buildings in 422 villages, towns and cities in the West Bank, Jerusalem and Gaza. This also includes the implementation of around 120 conservation projects in major towns and villages, 20 rehabilitation projects, the publication of 20 books on cultural heritage as well as a rich photo archive. Since 2006, however, RIWAQ's key vision has been to rehabilitate and re-enliven Palestine's 50 most significant historic centres via its 50 Village Project. This project not only shifted RIWAQ's work towards a village scale to include historic fabrics, alleys and outdoor spaces, but also challenged the fragmented geography emplaced by Israeli occupation through land confiscation, the West Bank border wall and checkpoints.[1] The project's vision is to link such fragmented geographies through its communities, beyond aforementioned physical obstacles. Looking into the histories of these villages, as well as their productions and interrelations based on agriculture, craft and trading, sets new potentials for reviving socioeconomic production within historic centres and their surrounding landscapes. In the context of Palestine, where cultural heritage is actively being destroyed by the Israeli occupation, RIWAQ reaches beyond traditional notions of heritage conservation to involve local community members in place-making activities and reconstruction. As such, this article will first discuss revitalisation of the cultural centre in the Palestinian village of Hajjeh, which is underpinned by community involvement, collective ownership and the principle of *al' Oneh* (reciprocity). It will then elucidate RIWAQ's 50 Village Rehabilitation Project, a large-scale cartography which reconstructs an alternative Palestinian map, binding together fragmented landscape towards new cooperative networks, thereby dynamically reimagining both heritage architecture and contested territorial boundaries.[2]

Hajjeh Village is situated in the northern region of the West Bank, 18 kilometres west of Nablus in the Qalqilya Governorate. Hajjeh is an Aramaic word, meaning 'market.' The village is surrounded by five neighbouring villages and is renowned for having an ancient Mamluk mosque that dates back to AD 1323.[3] As a result of the difficult political and economic conditions of the Palestinians, and during the migration of a number of Hajjeh's residents to other regions inside and outside Palestine (especially the city of Nablus, Jordan and the United States), the historic centre was abandoned and neglected. The capable residents constructed buildings seeking independence and modernity on the outskirts of the village, and those who had not been able to expand and build remained in the historic centre. When RIWAQ entered Hajjeh in 2012, the historic centre was partially abandoned, many buildings were deteriorating and semi-demolished, in addition to there being inadequate infrastructure. These conditions affected the residents and led to an inhospitable housing environment that pushed more residents to leave their old buildings at the first possible opportunity. The old town remained for the elderly, and to those who were not financially able to move. As RIWAQ's founder Suad Amiry asserts, too many villagers' historic centres are stigmatised for being neglected areas or for the poor; as such, it is the inherent tension between traditional physical structures of historic centres and contemporary needs for revitalisation that poses a major challenge for RIWAQ's work.

Building a stone home in Palestine between 1898 and 1946. Image courtesy of Matson Photograph Collection of The Library of Congress, 06014.

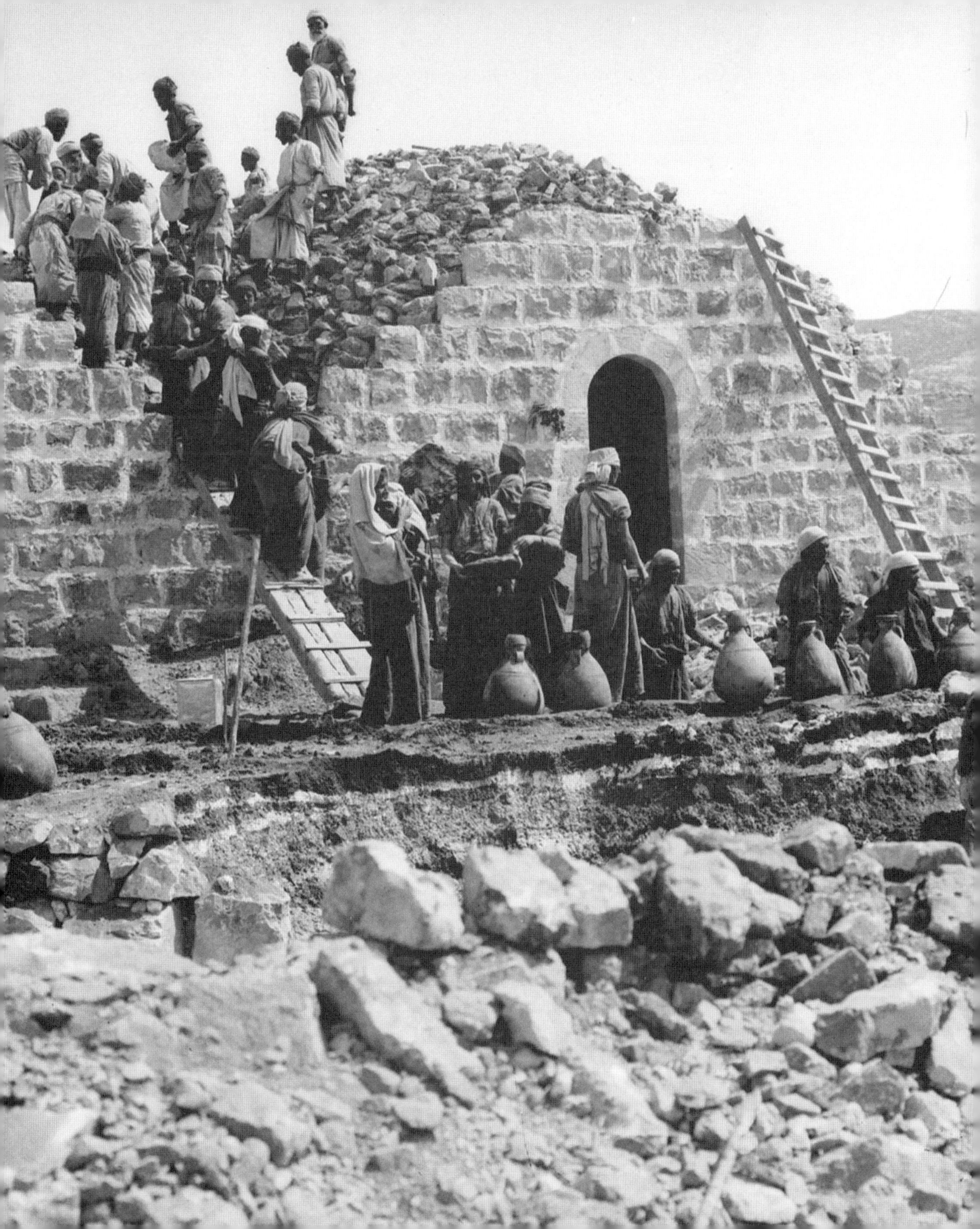

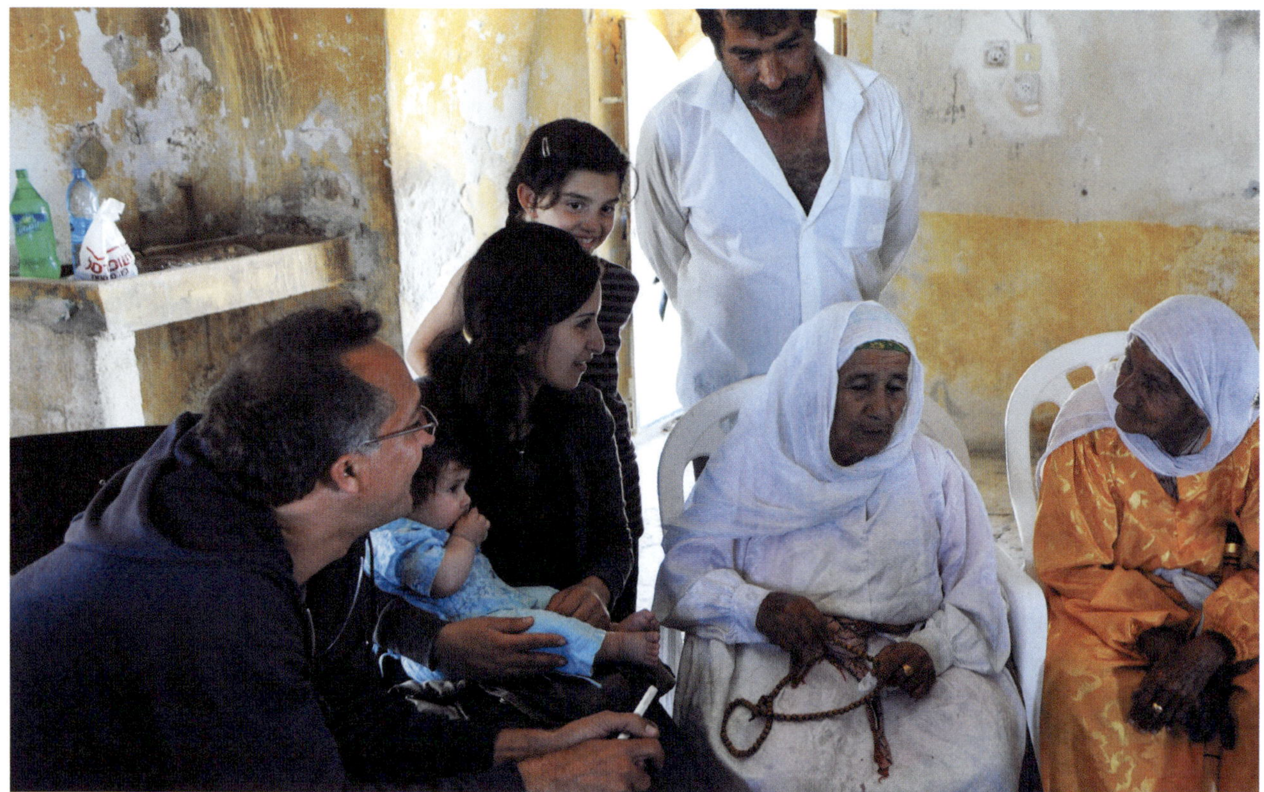

According to the update of RIWAQ's registry information in the year 2010, it was found that 23 historical buildings in Hajjeh are in poor condition, and 26 buildings are unusable.[4] In addition to many infringements on historical buildings, such as the addition of services, rooms without planning or consideration of their historical importance, have led to increased humidity within and the occurrence of cracks due to the additional loads. In the absence of a heritage law that protects such significant buildings, there have also been numerous cases of demolishing historic buildings (or parts of them) for the purpose of expanding streets and constructing public and private facilities; the last of which was recorded in the year 2011 with the demolition of an ancient religious shrine.

The revitalisation process of Hajjeh, as initiated by RIWAQ, is based on the principle of community participation, building local partnerships and building a shared vision with relevant parties. Through a partnership with the village council in Hajjeh as well as a group of local institutions, numerous visits and meetings were held for the purpose of introducing the project goal and building a participatory vision for the project that responds to the community's needs and aspirations. Given the project's limited financial resources, the first decision was to identify an area for intervention: the central area of the historic centre was chosen for its significance, potential and for the number of residents who would benefit from the work.

The project focused on three primary typologies: housing, public space and communal buildings; all the while underpinned by principles of collective dialogue, observation and willingness to learn. A range of formal arts and culture programs that convened community members regularly in the historic centre's public spaces were implemented; each of these activities required strong partnerships that fostered a sense of collective ownership and community empowerment. Ultimately for this project, the reclaiming of spaces and transfer of the project's ownership to its community was crucial. The housing component was driven by current residents interested in restoring their immediate environment, as well as by the larger community who

An oral history session organised by RIWAQ in Hajjeh in 2011, © RIWAQ Archive.

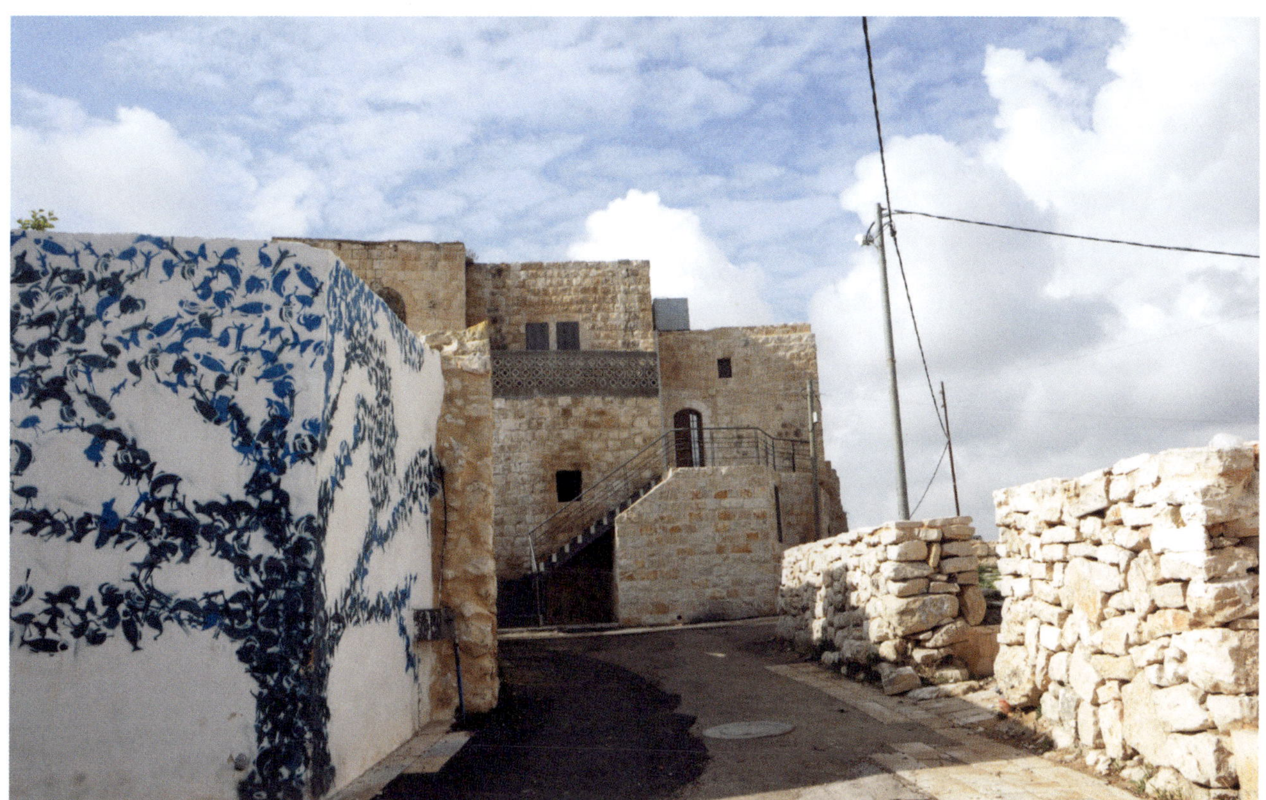

expressed interest in moving back to the historic centre if living conditions were to be improved. Unequivocally, housing was the primary engine for the project, which otherwise included the enhancement of public spaces, alleys and domestic gardens to provide a safe and comfortable living environment for residents, as well as for owners who wished to reuse their abandoned buildings. Importantly, RIWAQ's partnership with the local village council formed the main umbrella to facilitate communication between residents and the RIWAQ team, enabling the product of such conversations to be implemented within Hajjeh's historic fabric.

RIWAQ's work in Hajjeh was defined by the revival of a long-lived social practice in Palestine commonly associated with collective place-making activities and construction, called *al 'Oneh* (reciprocity). This is a traditional social solidarity system by which neighbours and relatives help each other carry out tasks otherwise difficult to pursue individually. This includes the construction of homes, the digging of water wells, feast preparations, and harvesting crops. The concept of *al 'Oneh*, in which social contracts are renewed and new community relationships are fostered, contributes to the fulfillment of RIWAQ's 50 Village Rehabilitation Project. For this project, a series of restoration and adaptation interventions were launched, which were designed in partnership with residents, responding to their unique aspirations. The projects were also implemented in partnership with residents via the principle of *al 'Oneh*: engineering designs and materials for the restoration work were provided by RIWAQ but implemented by owners, who in turn were supervised by RIWAQ. This collaborative back-and-forth approach yielded strong relationships. This project was RIWAQ's pilot housing project and it encouraged the organisation to adaptively reuse historic buildings for residential living as a key aspect for the rehabilitation process. Since 2011 to date, RIWAQ has been able to restore more than 50 historical buildings for the purpose of housing, alongside the partnership of its owners, in various areas including: Deir Ghassana, Abwein, Rantis, Bil'in (Ramallah), Beit Aksa and Jaba (Jerusalem), Jameen, Asira Al-Shamaliya (Nablus), and Al-Dhahirah (Hebron).

Preventive conservation and enhancement of public space in Hajjeh by RIWAQ in 2014, © RIWAQ Archive.

Economic feasibility and job creation

By adopting the practice of *al 'Oneh* via the owners' contribution and thereby halving restoration costs, RIWAQ was able to expand the work area and increase the amount of work accomplished without exceeding the available financial grant. Instead of restoring a single building, it could restore two or even increase the area of preventive restoration to include as many buildings as possible.[5] The project also frequently used locally produced materials to increase investment into local labour, avoiding imported or pre-made materials where possible.

Environmental impact and energy saving

Such locally-produced materials are inevitably extracted from natural resources in alignment with traditional building methods. When these methods are applied to housing, they provide adequate thermal insulation, which results in energy savings and thermal comfort for inhabitants. A key benefit of living in a passively heated and cooled restored historical building is that expenses otherwise spent on the installation and running costs of active thermal systems are eliminated.

Reflection

Presently, looking back at the Hajjeh Rehabilitation Project and revisiting restored buildings and spaces, one can only be proud of its experimental approach. As this project led RIWAQ's way towards adaptive reuse of historic buildings for housing, more needs for similar projects were realised. This experience has opened up our minds and challenged our egos as architects to better respond to the community's aspiration, tastes and aesthetic values. However, it is important to note that as the built environment of Hajjeh's neighbourhood improved, so too did the challenge of maintaining spaces within, given the poor economic resources of its residents. Many residents were happy with the restoration result and were trained on conservation techniques, yet could not afford to pay maintenance expenses. Ultimately, RIWAQ works as a catalyst for the rehabilitation process and has time as well as budget limitations that leave us with questions of 'what's next?,' 'who can be involved further?' and 'how can we collaborate with other partners in the fields of agriculture, infrastructure and economic development to circumvent scope and financial limitations?' To answer, RIWAQ's 2019-2029 strategy includes investing more efforts in partnerships. The rehabilitation process is a long term route that needs multidisciplinary involvement and most of all needs official commitment of the government and local and international donors. Such sponsorship is an investment into the socioeconomic development of Palestine's future generations; counterintuitively, latent within Palestine's heritage lies an alternative, hopeful future.

01 Suad Amiry, *Reclaiming Space: The 50 Village Project in Rural Palestine,* 2015.

02 Shatha Safi, "The Revitalization of Hajjeh," Chapter 9, *Reclaiming Space: The 50 Village Project in Rural Palestine.* (Ramallah: RIWAQ, 2015).

03 The Applied Research Institute (Jerusalem), "Hajja Village Profile, 2013," accessed June 2020, http://vprofile.arij.org/qalqiliya/pdfs/vprofile/Hajja_vp_en.pdf.

04 *RIWAQ's Registry of Historic Buildings in Palestine* (Ramallah: RIWAQ, 2006), accessed June, 2020, https://www.riwaq.org/ar/riwaq-register/district-town/416.

05 Khaldun Bisharah. *Tashgheel: RIWAQ's Job Creation through Conservation 2001-2011* (Ramallah: RIWAQ, 2011).

Top left: Youngsters from Hajjeh during an organized agricultural festival in Hajjeh by RIWAQ in 2013, © RIWAQ Archive.

Bottom left: Restored guesthouse in Hajjeh by RIWAQ in 2014, © RIWAQ Archive.

Top right: One of the main alleys in Hajjeh Historic Centre, by RIWAQ in 2011, © RIWAQ Archive

Bottom right: Organised voluntary work in Hajjeh in 2012, © RIWAQ Archive.

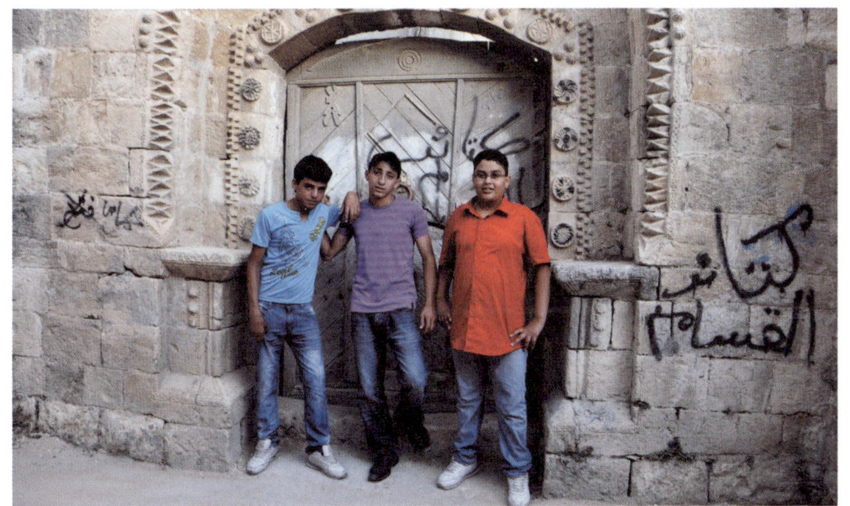
كتائب
القسام

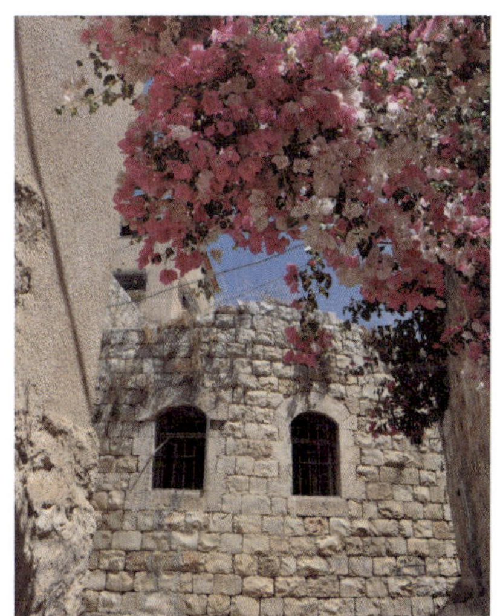

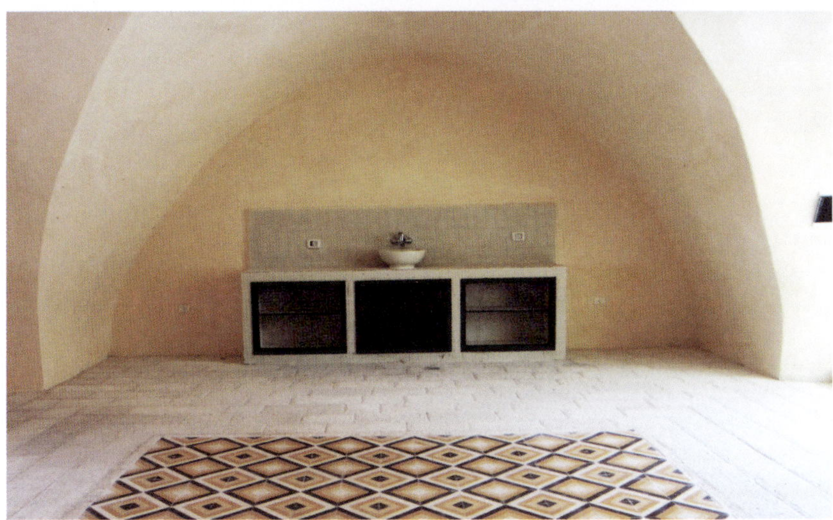

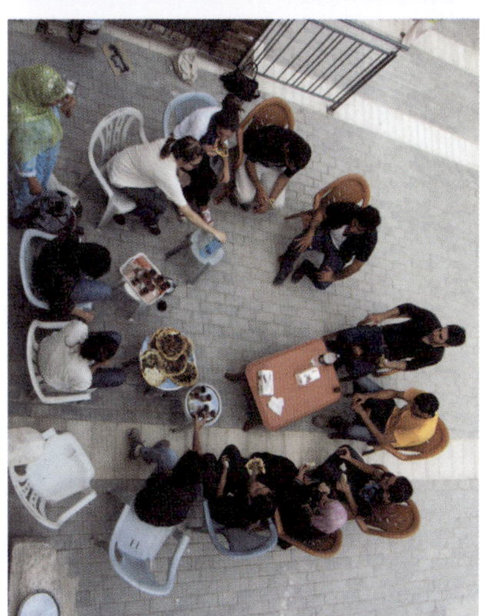

REPRESENTING THE COLONIAL CONTINUUM

THE CARTOGRAPHY OF SPACE-TIME DURING THE FRENCH STATE OF EMERGENCY

Léopold Lambert

In late 2015, I began research that aimed to investigate the colonial history of the French state of emergency. This piece of legislation allows the State to implement additional measures to the plethora already available to lead a counterrevolution: the bulk of them constituted by curfew, home searches, home arrests, police checkpoints, and the closure of gathering spaces. When I started this work, we had just entered a new episode of this violent legislation that was going to last for two years, only to stop when most of the measures enabled by the state of emergency were transferred into common law. This history covers three portions of what I call the French 'colonial continuum'—by 'continuum' here, I refer to a surface that embodies both time and space together. Representing this four-dimensional continuum is not an easy task, but it is an important challenge as this type of cartography can articulate an argument in a way that words could only suggest. However, it is also important to deconstruct various aspects of cartography to detach it as much as possible from its imperial origins. This discipline has been one of the most effective tools of the European colonial project, from the so-called 'discovery' of *terra incognita* (unchartered territory) to the tracing of lines that would materialise colonial borders in territories that did not need any . . . or at the very least, not clear-cut ones. Maps remain laden with codes that suggest this imperial visual domination of territories depicted within. It is therefore crucial to reduce these codes to a minimum. In practical terms, that can take the simple form of placing the North to the bottom part of the map to disturb normative imaginaries and therefore provoke a challenge of conventions.

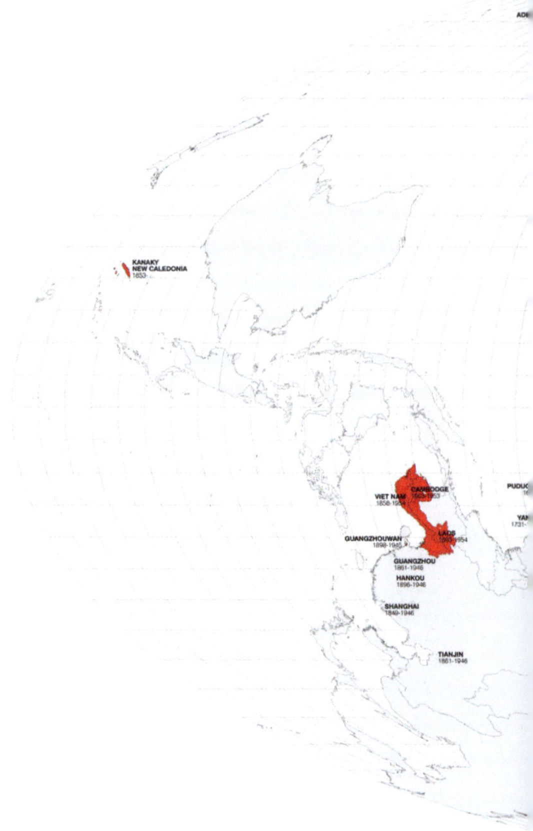

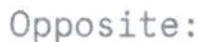

Opposite:
The Chronogeography of French Colonialism, with colonised territories shown in red. All images and diagrams by the author.

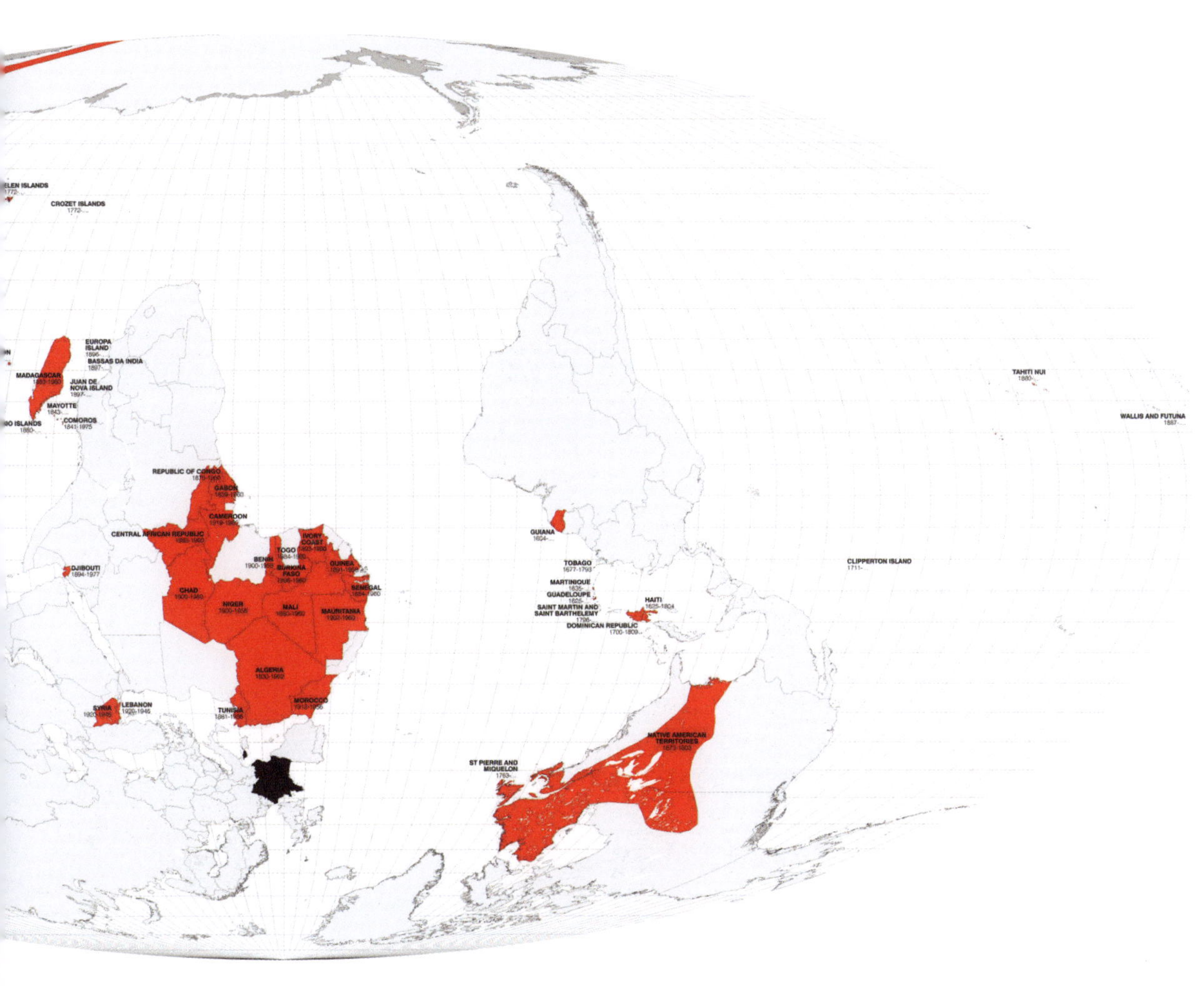
CROZET ISLANDS
1772-
EUROPA ISLAND
1896-
BASSAS DA INDIA
1897-
MADAGASCAR
JUAN DE NOVA ISLAND
1897-
MAYOTTE
1843-
COMOROS
1841-1975
REPUBLIC OF CONGO
GABON
CAMEROON
CENTRAL AFRICAN REPUBLIC
DJIBOUTI
1894-1977
IVORY COAST
TOGO
BENIN
BURKINA FASO
GUINEA
SENEGAL
CHAD
NIGER
MALI
MAURITANIA
ALGERIA
MOROCCO
TUNISIA
SYRIA
LEBANON
1920-1946
GUIANA
1604-
TOBAGO
1677-1793
MARTINIQUE
1635-
GUADELOUPE
SAINT MARTIN AND SAINT BARTHELEMY
1796-
HAITI
1625-1804
DOMINICAN REPUBLIC
1700-1809
NATIVE AMERICAN TERRITORIES
ST PIERRE AND MIQUELON
1763-
TAHITI NUI
WALLIS AND FUTUNA
CLIPPERTON ISLAND
1711-

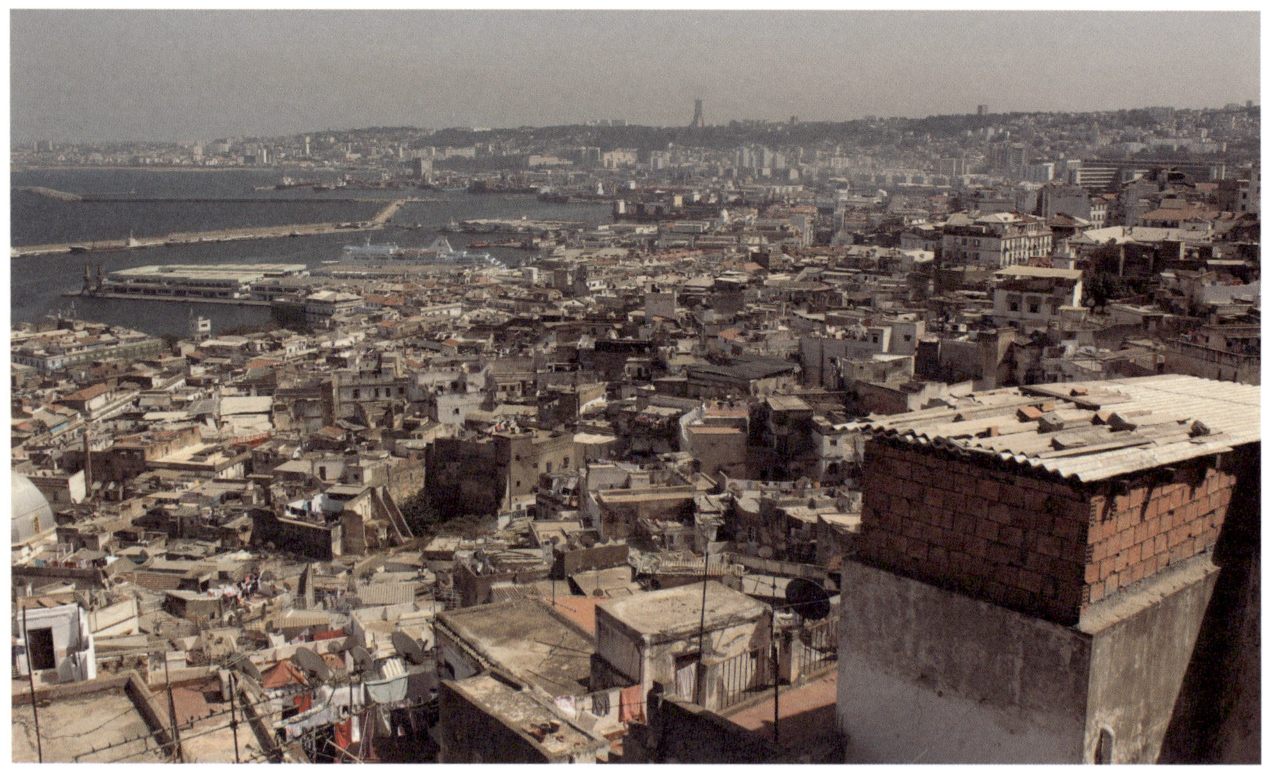

In order to understand the space-time cartographies presented here, one has to understand what is shown on them. The first of the three portions of space-time mobilised by the history of the French state of emergency, is a colonised Algeria during its Revolution (1954-1962), where the state of emergency was first drafted and applied by the French government. During these eight years of struggle to end French colonialism, the colonial authorities never ceased to implement legislation that would make legal its murderous counterrevolution on both sides of the Mediterranean Sea. The independence of Algeria in 1962 is interpreted in the French national narrative as the end date of French colonialism, despite the state still counting numerous colonies around the world—nevertheless termed 'overseas territories.' The state of emergency was later applied in one of them, the most paradigmatic example of French settler colonialism after Algeria: colonised Kanaky (New Caledonia) in Melanesia. Such measures were imposed against the Kanak insurrection of 1984-1988, which aimed at recovering Indigenous sovereignty and making the country independent. This struggle enabled forms of autonomy but still to this day falls short of actual independence. A third space mobilised by this history is rarely considered as colonised since it is situated in the core of France; yet, the logic of implicit sub-citizenship and an antagonistic relationship with the State most certainly registers it within the continuity of colonial rule. This space—or rather, these spaces—are the proletarian suburbs of French cities, what we call the *banlieues*, which are inhabited largely by French citizens or immigrants whose families were once colonised subjects, particularly in North and West Africa, as well as the Carribean. In 2005, when the *banlieue* youth revolted against the structural, discursive, and physical violence enacted against them on a daily basis by politicians, journalists, and the police, the state of emergency was declared against them too. Ten years later, when I started this research, the state of emergency promulgated after the bloody attacks of November 13 in Paris allowed for over 5,000 hyperviolent and traumatising police searches in Muslim homes, workplaces or mosques, as well as hundreds of house arrests of Muslim individuals.[1]

Algiers' Casbah where, in 1957, the Algerian National Liberation Front (FLN) organised the urban-side of the Revolution in the heart of the Algerian capital. Photo by Léopold Lambert (July 2018).

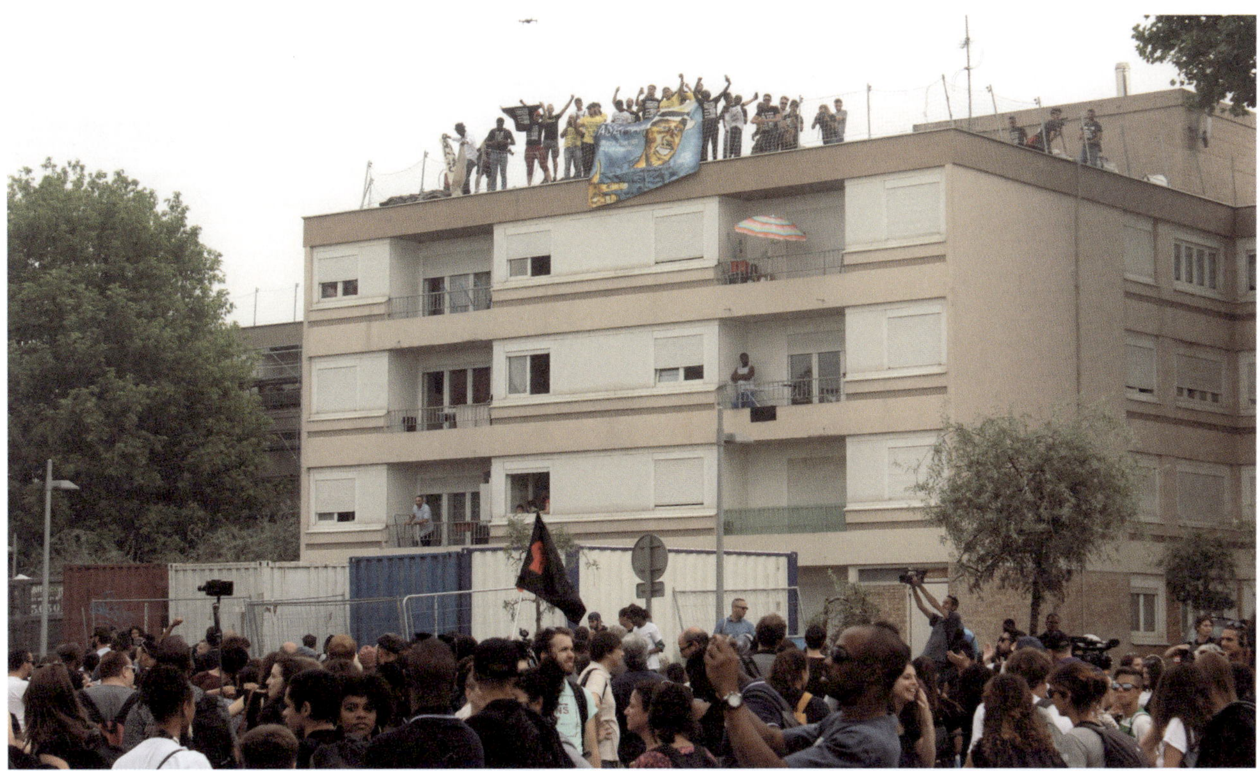

In describing this history in my forthcoming book *States of Emergency: A Spatial History of the French Colonial Continuum*, I wanted to show this French colonial continuum, which led me to drawing diagrams aiming to show different spatialities and temporalities together.[2] The challenge is greater than one might think. How do you show, not just space and time in a graphic document, but also the connection between them? The first diagram simply consisted in covering my office's wall with events scrawled onto post-its of various colors.

The result was somehow too linear in terms of time: I wanted to part from linearity as it would reproduce the way history is told by imperial powers. An encounter with a circular graph preformatted to register a factory's humidity levels gave me the idea for organising the next diagram in a similar way. This led to a chrono-cartographic synthesis of my book where the three main geographies (Algeria, Kanaky and France) are identified through colour, while time is indicated in a non-uniform manner: it is instead a metric that can be contracted (when the period considered is secondary in this history) or dilated (when, on the contrary, the period considered is crucial to the argument). This allows for crucial consequences of the various episodes of state of emergency (marked red on the diagram) to be clearly noticeable, even when one of these episodes was short-lived. For instance, the 1958 state of emergency only lasted two weeks but the events that accompanied it led to the change from the fourth to the fifth French Republic, a motion which resonates today. This exercise of time expansion could theoretically be pushed further, at times giving more importance to a single day (the massacre of over 200 Algerians by the Paris police on October 17, 1961 or that of 19 Kanak activists by the French Army on May 5, 1988 for instance) than to a decade.

Social housing neighbourhood in the distant Paris *banlieues* during the second commemoration of Adama Traoré's death in police detention. Photo by Léopold Lambert (July 2018).

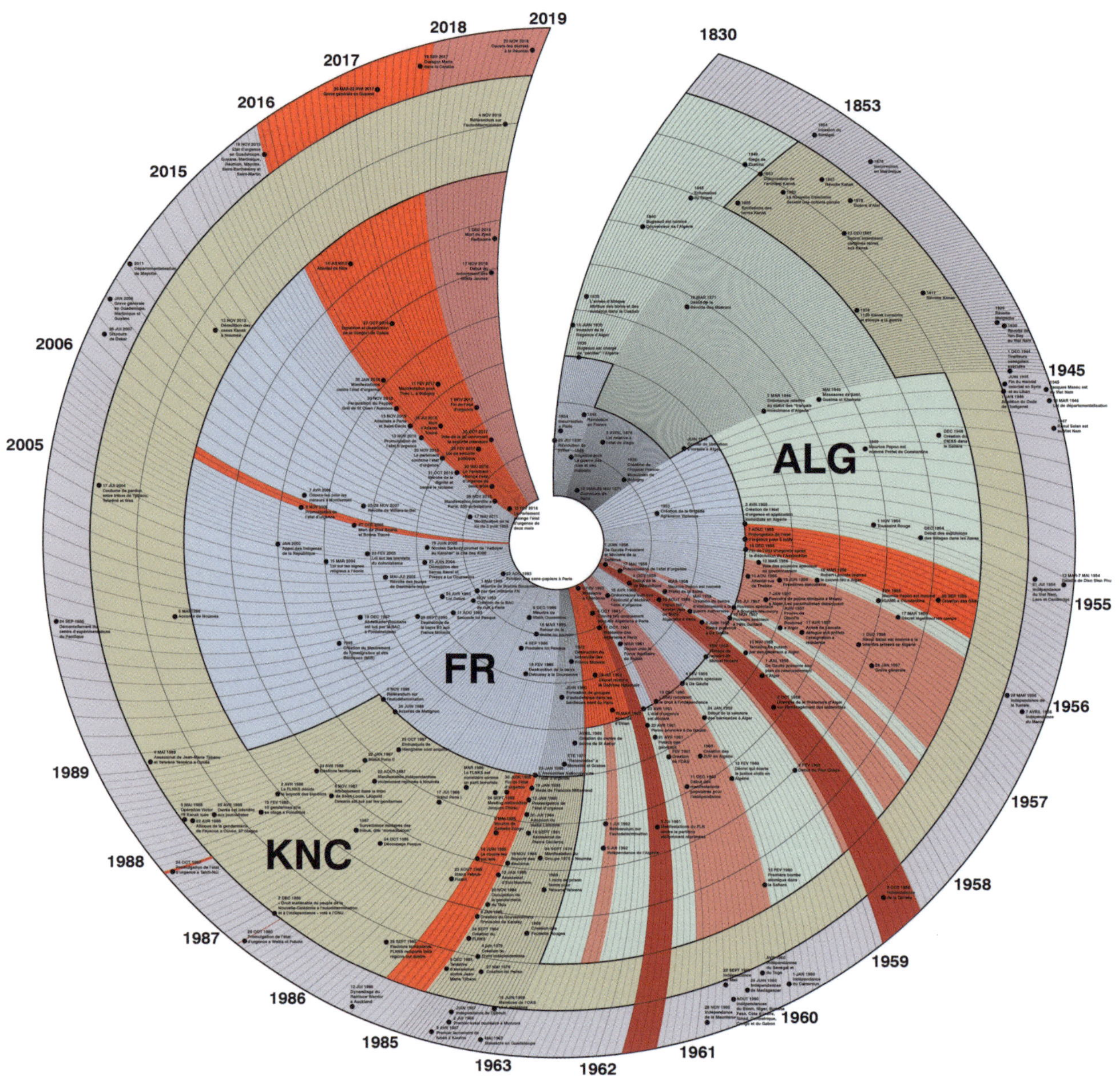

Chrono-cartographic diagram where the three main geographies (Algeria, Kanaky, and France) are identified through colour, while time is indicated in a non-uniform manner.

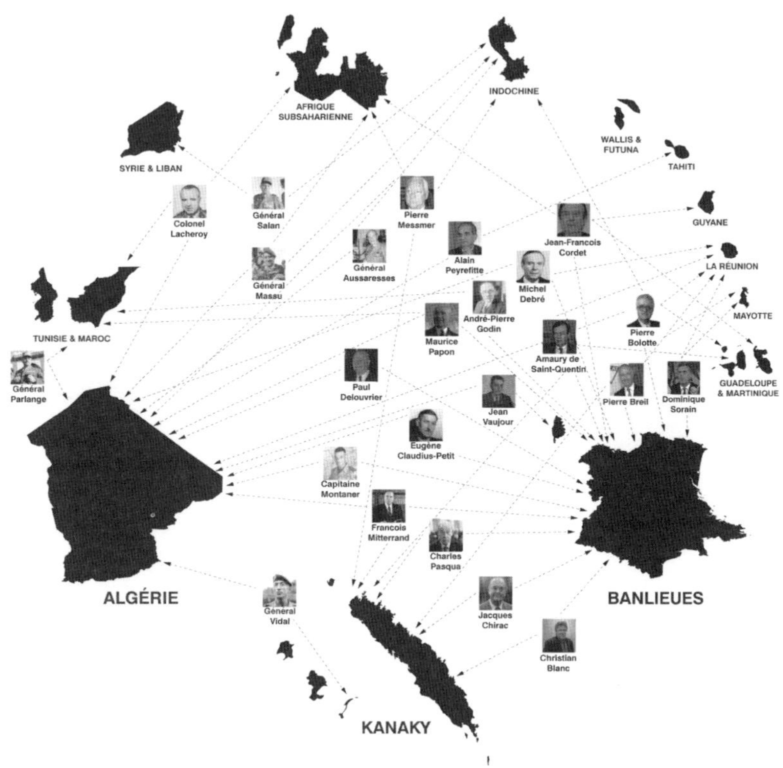

'The Men of the Colonial Continuum,' showing generals, prefects, administrators, experts, and ministers of French colonialism.

The colonial continuum is not only materialised by space and time, it also involves bodies navigating within it. This is the case of colonised bodies, of course, who willingly or forcefully move between geographies and time, but also of a certain number of colonial administrators and counterrevolutionary military officers. Such thinking led to a final map called 'The Men of the Colonial Continuum,' which catalogues the various colonised spaces (including the *banlieues*) in which these representatives of French colonialism obtained roles, thus acquiring skills in the field of population control and revolt suppression. Realising that the prefect of a French region that contains many *banlieues* is the same person who ordered the May 1967 massacre of Guadeloupean workers, or who declared a curfew in Reunion Island against demonstrators in 2018, draws upon the similarities of policy at work in these spaces. This map, like the others, is therefore conceived as a political tool.

One thing remains absent from these maps for the moment: the situation of recent months following the French government's response to political dimensions of the COVID-19 global pandemic: the state of sanitary emergency. Declared on the 23rd of March 2020, this legislation, just like its colonial elder, is centered on punitive measures for those who supposedly do not respect confinement. Like everywhere else in the world, these punitive measures almost always target racialised and proletarianised populations.[3] In the case of France, over these past months this has been the case. States of emergency are not states of exception; they are merely the exacerbation of structural and colonial violence already at work against those who never fully ceased being considered as colonial subjects. Exposing the colonial continuum allows for this argument to be made comprehensible. In order to do so, text is not enough: diagrams and maps, however difficult to be created, are indispensable.

01 Hassina Mechaï and Sihem Zine, *L'état d'urgence (permanent),* (Paris: Meltingbook, 2018).

02 Léopold Lambert, *Etats d'urgence: Une histoire spatiale du continuum colonial français,* (forthcoming, Paris: Editions PMN, 2021).

03 Léopold Lambert, "Introduction: A Short Colonial History of The French State of Emergency," *The Funambulist* No. 29 States of Emergency (May-June 2020).

PARTITIONING PERMANENCY

A REFLECTION ON 19TH CENTURY AND 21ST CENTURY MODELS OF CO-LIVING

Anwyn Hocking

The city provides the infrastructure for moments of permanency and impermanency. People travel, people stay, people move and people leave. These moments exist on a spectrum of human experience, yet our housing design and policy favour those who either settle down or pass through quickly. Permanency here takes on the dual meaning of physical permanency and permanency of the self, that one will find stable partnership, employment and housing, through which one's identity will be validated, respected and remembered. Housing options are so deeply embedded within these culturally contextual expectations that those who exist on the fringes are presented with housing choices that merely reinforce their perceived transience in society.

In the long-standing tradition of the urban lodging house for young, single, working individuals, this truth manifests. The architectural typology of the lodging house spans different extremes: the monastery, the prison, the boarding house and the student college. In all instances of this typology, the residents share one thing in common: they exist on the periphery of conventional lifestyles of partnership, family and home. However, while the monastery assumes permanence of its residents through obedience, the lodging house of past and present assumes impermanence through disobedience and discomfort. In London, the lodging house first appeared for poor urban migrants in 19th century lodging houses and has recently re-emerged as commercial co-living for affluent young students and professionals. The striking similarities between two representative buildings of the 19th century lodging house and 21st century co-living model in London reveal enduring social expectations, yet shifting social norms and the role housing plays in reinforcing extremes of permanency and impermanency.

The housing challenges faced by Victorian London parallel many of those experienced by modern London. With the rise of industrialisation, poor rural populations migrated to urban centres and, for the first time, the majority of the British population lived in cities. As the poor and working-class demographic rose, the affluent moved to new suburbs, leaving behind decrepit buildings for the less privileged and reconfiguring the city around new urban slums.[1] With deteriorating conditions and overcrowding, the urban slums became synonymous with "disease, immorality, pauperism, and crime," festering into a broader concern that these "contagions" would infect society at large.[2] As these concerns met the sentiments of social reformer authors, parliamentary measures and journalistic explorations, a new distinction between the 'deserving' and 'undeserving' poor appeared.[3] The deserving were viewed as those in relatively stable employment and the undeserving as the marginalised, often categorised as thieves, beggars and prostitutes. The distinction birthed the belief amongst the affluent that social stability would only be preserved by separating the deserving from the undeserving. It was this idea that precipitated the mid-19th century establishment of model dwelling companies by wealthy philanthropists to assist and house the deserving poor. The Metropolitan Association for Improving the Dwellings of the Industrious Classes (MAIDIC) was one of the earliest examples of these companies, aiming to "benefit the least fortunate class" through "improving the condition of those immediately above them."[4] Whilst such companies provided a variety of family and single-person housing options, the lodging house addressed a subset of the working-class population that posed a particular threat to Victorian morality: the poor single man. On this itinerant, untied and unwedded subset of the population all the fears of criminality, vice and immorality were projected. As described in Charles Booth's surveys of the London working-class, marriage was the norm and suspicion surrounded those who remained single, viewed as unable to progress with life in a socially acceptable manner.[5] Previously, such individuals were housed in communal style buildings, but the model dwelling companies captured the Victorian fear of the single individual and preference for privacy, modesty and individualism in the new typology of private rooms supplemented by communal

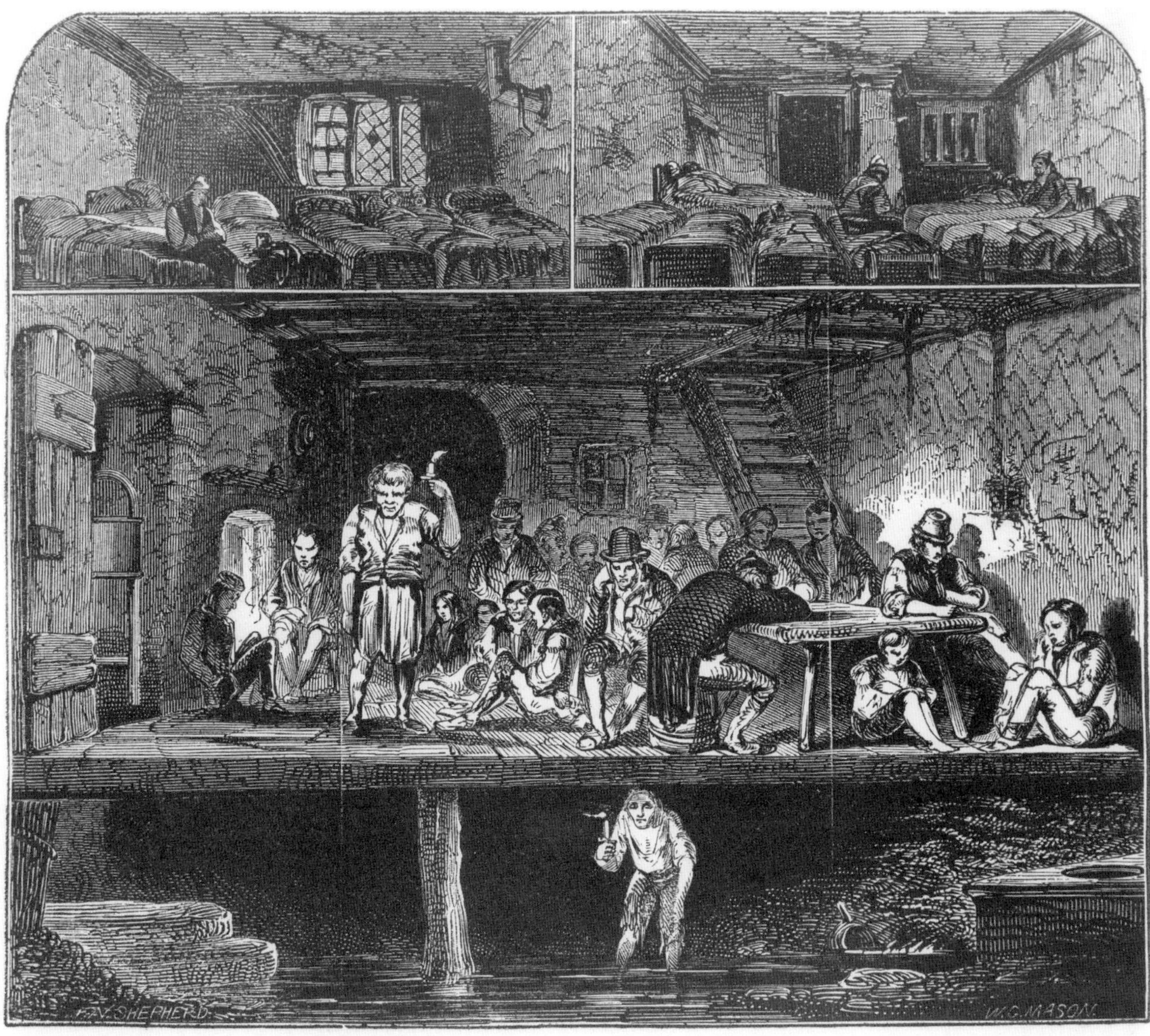

amenities. MAIDIC's first 1849 purpose-built lodging house in Spitalfields, Mile End New Town exemplifies this model. Albert Street Lodging House (ASLH) was a four-storey building accommodating 235 men in partitioned cubicles with supplementary communal spaces such as a library, coffee room and kitchen.

With globalisation, international education and jobs are more accessible today than ever before, creating unprecedented mobility of student and young professional populations. Many of these young people arrive in the education and commercial hub of London with no family, friends or broader community support. As with the influx of urban migrants in the 19th century, the increases in net migration have contributed to similar housing challenges with deteriorating and limited housing stock and the ever-increasing cost of living. Such challenges are compounded by changing social trends, as digitalisation fuels new modes of living, working and sharing, and millennials delay partnership and homeownership.
To counter these shifting norms, resultant housing challenges and an apparent decline in social cohesion, a communitarian response is promoted in urban discourse. As promoted by Robert Putnam, the communitarian response suggests that

Communal Lodging, Field-Lane Lodging House, The Poor Man's Guardian, 1847. Image released into public domain.

through recreating a sense of community, urban individuals will be able to work cooperatively to solve social, economic and environmental concerns.[6] In a similar way to the pre-welfare Victorian establishment of philanthropic model dwelling companies, commercial co-living companies have emerged in the past decade, drawing on such ideals to provide an affordable and convenient domesticated community for young, nomadic professional individuals, as typified by The Collective Canary Wharf (TCCW). The 21-storey building, located in the Isle of Dogs, was designed by SOM with 706 units and opened in 2019. The building is owned and managed by the UK's largest co-living company, The Collective, which aims to "build and activate spaces that foster human connection and enable people to lead more fulfilling lives."[7]

Improving the Marginalised

The socio-spatial similarities between the 19th century lodging house and 21st century co-living building capture lasting social norms of permanency and the role of housing in encouraging individuals perceived to be in a marginalised, transient phase of life toward more conventional lifestyles. In his lectures at the Collège de France, Michel Foucault describes this "conduct of conduct" as governmentality where an understanding of power expands to the organised practices through which populations are governed.[8] The strict organisation of the monastery, for instance, was not envisioned to replace life with a rule, but to embed the rule within the spatial arrangement of life in such a way that the rule would almost disappear. The spatial distinction between individual and collective, and the management of both past and present examples of co-living, serve to guide the health and wellbeing of residents. At ASLH, through the provision of services and amenities that hitherto had not been standard practice in housing, it was thought that many diseases would be avoided. As such ventilation, drainage, waste management, fire prevention and access to daylight were carefully incorporated in the design. Alongside the supposedly benevolent attempts to improve health, ran the darker and more judgemental codification of moral behaviour. In the 'Terms of Lodging Houses for Single Men' curfews determined a work schedule, with residents prohibited from their rooms between 10 a.m. and 8 p.m., while certain activities—including intoxication, card-playing, gambling, quarrelling, profane language and female visitors—were condemnatorily forbidden. The orthogonal spatial uniformity of the building also served this aim in purportedly suppressing crime through the eased surveillance of tenants and their potential misconduct.[9]

Whilst building codes attempt to ensure physiologically salubrious housing conditions today, under neoliberal governmentalities "moral autonomy" is quantified by "the capacity for self-care," as described by Wendy Brown in her reading of Foucault's biopolitics lectures.[10] It is little surprise then that the shared spaces and organised events of TCCW tend to be equated with the improvement of wellbeing. These facilities include a gym, spa, pool and an events programme focused on wellbeing and self-development with yoga as well as "breathing and mental health" classes. The programme of wellbeing extends into the convenience of cleaning and maintenance services, freeing residents' existence from the mundane distractions of chores and allowing a commitment to social connectedness and work. Again a darker side emerges in the building's tenancy agreement, which prohibits certain anti-social behaviours such as loud noises, smoking and obvious intoxication. The spatial arrangement also becomes central to this aim where orthogonal planning allows for easy surveillance from both staff and the CCTV system. Perhaps the strangest attempt to codify behaviour towards socialised expectations of partnership is the peculiar focus on partnership in a building that almost exclusively houses single occupants. Indeed, during the self-development events, one may just find one's next friend, lover or mentor. Such relationships are then nurtured by the advice provided by The Collective's blog about, for instance, 'How to be your authentic self in relationships' and 'How to build trust in the bedroom.'[11]

Although improved basic infrastructure at ASLH did contribute to general tenant health improvements, it is unclear if and how the moral character of tenants changed. Regardless, through improving the health of a working male population, being centrally located to sites of industry and demanding a degree of reliability in routine and behaviour, ASLH provided a reliable pool of employees for the surrounding industry that could be hired and laid off at short notice. The comparative success of The Collective's strategies for wellbeing and social connectedness is yet to be defined and observed. However, in being located within the commercial development area of the Isle of Dogs, a similar argument can be made of TCCW. The research associating wellbeing and improved productivity suggests that more than merely providing nearby housing for situated and freelance employees, TCCW allows for a life free from the mundane distractions of loneliness, stress and domestic chores to dedicate fully to the ethic of work, productivity and partnership.[12]

Reinforcing Transience

In responding to the socio-economic challenges of housing shortages and affordability, models of co-living today and in the past provide flexible and relatively affordable housing to a demographic displaced from community and yet to secure their position within society through partnership or homeownership. Through this, individuals are offered a degree of agency in their housing choice that may not otherwise be allowed in a largely unregulated and deteriorating private rental market. At ASLH, whilst the rent was more than the typical lodging house, it was cheaper than other housing options and afforded the security, privacy, and essential services not included in more communal typologies. In a similar way, TCCW is somewhat cheaper than other housing options, offering rooms and access to all amenities and events from GBP £330 per week in the Isle of Dogs, where the average rent price for a studio flat is GBP £415 per week.[13] In both past and present models of co-living, however, the ostensible benefits of flexibility and relative affordability are accompanied by payment systems and architectural constraints that preclude permanency and reinforce resident transience.

In the flexibility of the weekly tenancy payment system at ASLH, where tenants only had to give one day's notice to leave, the possibility for planning longer-term tenancy was eliminated. Alongside this flexibility was a rigid tenancy agreement that ensured tenants had no jurisdiction over personal or communal spaces and building management could take possession of rooms at any time in terminating tenancy and undertaking maintenance. The extreme spatial constraints of individual rooms, approximately three square metres, also limited self-expression by restricting personal possessions, and what tenants did own had to be stored away in small designated lockers.[14]

Similarly, in promoting complete flexibility, the tenancy arrangement at TCCW operates a "dynamic pricing model," where room rates can vary daily. Tenants are charged a nightly fee invoiced at the end of their stay or every month and are on a maximum 90-day license agreement, rather than a rolling lease. While longer tenancy is rewarded with cheaper rates, certain regulations mean that tenants are unable to consider their life at TCCW permanent. For example, tenants are not able to register for Council tax or enrol on the electoral roll using the TCCW address. Residents are also not permitted to establish or set up individual utilities and do not have exclusive possession of their private room, meaning management and security can enter at any time.[15]

Whilst tenants at The Collective boast a full 12.5 square metres of space in the standard private room, the fully furnished and decorated room with double bed, kitchenette, bathroom, and desk likewise provides limited storage and little space for personal possessions. In his 1903 essay 'The Metropolis and Mental Life,' Simmel warned of the "atrophy of individual culture" and that the "deepest problems of modern life derive from the claim of the individual to preserve the autonomy and individuality of his existence."[16] For Simmel, modern life is characterised as a continuous individual struggle to preserve one's sense of individuality. In the context of both the 19th century lodging house in industrialising London and 21st century commercial co-living in today's advanced industrial London, the struggle against standardisation comes to the fore as tenancy agreements impede individual identity by ensuring an aesthetic uniformity across all domestic space and limiting the usual means of agency and self-expression.

A Model For the Future?

The twenty years following Albert Street Lodging House's construction proved, as with other 19th century model lodging houses across London, that the typology was unsuccessful. The spatial constraints and tenancy regulations had little appeal, and many men preferred the camaraderie of previous, typical lodging houses. Whilst the building could accommodate 234 men it rarely had more than 157 lodgers. In 1869, after it became clear that MAIDIC could no longer continue such an unprofitable venture, the building was converted into longer-term family dwellings. The partitions were removed, and the open dormitory hall subdivided into family units.[17] The enhancement of social control through a focus on privacy, surveillance and individualism was resisted by the male working population in favour of more communal and flexible housing approaches. The company's view of the single poor working individual did not align with the lived reality and identity of these individuals.

Whilst time is required to assess the success of co-living, the growth of the industry and its apparent popularity demonstrates changing social norms of partnership with the increase of single-person housing options, and urban transience as more people seek convenient, affordable and short-term housing. Although this article has focused on London, the co-living model is currently being disseminated across cities of the Global North. The Collective, for instance, now has buildings in the United States and current planning applications in cities across Europe.

The paradox between the 19th century poor single working men who defied institutional attempts to control their behaviour and the more privileged class of 21st century young professionals who ostensibly relinquish a degree of freedom in favour of convenience, demands reflection on the future of urban impermanency. Existing in the fringe between individuality and community, isolation and globalisation, the co-living model promotes a lifestyle of transience, unrooted and untied to place by possessions or permanent community. In so doing, co-living supports international education and employment opportunities with a mobile and easily accessible domesticated community for a young demographic with increasingly precarious social connections and economic circumstances. Although the current model of contemporary co-living nurtures the 'atrophy of individual culture' that Simmel warned against in the presumed transience and uniformity of individual experience, it simultaneously allows for greater freedom in housing options. Beyond merely reinforcing transience, contemporary models of co-living provide a foundation from which we can and should develop more equitable housing options on the spectrum of experience between permanency and impermanency in the urban landscape.

01 John Tarn, *Five Per Cent Philanthropy* (London: Cambridge University Press, 1973), 41.

02 Robert Rawlinson, *The Social and National Influence of the Domiciliary Condition of the People* (London: P.S. King & Son, 1883), 37.

03 For instance, see the writings of Charles Dickens, Elizabeth Gaskell, Charles Kingsley, the reports of the 1942 Poor Law Board, e.g.: *Report of the Sanitary Conditions of the Labouring Population and on the Means of Its Improvement*, and journalist Henry Mayhew's 1849-1850 *Labour and the Poor*. For more: Gertrude Himmelfarb, "Mayhew's Poor," *Victorian Studies* 14, no.3 (1971): 309.

04 Charles Gatliff, "On Improved Dwellings and Their Beneficial Effect on Health and Morals," *Journal of the Statistical Society of London* 38, no.1 (1875): 33.

05 Rebecca Probert, "Living in sin," *BBC History*, accessed November 2016, https://www.historyextra.com/period/victorian/living-in-sin-unmarried-relationships-in-victorian-britain/.

06 Robert Putnam, *Bowling Alone* (London: Simon & Schuster, 2000).

07 "About the Collective," *The Collective*, accessed November 2019, https://www.thecollective.com/about-us.

08 Michel Foucault, *Security, Territory, Population: Lectures at the Collège De France*, 1977-78 (New York: Palgrave Macmillan, 2007).

09 MAIDIC, "Healthy Homes," *LSE Selected Pamphlets* (1854): 33-35.

10 Wendy Brown, *Undoing the Demos: Neoliberalism's Stealth Revolution* (New York: Zone Books, 2015).

11 *The Collective Journal* (blog), accessed October-2019, https://thecollective.com/the-journal/how-to-be-your-authentic-self-in-relationships; https://thecollective.com/the-journal/how-to-build-trust-in-the-bedroom.

12 Rand Europe, *Health, wellbeing and productivity in the workplace* (Cambridge: RAND Corporation, 2015).

13 "Rooms & Prices," *The Collective Journal*, accessed November 2019, https://thecollective.com/locations/canary-wharf.

14 William Beck, "Plan of Lodging House for Single Men, in Albert Street, Mile End NewTown," in *Healthy Homes: Report*, delivered by M. D. Hill, MAIDIC, LSE Selected Pamphlets (1854): 42.

15 *The Collective Canary Wharf Management Plan*, submitted to Tower Hamlets as part of PA/18/01782/NC Planning Application for 36 Limeharbour, London, July 13, 2018.

16 Georg Simmel, "The Metropolis and Mental Life," in *On Individuality and Social Forms*, ed. Donald N. Levine (Chicago: University of Chicago Press, 1971), 52.

17 "Mile-End-New-Town," *British History Online*, accessed November 2019, http://.british-history.ac.uk/survey-london/vol27/pp265-288.

KIEWA: ENCOUNTERING THE HYDROELECTRIC MARGINS

Jonathan Russell

Stand in the centre a while and consider the edge. From 699 Bourke Street in Melbourne's CBD, the view stretches west towards the horizon and the urban boundary. But where is the edge of Melbourne? Is there a hard outer limit to the city, or is this edge greyer, less easily defined? Like every city, Melbourne sits at the centre of a broad hinterland in which human and natural systems intermix. Studies of urban metabolism have sought to quantify this mixing, measuring the movements of matter and energy as a proxy for the relationship between a city and its surroundings.[1] This quantitative method, while useful, tells us little about the nature of the boundaries created by the interaction of city and hinterland. It is difficult to interrogate the edge from the centre—instead, we need to follow the capillaries that spread across the landscape, long threads that tie the city into its context.

The office building at 699 Bourke Street is the near end of one such thread. In a control centre here, AGL, Australia's largest energy company, remotely operates ten hydroelectric power plants spread throughout Victoria.[2] Primary amongst these is the Kiewa Hydroelectric Scheme, located in the Alpine National Park more than 300 kilometres northeast of Melbourne. First proposed in 1911 and constructed between 1938 and 1961 (with further additions in 2009), the Kiewa Scheme remains the state's largest hydroelectric power source.[3] In Victoria, the vast majority of electricity is generated far from its point of consumption. Every household in Melbourne is directly, physically connected to this far-flung system of generators through a network of conduits, transformers and high-voltage power lines. These generators, in turn, are operated from control rooms like the one here on Bourke Street—functionally, the power station is a remote appendage of the city, the far-flung reaches of an urban border. What happens at this edge? When natural and artificial systems are superimposed, what kind of hybrid landscape emerges?

A note on terminology: boundary and border are sometimes used interchangeably, however there is value in untangling the two. Taking his cue from biologist Steven Gould, Richard Sennett writes that "The boundary is an edge where things end; the border is an edge where different groups interact."[4] Sennett applies these concepts primarily to urban planning, but they provide a useful framework for interrogating any edge condition, including the margins of a city: if the edge between inside and out is solid, easily defined and exclusionary it is a boundary. If the edge is porous, allowing for interaction between inside and out, it is a border. While not universally adhered to in the literature, the difference between a hard and porous edge is key to understanding the relationship between the city, the Kiewa Scheme and the wilderness beyond.

Gateway to the High Plains

The Kiewa Valley is a picturesque region four hours northeast of Melbourne at the foot of Mount Bogong, Victoria's highest peak. The area has been inhabited for thousands of years by First Nations peoples, with graziers and gold prospectors first arriving in the 1850s.[5] The Valley's largest settlement, Mount Beauty, was founded in 1946 by the State Electricity Commission (SEC) as a state-run model town, closed off for years to the outside world. The SEC, a state government entity, was the controlling authority for electricity in Victoria from 1921 to 1993. For much of this period, the Commission planned, constructed and operated all of the state's electrical infrastructure, including the Kiewa Hydroelectric Scheme. Today, Mount Beauty remains the gateway to the Bogong High Plains and the monumental power-generating infrastructural complex spread across these mountains.

In *Organization Space: Landscapes, Highways, and Houses in America*, Keller Easterling profiles Benton MacKaye, a 20th century American planner and theorist of infrastructure. Mackaye was influential in the early years of the Tennessee Valley Authority (TVA), a Depression-era superproject with interesting parallels to the Kiewa Scheme.

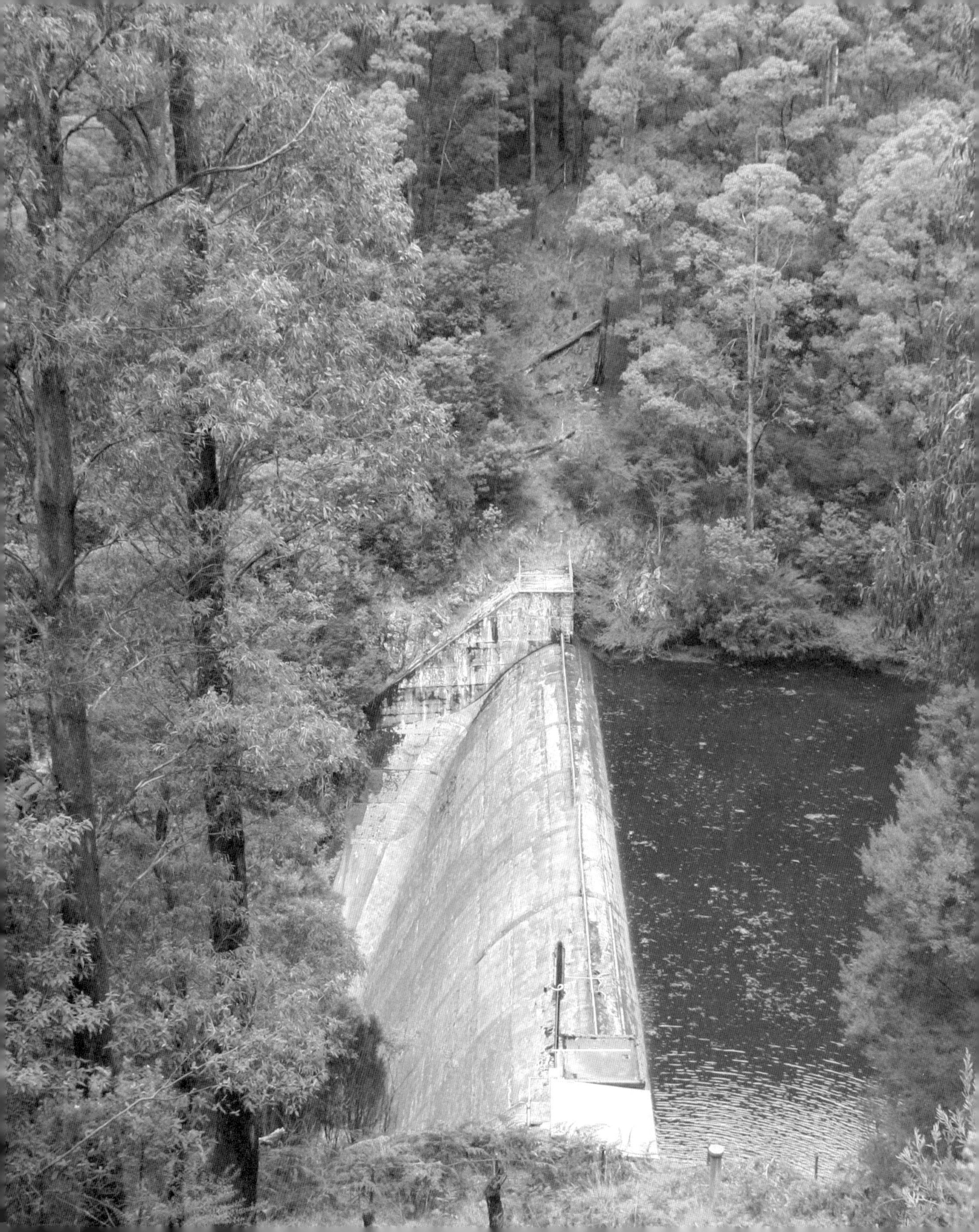

Specifically, the TVA illustrates Mackaye's interest in conceptualising space as defined by functional relationships rather than political boundaries. In Mackaye's ideal, for any given system, "the external boundary criteria depended on an emanating generative activity and was often an elastic condition."[6] The relationship between Melbourne and the Kiewa Scheme can be thought of through this lens. In Easterling's terms, the emanating generative activity was Melbourne's burgeoning demand for power. This led the city, under the auspices of the SEC, to reach out into its hinterland and the Kiewa Valley. The border between inside and outside the city is, again as per Easterling, an elastic condition: the functional relationship (power generation and transmission) between the Kiewa Valley and Melbourne allows us to see them as a single, connected entity despite their physical separation.

Climbing the Kiewa Valley

The Bogong High Plains Road winds out of Mount Beauty and into the Alpine National Park. The valley narrows and folds as it climbs, and soon the view is of tall Alpine Ash forests laid across the gullies and foothills of Mount Bogong. A fifteen-minute drive out of town the road dips to meet the Kiewa River, and an incongruous site emerges from the bush. A concrete bridge crosses the river to an industrial building nestled in a forested gully. This is Clover Power Station, completed in 1945 and the oldest of the four generators in the Kiewa Scheme. Built during World War II, it is functional and unadorned but tectonically rigorous, clad mostly in corrugated fibre-cement sheet due to wartime concrete shortages.[7] Clover is the most visible of the four stations in the scheme, the others being mostly buried underground. It is a large, almost brutal building, but here—enveloped by forest in the steep foothills—it is dwarfed by its context. A short way downstream, Clover Dam is similarly inconspicuous. A reinforced concrete gravity dam built in 1954, in the decades since, the bush has regrown and surrounded it, the ogee profile of the dam wall stained and spotted with moss. (Fig. 1) This is an integral, still-functioning part of the Kiewa Scheme, but time has softened it into its context, and today an abandoned atmosphere pervades the place.

It is worth pausing here to consider the name and nature of the Kiewa Hydroelectric Scheme, and dwelling particularly on the idea of a hydroelectric 'scheme.' Hydroelectric power generation dates back to the 1870s and has existed in Australia since at least 1895.[8] The basic operation in all cases is the same: transmuting gravitational potential energy into electricity. Water at a high point falls by force of gravity and is directed at pressure towards a turbine. The momentum of the falling water rotates the turbine, which is connected to a generator. Powerful magnets in the generator convert this kinetic energy into electricity that feeds into the wider grid. The generating capacity of any hydroelectric system is driven by two fundamental variables—the volume of water passing through the system and the vertical distance that water falls. Prior to construction of the Kiewa Scheme, officials from the State Electricity Commission conducted study tours, which included tours during the construction of the massive Hoover and Grand Coulee dams in North America.[9] These dams, along with most of the world's largest hydroelectric projects, collect and generate electricity at a single site. In this configuration, water is released to turbines either inside or below one large dam, with the overall drop (and hence the energy of the water) equal to the height of the dam. The Kiewa Scheme operates somewhat differently. The East and West Branches of the Kiewa are low volume, fast-flowing rivers that drain a mostly-flat mountain plateau, the Bogong High Plains. From top to bottom, the Kiewa Scheme falls around 1200 metres, but no single power plant harnesses the energy of the whole drop. Instead, water passes from dam to tunnel to turbine before flowing to the next station at a lower elevation, repeating the process to turn as many as four generators on its way down the valley.

The SEC's 1960s-era illustration of the scheme is a useful guide to the hydrological sequence of the Kiewa Scheme. (Fig. 2) On the High Plains, Pretty Valley and Rocky Valley reservoirs collect streams and seasonal snowmelt and pass the water through a tunnel and pipeline to the underground Mackay Creek Power Station. Water released from the Mackay Creek Station is diverted underground to Bogong Power Station, long planned but only completed in 2009. Bogong's release is captured behind Junction Dam and released by underground pipeline to Clover Power Station, its incongruous above-ground generator hall dwarfed by the surrounding mountains. Clover Station releases to the adjacent Clover Dam, which diverts water to West Kiewa Station, buried 140 metres below ground. The Kiewa, then, is not any single place or facility, but a scheme: an integrated yet diffuse infrastructural complex, with individual components scattered throughout the mountain landscape. Why does Clover Station seem so dwarfed? At least in part because the Kiewa Scheme is a stealthy kind of infrastructure: its component parts are spread so widely across the landscape that it is never perceived all at once.

Fig 1 (Opposite): Clover Dam. All images by author unless otherwise stated.

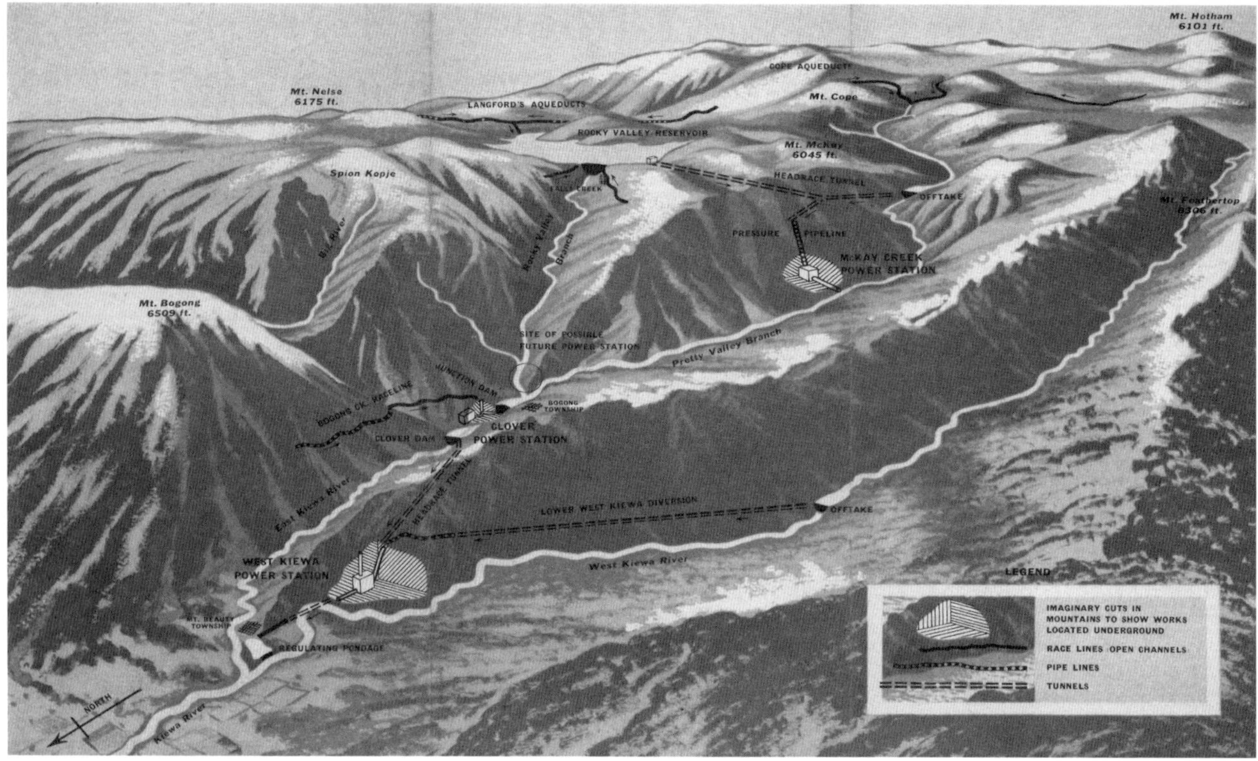

Stream Gauges and Aqueducts

Fundamentally, the Kiewa Scheme is driven by the natural hydrology of the Bogong High Plains. Since the early 20th century, the distant Kiewa watershed was considered the best site in Victoria to generate hydroelectric power.[10] A successful scheme requires the efficient exploitation of natural hydrological processes—harnessing and redirecting flows of water in order to use their embodied energy. The Kiewa, which forgoes the simplicity of a single large dam in favour of a distributed infrastructural landscape, is more complex again, and its development began only after decades of hydrological research. High on the Bogong Plains, the oldest fragments of the Kiewa Scheme are a network of stream depth, snow and rain gauges dating as far back as the 1920s. These instruments still operate today, dotting the treeless alpine landscape. (Fig. 3) Encountering a lone iron shed standing sentinel on the High Plains is a reminder that this is not a pure, untrammelled wilderness. Rather, it is a carefully monitored landscape whose natural hydrological processes have been measured, quantified and modelled for more than 100 years. The shape and operation of the Kiewa Scheme has been formed by these natural processes, a vast human undertaking pressed and moulded by the contours of the mountain landscape.

Fig 2 (Above): State Electricity Commission of Victoria, Diagram of Kiewa Hydroelectric Scheme, 1960. Image released into public domain.

Behind Clover Power Station, the hills rise sharply towards Mount Bogong. But this backcountry, at first glance an impenetrable wilderness, bears marks of human activity. High above the power station, passing bushwalkers might stumble on an abandoned rail yard, rusted-out rolling stock and overgrown tramway tracks alongside a deep concrete-lined channel. (Fig. 4) This is the near end of the disused Bogong Creek Raceline, a 9.3 kilometre long aqueduct completed in 1954 that once drained 23 square kilometres of these foothills, redirecting the water into Clover Dam and, ultimately, the West Kiewa Power Station.[11] The abandoned rail twists and turns alongside the aqueduct, across spurs and mountain gullies. Large sluice gates stand permanently open where water that would once have passed through the raceline now flows down to the Kiewa River. Over 40 kilometres of aqueducts and racelines were built for the Kiewa Scheme, and they tell an important story about the intertwined relationship between the natural and artificial processes at work here. An aqueduct is an artificial subversion of a pre-existing hydrological system. In the Kiewa Scheme, aqueducts intercept creeks and streams of all sizes, capturing

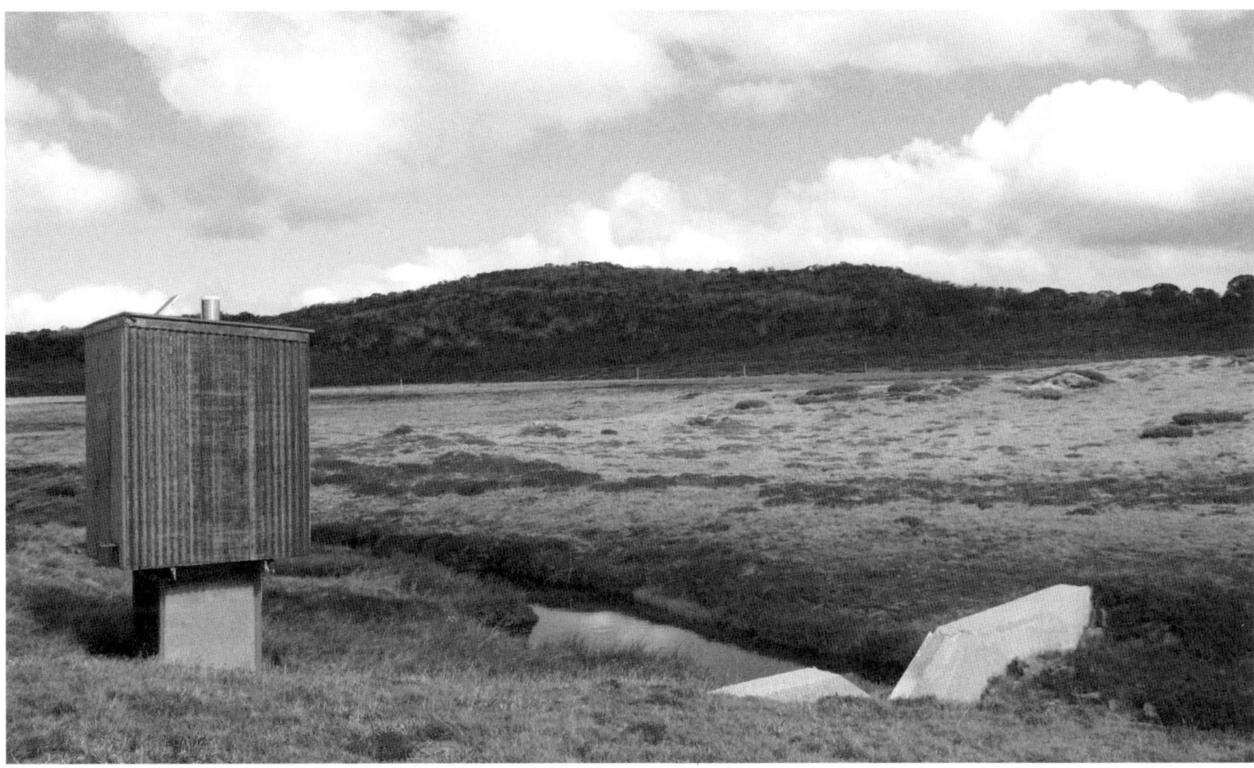

water and redirecting its flow, draining it into the system's pipelines and power stations. In this way, the total runoff into the Scheme (and hence its generating capacity) is increased and the total runoff into adjacent watersheds is decreased. These aqueducts are less visible in the landscape than power stations, reservoirs and transmission lines, but they represent something important: the subtle yet powerful human hand reshaping the hydrology of the Kiewa River.

Stream gauges and aqueducts, then, stand as contrasting totems of the relationship between natural and artificial in the Kiewa watershed. Every stream gauge tells the story of an artificial system adapted to the contours of a natural hydrological process. Every aqueduct tells the inverse story: of humankind bending natural hydrologies, reaching out and altering the landscape for its own benefit. Through these lenses, we can see that the Kiewa Hydroelectric Scheme is a hybrid system operating at the border of wilderness and city, tying them together in ways that blur distinctions between the two. William Cronon, in his essay 'The Trouble With Wilderness,' argues that we need a more nuanced conception of wilderness that accounts for this grey area: the human influence on 'natural' processes and the natural influence on 'human' processes.[12] The incongruity we feel when encountering a power station in the middle of a national park emerges at least in part from our tendency to categorise the human and the natural worlds as fundamentally opposed, and to imagine hard boundaries between the two that rarely, if ever, exist. When we encounter the margins of the Kiewa Scheme, we are also standing at the border of a much larger system—the city itself—that is not diametrically opposed to the wilderness but fundamentally, constructively dependent on it.

Fig 3 (Above): Stream Gauge at Cope Creek.

Following Flow Lines

The Kiewa Scheme, by virtue of its diffuse nature, is sewn tightly into the landscape it occupies. The intermingling of natural and human systems that occur at its edges can be sketched by following a single stream through the mountains to Power Station Number 1 at Mackay Creek. In the backcountry of the High Plains, a dead-end vehicle track follows the Cope West Aqueduct along the 1700 metre contour line to a lonely weir. (Fig. 5) Here, the High Plains Creek is prevented from falling away into the Bundara River and is redirected back into the Kiewa watershed. Along the way, the aqueduct collects countless tiny rivulets, each becoming part of the greater Kiewa Scheme. At a low saddle, the aqueduct flows into Cope Creek, a well preserved natural

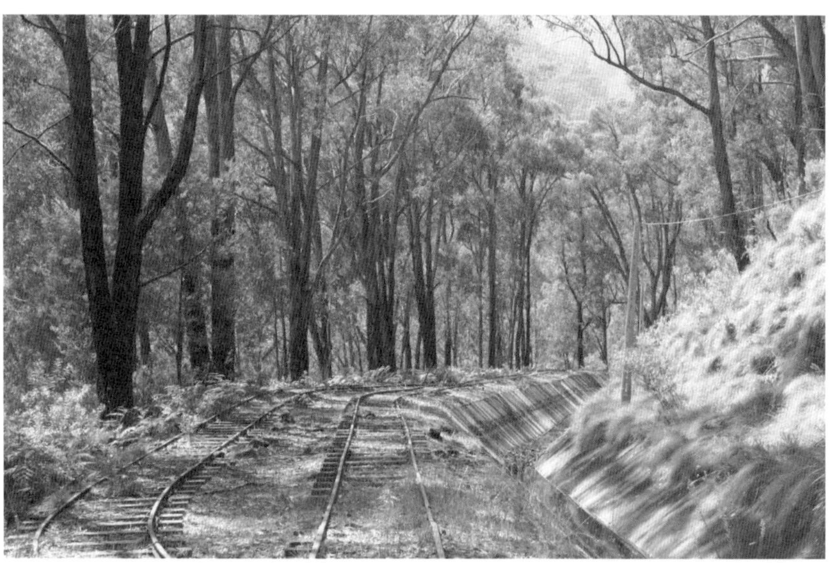
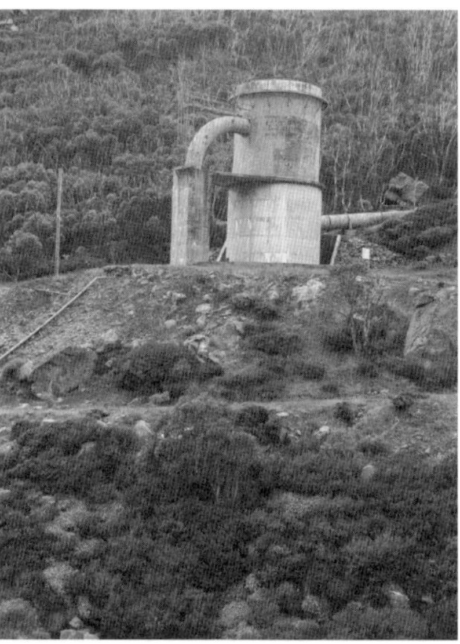
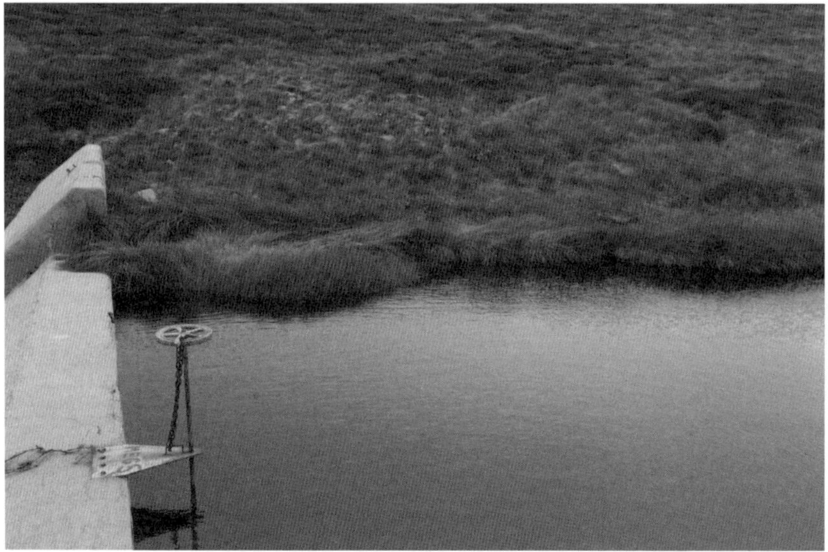
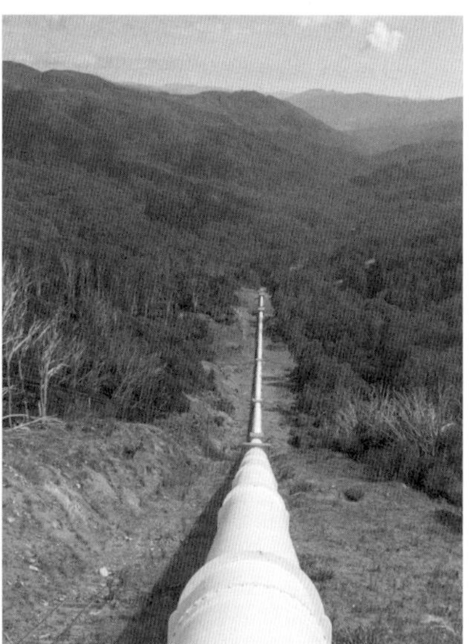

Fig 4 (Top Left): Bogong Creek Raceline.

Fig 5 (Bottom Left): Weir at High Plains Creek.

Fig 6 (Top Right): Pretty Valley Vortex Tank at Damsite Hill.

Fig 7 (Bottom Right): Mackay Creek Headrace Pipeline.

watercourse supporting moss bed ecosystems untouched since European arrival.[13] Cope Creek drains into a small man made reservoir, the Pretty Valley Pondage, which in turn discharges down a narrow valley below an outcropping named Damsite Hill. A 1947 plan for the Kiewa Scheme envisioned a massive concrete dam across the throat of this gully, but plans were cancelled during an economic downturn in 1951.[14] Today, remnants of the dam's foundations sit in the gorge, but water is instead diverted through a tunnel under Mount Mackay. At the head of this tunnel, another incongruous piece of Kiewa infrastructure stands partway up the face of the gorge. (Fig. 6) A massive steel tank, with once-bright orange paint faded and flaking, stands where the Pretty Valley Pipeline turns underground. Several storeys high, the tank is nonetheless dwarfed by the mountains, and like much of the Kiewa infrastructure appears to be slowly disappearing into its context. On the opposite side of Mount Mackay, the tunnel emerges into a wide steel pipeline that marches down the mountainside, cutting a scar through the forest. (Fig. 7) Built to save the delay of tunnel construction, the Mackay Pipeline is the least-camouflaged part of the Kiewa system—the bright-white tube has never faded into its context.[15] At the bottom of the Pipeline lies Mackay Creek Power Station. The Mackay Creek turbine hall is far underground, leaving only an unassuming concrete depot visible on the surface. Beside it, giant transformers fill the air with a constant low buzz, a characteristic 98Hz G note driven by the frequency of the power grid. Here, at the start of the long transmission network, you can imagine the path back to the city: hundreds of kilometres of wire routing back to 699 Bourke Street and completing the circuit between city and hinterland, centre and periphery.

What can we learn about the relationship between a city and its hinterland by encountering the margins of the Kiewa Scheme? First, that the edge of the city does not lie along any imagined municipal boundary line. Easterling and Mackaye ask us to expand our perspective and think about functionally organised divisions of space. This functional perspective focuses our attention on the dynamics of the expanded city. Flows of electricity and water, yes, but also flows of people and information and capital pass constantly back and forth between the centre and periphery. If on this basis we consider the Kiewa Scheme part of the city, then one edge of the city lies along the watersheds, aqueducts and pipelines scattered through the mountains. Using Sennett's terminology, this is not a boundary but a border—a rich site of movement and exchange between inside and out. Water flows into the Scheme from a thousand tiny rivulets, forest grows up around decades-old structures, camouflaging them in the visual language of wilderness. Infrastructure dots the landscape, warping and reshaping hydrological systems millions of years in the making. The Kiewa Scheme is a giant machine, operated by remote control from hundreds of kilometres away and sewn deeply into the landscape. The work of William Cronon asks us to question our assumptions about wilderness and untouched nature, and the Kiewa Scheme provides an opportunity to do that. The Bogong High Plains and the Kiewa Valley today are, fundamentally, a hybrid landscape: neither entirely wild nor entirely controlled, neither entirely natural nor entirely artificial. This hybridity is more obvious here in the mountains, where the juxtaposition between monumental works of engineering and spectacular natural landscapes draw our attention. But perhaps the Kiewa Scheme is only an extreme example of a fundamental truth about the relationship between a city and its hinterland: that from the very centre to the outermost edge, every landscape is shaped by a complex, dynamic mix of human and natural forces.

01 Christopher Kennedy, John Cuddihy, and Joshua Engel-Yang, "The Changing Metabolism of Cities," *Journal of Industrial Ecology*, 11, no. 2 (February, 2008): 43-59.
02 AGL Hydro, "Hydroelectric Power Stations," accessed April 9, 2020, https://www.agl.com.au/about-agl/how-we-source-energy/hydroelectric-assets.
03 Graham Napier and Geoff Easdown, *The Kiewa Story* (Melbourne: State Electricity Commission, 1993), vi-ix.
04 Richard Sennett, "The Open City," 2013, accessed April 9, 2020, https://www.richardsennett.com/site/senn/UploadedResources/The%20Open%20City.pdf.
05 Ruth E. Lawrence, "The interaction between the environment land use and hydrology of the Bogong High Plains area from 1850 to 1985" (PhD Thesis, University of Melbourne, 1990), 5.
06 Keller Easterling, *Organization Space: Landscapes, Highways, and Houses in America* (Cambridge: MIT Press, 2001), 58.
07 Napier and Easdowne, *The Kiewa Story*, 78.
08 "A Brief History of Hydropower," International Hydropower Association, accessed April 11, 2020, https://www.hydropower.org/a-brief-history-of-hydropower.
09 Napier and Easdowne, *The Kiewa Story*, viii-ix.
10 Parliament of Victoria, *Votes and Proceedings 1920* (Melbourne: Parliament of Victoria, 1920), 46.
11 Lawrence, "The interaction," 143.
12 William Cronon, "The Trouble with Wilderness; or, Getting Back to the Wrong Nature," in *Uncommon Ground: Rethinking the Human Place in Nature*, ed. William Cronon (New York: W.W. Norton & Co., 1995), 69-90.
13 Lawrence, "The interaction," 24.
14 Ibid., 575.
15 State Electricity Commission of Victoria, *Kiewa Hydro-electric Scheme: General Development 1911-1961* (Melbourne: State Electricity Commission, 1973).

CONSTRUCTION OF THE GARDEN AND THE PEOPLE

Wang Shu
Translated from Mandarin by Han Jiang and Ester Leung

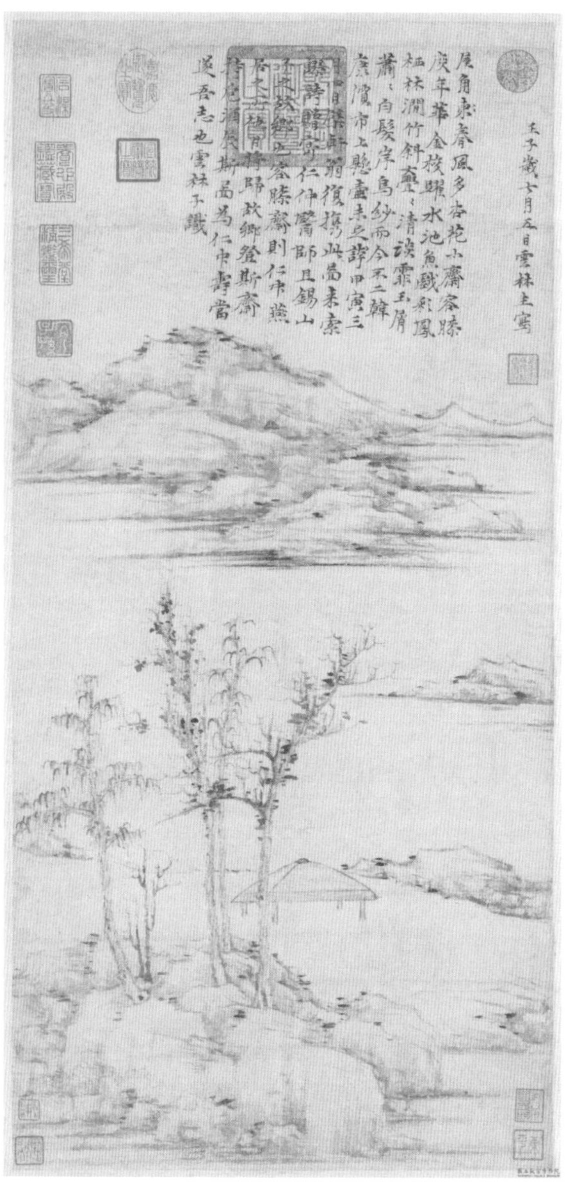

For the past few years I have been teaching while designing houses, and there are always students around me. There are three things I will often tell them about my attitude towards designing architecture. First of all, before an architect, I am first a literati. Secondly, I suggest that one not prioritise the most important thing, but rather the most tasteful thing. Finally, building a house translates to constructing a small world. After all these years of instilling knowledge in students, I am still not sure how much they understand.

Every spring, I take my students to experience the Chinese gardens in Suzhou. I particularly remember in 2006, an artist friend called me and asked: "why are you still visiting those classical gardens even when you have been there hundreds of times? Are you not getting tired of them?" I remember I told him that I am slow-witted so I need to visit them again and again. At this time, when the world is fraught with clamour and impetuousness, matters that are serene, such as gardens, require attention.

Constructing gardens has always been a favoured activity of the traditional Chinese literati. In recent years, I often start my lecture on building gardens with the painting Rongxi Studio, by Ni Zan, an artist of the Yuan Dynasty.[1] (Fig. 1) It is a typical Shan shui.[2] The top section depicts mountains in the distance, with patches of wintry forests; the middle section represents water features, which are always left as blank by Ni; and a couple of timeworn trees occupy the front of the scene. A pavilion is placed under the trees, with four simple, delicately thin columns, hardly holding any weight, but supporting a thatched roof above. If we treat the boundary of the painting as a wall, with a pavilion, pond in the middle and trees or stones in front, it is considered a typical Chinese garden layout. However, what I am trying to emphasise is the attitude.

Fig 1: Rongxi Studio, Ni Zan (Yuan Dynasty). Collection of the National Palace Museum, Taipei.

The interesting fact is that the reactions to lectures vary dramatically by different audiences. For domestic Chinese students, Rongxi Studio raises a discussion mainly about value systems. This is of course vitally important; if there is no value judgement of building houses in advance, one can easily lose their direction. I used to conduct lectures at American universities and the professors there were always excited, saying that they got to know a completely different architectural theory from what they were familiar with. Attitude towards the world is more crucial than knowledge. This reminds me of Mr. Tong Jun. He was an overseas student at the University of Pennsylvania and a recipient of the Boxer Indemnity Scholarship.[3] He had travelled around Europe and had a solid foundation in Western architecture. However, unexpectedly, once he returned to the motherland, he switched his focus to the study of traditional Chinese architectural history, especially the history of Chinese gardens. This shift of direction in his academic pursuits signified the change in his thinking and values. Mr. Liu Dunzhen wrote in the preface of Mr. Tong's book *Glimpses of Gardens in Eastern China*:

> Before the war against Japan, Mr. Tong visited numerous classical gardens in South Eastern China during his spare time, but all he witnessed was ruin and decay. Thinking about how rich people indulged in the constructions without protecting the classical gardens and sensing there was a danger of losing this traditional art of building classical gardens, he decided to investigate further and write a book about them.[4]

Reading this now, it feels like a reflection of what is happening in China today. There is no doubt that Chinese gardens will disappear if we do not preserve them. It is even worse if we destroy them in the name of inheritance by not doing a literary study of them.

Differing from the later scholars who would study classical gardens, Mr. Tong truly had the temperament and charm of a master literati. He was well-read, knowledgeable, and worked tirelessly and rigorously, which made him both admirable and respectable. However, what touched me most was what he once said: "Nowadays architects are not capable of poetic garden construction because they prioritise construction technology over sentiment."

'Sentiment'—such a weightless word, yet it distinguishes real culture differences. For Chinese literati, 'sentiment' arises from learning through nature, which holds higher philosophical value than human society. Individuals need to study the principles of nature rigorously to have the chance of ever possibly reaching its balance and harmony, and the degree of one's enlightenment differentiates one's 'sentiments.' Classical gardens, as a construction practice through which literati directly participated in the real world, showcase some of the philosophical perspectives of Chinese people. The importance of the literati's involvement in the real world is not only in their participation, but also their criticism. Indeed, the set of paintings by Wen Zhengming for the Humble Administrator's Garden is still carved in the Garden's hallways.[5] (Fig. 2) Compared to the tremendous scale of the Garden and complexity of buildings within, Wen's paintings delicately focused on the simplicity of bamboo fences and modest thatched houses. In my opinion, this is a gentle criticism of the Humble Administrator's Garden itself. Certainly, throughout the history of constructing Chinese Gardens, criticism from literati remains constant. These criticisms prolong and sustain the life of tradition. The aspect of Tong Jun that I respect most, apart from his understanding and contribution towards the scholarship during his life, is his determination to stay away from an era of fickle architecture during his later years. This makes him a representative figure in the history of modern Chinese architecture on a new spiritual level. I have seen a photograph of him in his later years: Tong was in a terribly old but clean white shirt, eyes wide open, staring at me as I peered into the photograph. He was standing next to a pine tree and looked like a true gentleman from the ancient paintings. Among the four fundamental architectural masters in modern Chinese history: Liang Sicheng, Yang Yanbao, Liu Dunzhen and Tong Jun, Tong was the only one without any official obligations, and the last one to appear at public occasions. But he would be the most profound influence for students like me. Not only because of his academic achievements, but also due to his strength of character and sentiments belonging to the tradition of Chinese literati.

I often feel that Mr. Tong must have regrets in his heart since he devoted his life to garden research, but never got the chance to practice it during his lifetime. However, if there was to be an opportunity, how would Mr.Tong build a garden? Perhaps the clues can be seen in his article, 'Essay about the Sui Garden.' The owner of the garden, Yuan Mei, is a gifted scholar from Hangzhou. He became a Jinshi at the age of 25 (the 4th year of the Qianlong Emperor) resigned at the age of 34, and built the Sui Garden in Nanjing.[6] Having lived in the garden for nearly 50 years, he is one of the few Chinese literati who enjoyed a long life and the happiness of living in a garden. As written by Mr. Tong, Yuan bought himself the deserted garden, which was named after its former owner's surname Sui. Rather than formulating massive architecture to make the garden impressive, Yuan instead only trimmed the

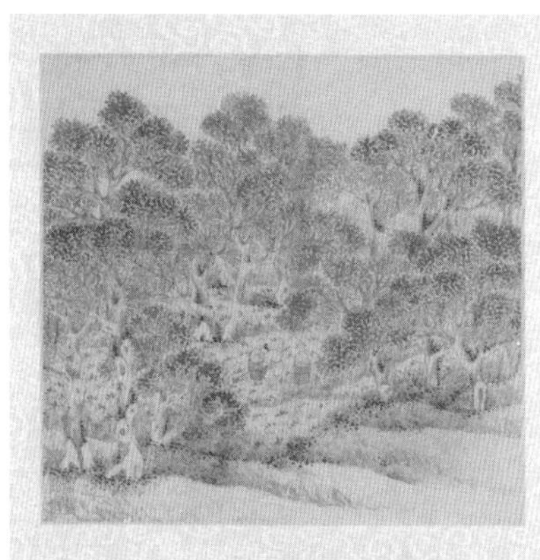
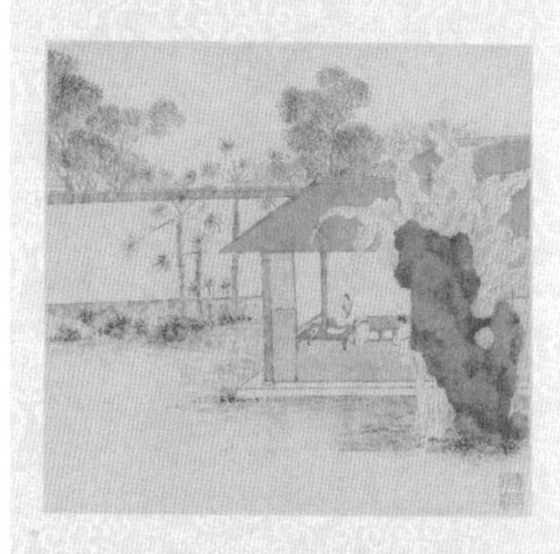
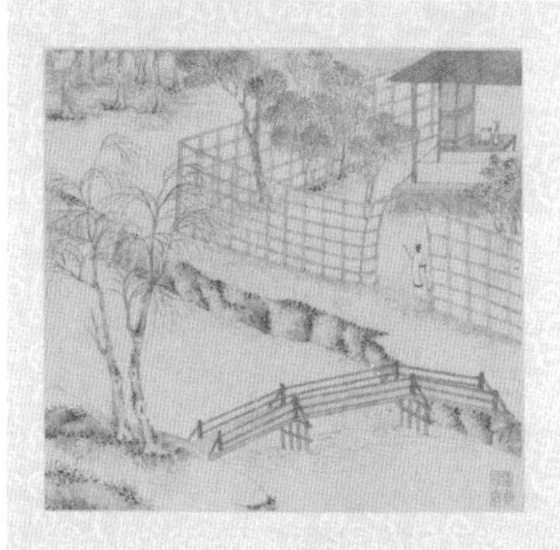

garden's excess weeds and branched to accentuate its existing features. He used the gestures of trees to form a kiosk, extended the cypress to be the pavilion, and did not build any walls so the garden would be open to the public. Parallel to his garden construction, Yuan Mei stopped pursuing his political career to read, write, and earn himself a decent reputation by his numerous tasteful papers and books with other literati. Attracted by his fame, many literati came to visit him for discussion.[7] Interestingly, Yuan truly influenced the society by distancing himself from it with a precisely new way of living. As Yuan explained, rather than changing the name of the garden, he changed the meaning of the name instead. For the word and surname 'sui' means 'follow,' so he simply 'followed' the natural environment of the old garden, rather than forcing his own ways onto the garden's development. In Tong Jun's book on gardens, he wrote a specialised article about the Sui Garden which showed what style he really admired and the implicit, but confident, values he held for building gardens. Mr. Tong specifically mentioned in his writing that Yuan was very broad-minded. At the end of his life, he told his two sons that his wish was to keep the Sui garden as it was for at least another thirty years from his passing. Thirty years flew by, one of Yuan's friends visited the garden—it had become desolate and was used as a wine shop. Yuan had been maintaining the garden for over 50 years, which was similar to nurturing a life. As the old saying goes: "constructing a garden is difficult, maintaining one is even harder." Building a Chinese garden is such a special kind of architectural activity. It completely differs from today's architecture and urban construction programme, which no one cares about after completion. The garden is a living creature. The gardener, the resident, and the garden grow and evolve together, rising and falling like natural beings. This is indeed an important inspiration for today's architectural and urban design.

Constructing gardens represents a completely different kind of architecture that we are pursuing today. It is an architectural activity that is especially local and spiritual. In an age of cultural disorientation, it is hard to capture uncertainties, and that is why it is so hard to build gardens, especially when gardens are alive. Mr. Tong wrote in 1937 after he visited a garden that "the plans I drew of this garden are not very accurate, but approximate dimensions. That is because the arrangement is not limited to rules and methods. The garden is full of vitality and flexibility, I do not think it is of importance to know its exact measurements." I doubt how much Mr. Tong's words are understood by people nowadays. Building gardens represents a vital culture that is not restricted by rules and traditions; it relies more on the people who cultivate them; on their knowledge, taste and understanding of gardens. To some extent, the garden is there because the people are living with it—without the people, the garden is dead too. Furthermore, in my mind, gardens do not just belong to the literati, but also a constructed image of the Chinese homeland today. Discussion about gardens is to find the way to construct the Chinese homeland, as well as how to rebuild its cultural confidence and local values. I know that with the education of our generation, it is somehow difficult; however, there must be someone to do such things which requires concentration and persistence. We would be reshaped through things like building gardens.

Fig 2 (Above): The Booklet of the Humble Administrator's Garden, Wen Zhengming, the Ming Dynasty.

Discussion on 'sentiments' for constructing gardens should never be this heavy. China has too many scholars with idle hands. Li Yu is another literati who I admire and who was able to build gardens by hand. His essays cover a broad range of topics, including dining, living, make-up, construction, even toilets, and what pattern should be used on the windows of boats in the West Lake. He was similar to Yuan Mei, who prioritised strength of character and dared to take on critics and rumours, as well as being open to life and embracing its possibilities while being a rebel in society. These literati were capable of building gardens and our society today needs such literati to participate in architectural activities. However, it is hardly achievable for the universities nowadays to cultivate these kinds of people, who are the vibrant carriers of a local culture.

Things are not as negative as they seem. In fact, profound and subtle ideas in Chinese culture have never relied on the public at large, but instead on the enlightenment of a few. Yesterday afternoon, I felt that I could not write anything. So I went to the West Lake with my wife to have tea. Looking at the picturesque distant mountains across the lake, I remembered my friend Lin Haizhong. Knowing that he had opened a new painting studio by the lake, I called him to see if we could visit it. He told me on the phone that he had already left on a solo trip in the mountains of Fuyang. Haizhong is younger than me. He has a gentle temperament and open-minded personality, as well as outstanding talents in drawing Shan shui of the wintry forests. Another young friend of mine, Wu Gan, is very skillful and knowledgeable in analysing calligraphy and painting. He once commented on Hai Zhong's xiaokai, saying that Zhong is able to portray the delicate senses of how many hairs are on the tip of the brush.[8] A minimal error or deviation may result in wide divergence and one false step will make a great difference. I thought of Hai Zhong once telling me that he was sketching in Guoqing Temple Mountain, and his painting style turned out a little like Li Cheng (the painter of the early Song Dynasty).[9] Thinking of these I feel very pleased, knowing that the spirit of the literati still exists and so the making of gardens will be possible.

01 《容膝斋图》 Literal meaning: a painting of the house named Rongxi. Rongxi means accommodating the knees, describing the house as comparatively narrow. In Chinese culture, physical limitations are adopted as a device which, by negation, suggests broadness of the mind.

02 Shan shui (literal translation: 'Mountain-water') refers to a style of traditional Chinese painting that depicts scenery or natural landscapes, via brush and ink. Mountains, rivers and waterfalls are prominent in this art form.

03 The Boxer Indemnity Scholarship was a scholarship program for Chinese students to be educated in the United States. In 1908, the U.S Congress passed a bill to return to China the excess of Boxer Indemnity in the form of the scholarship program, amounting to over 17 million dollars.

04 From 1932 to 1937, Tong Jun investigated and researched 109 private gardens in 27 cities in Jiangsu and Zhejiang provinces, and completed the manuscript of *Records of Gardens in South Eastern China,* which founded a new and profound direction for analyzing gardens in the contemporary context. Mr. Tong re-wrote the book again in English until his death in 1983. Only until 1997, Glimpses of Gardens in Eastern China was published, carrying Tong's lifelong research about classical gardens.

05 The Humble Administrator's Garden is one of the most famous gardens of Suzhou. The garden was initially constructed during 1131-1162 in the Southern Song Dynasty. Since then, it has continually changed ownership, been destroyed and also modified. The Chinese name for this garden may also be translated as the Garden of the Inept Administrator. In Chinese culture, 'inept' has a delicate meaning. The great and wise people tend to be recognised as gentle, broad-minded and humble-they are portrayed as being plain and 'inept.'

06 Jinshi was the highest and final degree in the imperial examination in Imperial China. The examination was usually taken in the imperial capital in the palace, and was also called the Metropolitan Exam. Recipients are sometimes referred to in English-language sources as Imperial Scholars.

07 Literati's communication is of significant importance in Chinese culture. The philosophy behind this activity was first described in the Book of Rights, of which the history could be traced back to the 1st century BC. It said that a lack of alumi's communication during the study process will inevitably lead to the narrowed version of knowledge. More famous and respectful the literati is, more others will visit and consult with him.

08 Literal translation is 'Small Regular Script,' one of the most popular types of calligraphy.

09 Li Cheng, Fan Kuan, and Guan Tong together became known as the "three great rival artists." Cheng did many landscape paintings with diluted ink, known as "treating ink like gold," which gives the appearance of being in a foggy dream. He was considered the best landscape painter of all time.

REFUGEE SPACE-TIME

Jennifer Ferng

Unique faces of the global refugee crisis have been rendered anonymous by the recent COVID-19 pandemic, which has exacerbated forced displacements due to war, famine, natural disasters, and religious persecution. Refugee camps like Za'atari in Jordan have been trying to maintain appropriate levels of sanitation and hygiene. Vulnerable individuals, such as those featured as part of the United Nations High Commission for Refugees' (UNHCR) emergency appeal report, are depicted wearing disposable face masks. Given this pandemic, human suffering in the form of inequality, exclusion and global unemployment has been more widespread for refugees, migrants, those in poverty, homeless, and indigenous peoples. The impact of COVID-19 has been felt acutely in refugee camps and cities in over 196 countries where resettled refugees struggle to access essential services. Yet, the UNHCR must navigate difficult health systems at international and local levels, amidst complications about who must take responsibility for refugees and the stateless.[1]

Given these turbulent times, the UNHCR remains a critical organisation that guides state governments in their treatment of asylum seekers and refugees. This essay revisits two landmark documents authored by the UNHCR in order to demonstrate the entanglements between architecture and law when it comes to the current refugee crisis. The 1951 Refugee Convention and 1967 Protocol determined who could be considered a refugee. Today, the spatial and temporal borders of this political category have expanded immeasurably. Anthropologists, lawyers, and sociologists have had significant roles in shaping policies related to refugee migrations, but more recently, the expertise of architects and planners is slowly being acknowledged in the construction of refugee camps and housing solutions. Architects have embraced the creation of humanitarian shelter often with mixed consequences, imposing Western-centric values on other regions of the world. At the same time, refugees' global movements have collapsed conventional notions of geography and generated new models of law where international, national, and local governance overlap. A sense of place is no longer experienced by refugees, and we have witnessed how local communities have become eroded by third country offshore processing and immigration detention.

Global movements of refugees are also becoming more intractable in the 21st century, with refugees crossing more continents and staying longer in transit than ever before; the UNHCR's self-standing tent is but one design example that has tried to cater for worldwide instability (Fig. 1). The UNHCR has estimated that around 70.8 million people were displaced at the end of 2018. Within this particular number, at least 25.9 million were considered refugees, and 3.5 million were asylum seekers; almost 57% of the refugees covered by the UNHCR originated from within Syria, Afghanistan, and South Sudan.[2] Even during a health pandemic, vulnerable members of society are prone to greater upheaval when visas are due to be cancelled and national borders are closed to non-citizens.[3] Sociological experts claim that the international refugee regime is "fundamentally broken," and the "crisis of confinement" around refugees remains ineffective, leaving millions of people in search of shelter.[4] Mass migrations of refugees have made current systems of healthcare, education, and housing ineffective. In terms of solutions for responding to the crisis, 'responsibility by proximity' can assist in distributing the ethical responsibility of hosting refugees. What immigration law scholar Alex Aleinikoff calls an "arc of protection," once extended only to refugees, is now used as a commonplace legal term that covers other types of displaced persons as well.[5]

The UNHCR's 1951 Refugee Convention defined anyone who might be labelled a refugee in legal terms, and the 1967 Protocol later removed any geographic and temporal restrictions on who could be considered a refugee. Both the multilateral treaty and protocol generated refugees as a new type of political subject who could come from anywhere at any period of time. These two critical pieces of legislation have determined how state governments have treated, hosted and resettled asylum seekers and refugees for the past 70 years. Both of these legal documents have not been extensively revised since 1967. I treat both of these legal documents as part of a potential archive that links the built environment to law through the political subject of the refugee. The dissolution of any *space-time* continuum frames refugees as being political subjects lacking any connection to place, nationality, or historicity. Their temporality, which reaches back into the past and extends into the present day, also affects local communities in which they reside. This sense of timelessness, based on a refugee's status, transforms camps and cities into sites devoid of law, architecture, and more importantly, time. Geographic places are rendered secondary as legal definitions of citizenship and residency become more important in determining basic human rights.

Space-time refers to the physical limits of both geography and place when considering the plight of asylum seekers and refugees who are travelling further and staying longer in third countries. This term addresses how refugees consider their own lived experience as they move from country to country, from states of impermanence to resettlement. Conventional models of *space* or *time* no longer apply to the international refugee regime, and the constant conditions of being simultaneous and on the move characterise contemporary refugees as they navigate various legal systems in order to seek asylum. As stateless subjects, refugees experience *simultaneity* (being confined in one place) and *movement* (being on the move and not being allowed to stay or settle) throughout their journeys: two conditions which underscore refugees' spatial and temporal experiences as perpetually changing. This essay's title refers to Sigfried Giedion's concept of *space-time* in architecture—a definition of physical space that included a notion of time within architecture. Giedion defined *simultaneity* as a mode of seeing various aspects of an object without moving and *movement* as a mode of understanding an object by moving around it.[6] *Refugee space-time* thus represents a new political state where asylum seekers and refugees are defined by their ability to understand their own situation in one place and to continue moving onto new locations in order to receive refugee status.

The brief example of Syrian, Iraqi and Iranian refugees who have resettled in Australian cities illustrates how conditions of *simultaneity* and *movement* complicate refugees' lives in a new country, when they begin to pursue permanent residency and citizenship. Not surprisingly, the legal processes that state governments and organisations like the UNHCR use to determine a person's status are closely tied to the built environment; legal residency and permanent status of resettled refugees dictate whether or not they qualify for temporary accommodations or more permanent housing in Australian cities. I explore how the dissolution of spatial coordinates, or a permanent attachment to one place, becomes embedded within the legal processes of refugee determination.

Legal definitions of refugees reciprocally shape how these vulnerable populations are spatially constructed—that is, political subjects not tethered to places or historical periods are circumscribed by legislation that dictates their position in *space* and *time*. As subjects, refugees are both timeless and endless, meaning that their citizenship from a certain country is always superseded by the category of refugee. *Refugee space-time* thus makes architecture and its physical manifestations obsolete when discussing mass migrations, and in re-reading legal documents from the UNHCR, architecture in the traditional sense becomes reconnected to definitions of illegality and legality, shaping how refugees and the stateless may be considered.[7] Conventional interpretations of the built environment are thus remapped in radical ways, reflecting refugees' trajectories within complex legal systems of determination and resettlement.

Re-reading the Law

Refugee camps are the most obvious example of spatialised resettlement, but cities pose a greater challenge since access to temporary housing must be balanced against the rights of permanent citizens in dense urban communities. 21st century spatial and temporal definitions of legality faced by asylum seekers and refugees are now regulated by international conventions, national borders, and local ordinances that govern the lives of migrants in cities. Definitions of legality and illegality have grown more complicated now that humanitarian organisations and NGOs operate services within the borders of nations as third-party contractors. Legal conventions created in the early 20th century by the UNHCR are no longer adequate to describe the complexities and flows of people moving between countries today. Among the most affected are developing countries where at least 86% of asylum seekers and refugees are hosted in the Global South.[8] In light of these circumstances, boundaries no longer function strictly as borders—that is, they are no longer territorial lines that admit or restrict groups of people entering a country. Instead, borders now operate as greater elastic zones determined not by physical geography or proximity, but by

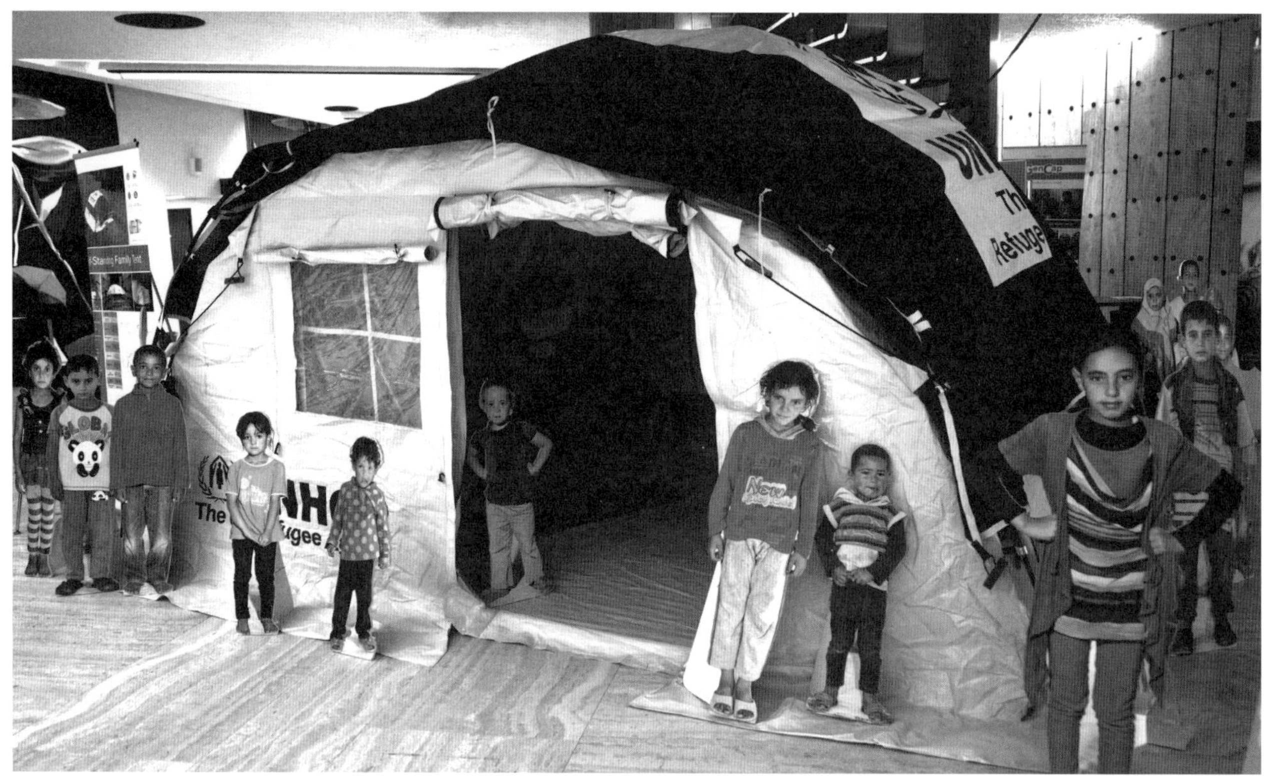

modes of political sovereignty, permanent residency, and citizenship. Geographic boundaries have been transformed into intersectional zones defined by First World nations with financial resources, bartering with developing countries that have large populations of refugees.

The 1951 UNHCR Refugee Convention remains the standard by which most international countries define their treatment of asylum seekers and refugees. Endorsed as a 'key legal document,' the Refugee Convention was ratified by 145 state parties in response to the European displacement of citizens after World War II. Australia was one of the original 26 state parties who signed the 1951 Refugee Convention. Refugees like Alexander Ranezay became one of the first to be resettled in the United States in 1951. As a result, Eastern Europeans, Germans, and Jews sought secure homes after the end of the war and were welcomed in places like New York (Fig. 2).

The Refugee Convention defines who may be considered a 'refugee,' outlining the rights of the displaced and the legal obligations of states to protect them. The core principle behind the Convention relies on *non-refoulement*, or the act of not returning refugees to places of harm.[9] In essence, the UNHCR as a humanitarian organisation serves as the 'guardian' of the Convention and uses a single definition to encompass who may be considered a refugee: "a refugee is someone who is unable or unwilling to return to their country of origin owing to a well-founded fear of being persecuted for reasons of race, religion, nationality, membership of a particular group, or political opinion." The Convention lays down minimum standards for how refugees can be treated: "without prejudice to States granting more favourable treatment."[10] Such legal rights include access to courts, primary education, work, and the provision for documentation, including a portable travel document ('Nansen passport,' named after the first commissioner for refugees and used between 1922-38).[11] Refugees cannot have committed any crime, crimes against humanity, or any serious non-political crimes.

Fig 1 (Above): Self-standing tent of the UNHCR, 22 June 2017, Geneva, Switzerland. UN Archives, New York.

Fig 2 (Opposite): New Yorkers welcome a group of refugees arriving on board of S.S. General K.M. Blak (1951). UN Archives, New York.

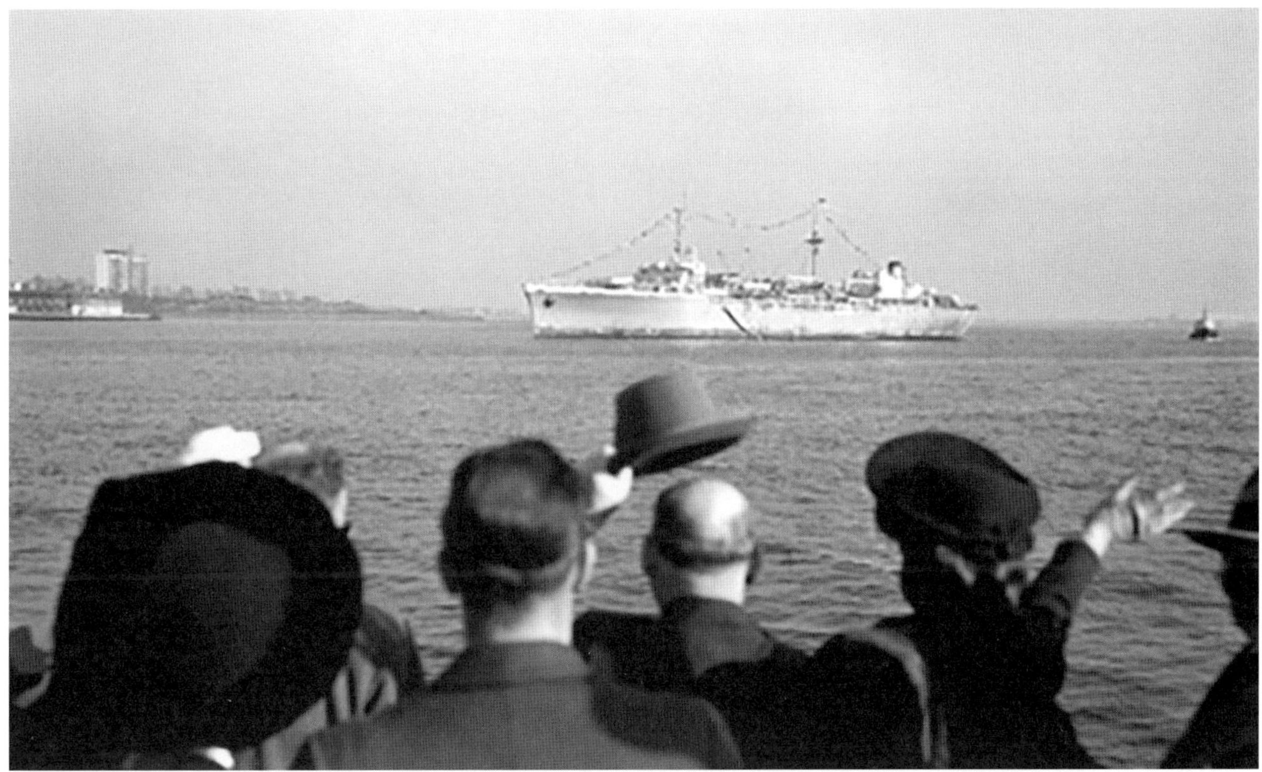

The Convention, however, does not apply to refugees covered by any different policies, such as the United Nations Relief and Works Agency (UNRWA) for Palestine, nor to those who hold the equivalence of being nationals in their country. Established by the United Nations General Assembly, the UNRWA set out its own working definition of who could be labelled as a refugee in 1949. In particular, Palestine refugees were "persons whose normal place of residence was Palestine during the period 1 June 1946 to 15 May 1948, and who lost both home and means of livelihood as a result of the 1948 conflict" (Fig. 3).[12] In this case, the temporal and spatial scope of who could be considered a refugee was limited only to two years and those who were affected by the Arab-Israeli War (1948).

The *space-time* paradigm becomes most evident in how the scope of the 1951 Convention was established—section D of the 1951 Refugee Convention relates to international cooperation in the field of asylum and resettlement, while section E addresses the treatment of refugees. The 1951 Refugee Convention stipulates that international cooperation is required in order not to place "unduly heavy burdens on certain countries." Article 1 initially pinpoints a set of historical origins for refugees—those who had been considered refugees in the 1920s, for example, were grandfathered into the present-day definition. Any historical events occurring before the 1st of January 1951 were erased as a precedent for refugee determination, thus making any specific dates irrelevant. While article 26 details freedom of movement, refugees were able to choose where they wanted to settle within a given territory.

Subsequently, the UNHCR 1967 Protocol was later intended to cover the new refugees who had emerged since the signing of the 1951 Refugee Convention. In the first article, the last two sections of the Protocol are particularly relevant and worth mentioning:

> 2. For the purpose of the present Protocol, the term 'refugee' shall, except as regards the application of paragraph 3 of this article, mean any person within the definition of article I of the Convention as if the words "*As a result of events occurring before 1 January 1951 and . . .* " and the words " *. . . as a result of such events,*" in article 1 A (2) were omitted.

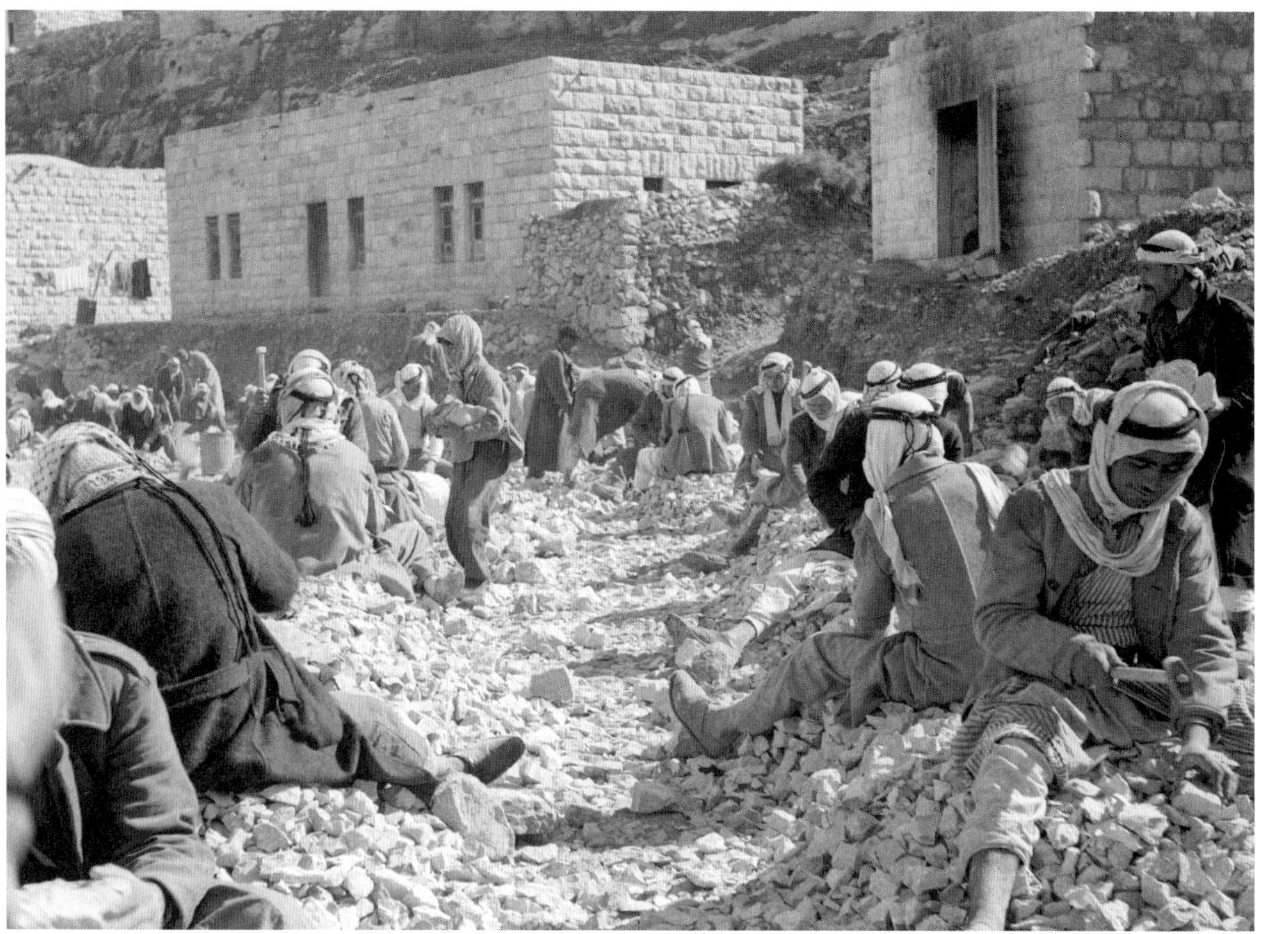

3. The present Protocol shall be applied by the States Parties hereto *without any geographic limitation*, save that existing declarations made by States already Parties to the Convention in accordance with article I B (I) (a) of the Convention, shall, unless extended under article I B (2) thereof, apply also under the present Protocol.[13]

The second section releases the term 'refugee' from any temporal restrictions so that the category of refugees can include any individual outside of the date 1st of January, 1951. In the 1967 Protocol, the lifting of geographic and temporal restrictions framed refugees as a new type of political subject that existed beyond the borders of any given country or historical time period.

More recently, the Global Compact released by the UNHCR in 2018 expands humanitarian networks to reinforce refugees as a universal subject; it emphasises international cooperation "in solving international problems of a humanitarian character" and the need for "more equitable sharing of the burden and responsibility for hosting and supporting the world's refugees."[14] The Global Compact is also not legally binding and represents "the political will and ambition of the international community as a whole for strengthened cooperation and solidarity with refugees and affected countries."[15] Given the Protocol's list of humanitarian actors that are involved with refugee determination (faith based actors, public private partnerships, and the accommodation of refugees), architecture under the headings of accommodation and environmental impact can be interpreted here as a function of law—architects and planners can offer valuable resources and expertise to strengthen the infrastructure of host countries.[16]

Fig 3: Palestinian refugees, Middle East, 1951. Refugees here are building a road but only 10% of able-bodied men obtained temporary employment.
UN Archives, New York.

To reiterate, Giedion's notion of *space-time* suggests how we can think about refugees as political subjects existing outside the normative limitations imposed by geography and citizenship. If the legal documents from the UNHCR set forth detailed definitions of who might be a refugee, they are also responsible for determining *when* and *how* these subjects may address and navigate political sovereignty. Syrian, Iraqi, and Iranian refugees who are resettling in Australian cities exemplify how the UNHCR Convention and Protocol have had little impact on the resettlement process in Australia. The Australian government enforces a stringent immigration processing policy where average processing times for refugee determination match those of other Western countries, with applicants waiting up to five years. Supranational laws like those set forth by the UNHCR operate only as recommended guidelines for resettled refugees, and the process of resettlement becomes more complex after refugees are granted refugee status by the Australian government. This path towards resettlement contrasts with the situation of unauthorised maritime arrivals who cannot apply for a protection visa.[17]

Resettlement in Australia

Asylum seekers waiting on their determination from the UNHCR face insurmountable challenges when trying to access temporary accommodations or rental housing in Australian cities. In Australia, the UNHCR designation of being a refugee determines access to financial resources and social assistance as well as temporary accommodations. Despite this label, such designations do little to ameliorate how national and local resources are parcelled out to resettled refugees. Refugees are often associated with other cultural categories given over to agricultural workers, migrant laborers, backpackers, and students: all of whom reside in the country on a temporary basis.

Resettlement success, for lack of a better word, depends on reliable access to secure housing in Australian cities. Refugees, as political subjects lacking any spatial or temporal definitions, are transplanted to a new country where their assigned nationality means little in a legal system that only acknowledges their visa status as the gateway to public services. The legal definition of a refugee, thus, determines if a family or individual will receive temporary housing. Here, the temporal aspects of *space-time* become relevant again—asylum seekers may be granted a refugee visa, but in practical terms, this does not make their liminal status as refugees any better. Rather, their assignment to Australian cities is determined by visa status or available employment offered in regional towns that may need to boost their local population(s). Likewise, the amount of time remaining in Australia is dependent on the bridging visa given to an individual. But these spatial and temporal limits are already decided for them, derived from the refugee determination process enforced at state level. In this sense, refugees' experience of *space* and *time* becomes indefinite since the humanitarian organisations who assist them do not have any control over these legal processes.

Emerging from both of these situations—it is clear that legal rights remain quite central for how asylum seekers and resettled refugees are able to establish a stable existence in Australian cities like Brisbane, Melbourne, and Sydney. Refugee law in Australia, for example, defines a refugee as someone who "has a well-founded fear of being persecuted for reasons of race, religion, nationality, membership of a particular social group or political opinion, is outside the country of his nationality and is unable or owing to such fear, is unwilling to avail himself of the protection of that country."[18] This description resonates with the definition of refugees mentioned in the UNHCR 1967 Protocol. Refugees who are living outside their country of origin cannot depend on legal protection covered by their original citizenship.

At the House of Welcome in Granville NSW, for instance, asylum seekers who have been granted refugee status can access limited options for temporary accommodations. Humanitarian managers and volunteers who work in this sector have stressed that legal rights are crucial to obtaining housing for asylum seekers and refugees. Asylum seekers, who have not been designated as refugees, remain the most vulnerable since they cannot access Centrelink payments (unemployment benefits) nor are they able to sign a year-long or even monthly lease for an apartment. Syrian and Iraqi asylum seekers typically rely on temporary accommodations offered by the local diocese or organisations like the House of Welcome; these temporary accommodations consist of donated buildings owned by the Catholic diocese or other properties that have been offered by congregation members. Most of these accommodations are already pre-furnished and are scheduled back-to-back with multiple families or individuals waiting for an apartment or spare room to become available.

Domestic violence complicates access to housing for many women who are either asylum seekers or resettled refugees. Women who have children try to leave their homes in order to seek out more stable accommodations away from abusive spouses. Women in these situations typically do not control their family income and in traditional families, such decisions are left to the male head of the household. Housing managers and volunteers, who must locate emergency housing for women and children, have witnessed this imbalance of financial power within certain Syrian, Iraqi, and Iranian families.[19] Due to cultural conventions, many of these women often end up returning to their households, perpetuating a cycle of abuse that keeps them out of permanent and stable housing.

Destitution and homelessness among asylum seekers are also quite common once income support and housing are cut off. Legal visas provide access to fundamental services needed by asylum seekers (such as Bridging Visa E) who are connected to financial benefits provided by the Australian government. Like the House of Welcome, third-party service organisations such as AMES (Accommodation Services Australia) only come into play after refugees have been awarded an official visa confirming their refugee status. Resettled refugees often do not have a documented rental history, struggle with language barriers, and have low incomes due to being on Centrelink or limited stipends offered by non-profit organisations. Their lack of official documents like birth certificates, bank statements, work recommendations, school transcripts, and other paperwork proves to be another barrier when applying for temporary accommodations.

Architecture as another legal apparatus, or access to temporary housing, is dependent on visa status and refugee determination. But temporary accommodations offered to many asylum seekers are part of a city's rental market and only provide short-term shelter. Even the leases given to such families are precise in their wording, detailing the termination of leases, good tenant behaviour, and time of residency guaranteed by a sponsor or non-profit organisation. Western Sydney has remained one of the more popular places for resettled refugees from many ethnic enclaves; families and individuals have access to community resources like day care, elementary schools, healthcare, and public transport. The conditions of simultaneity and movement prompt self-reflexive questions around what constitutes a home, security, and economic stability. Refugees, who were deemed legal by the Australian government after spending time in detention centres on Manus or Nauru, have been outspoken about their need for greater legal protection. These same resettled refugees must navigate the Australian legal system and their position of being placeless and timeless is only exacerbated while waiting for these public services. Refugees are perpetually reassessing their situation in one place for a long period of time, and trying to understand where they will go next.

For the House of Welcome, it may take weeks to several months to locate suitable housing for a family or individual. Asylum seekers and resettled refugees do not have a choice of accommodations and must accept what is being offered. Non-profit organisations have even resorted to using hotel rooms when their own properties are full with other tenants. Refugees as subjects are representative of our contemporary age, where basic human rights are connected to forms of legal protection. Subsequently, we must also reposition architecture and law in order to understand these contemporary notions of citizenship, permanent residency, fixity, and movement.

Simultaneity and Movement

In conclusion, legal documents such as UNHCR's 1951 Refugee Convention and 1967 Protocol have altered the public perception of refugees, their fundamental rights, and their settlement in local communities. Popular media outlets lump refugees into a single category, and they no longer represent a specific ethnicity, nationality, country, or place. Refugees in Australia and overseas are only identified by their category of visa, or by their type of arrival into a country. The term 'refugees' suggests a singular group requiring special protection. But there are now other types of refugees to claim public attention as well: climate refugees (e.g. Kiribati citizens moving to Fiji and New Zealand) as well as economic migrants (e.g. Cameroon teachers fleeing violence for the US or Japan) who have tried to use the asylum system to access better opportunities in democratic countries.[20] Internally displaced persons and the stateless now mix together, foregoing any claims to a particular place or fundamental set of legal rights.

The UNHCR 1967 Protocol portended what we are experiencing now—that legal definitions of displaced persons have become more significant than ever, and if anything, the built environment in which refugees must endure has been reduced to a few lines of international legislation. But strangely enough, *space* and *time* are far from being obsolete concepts since between the lines of these legal documents, there exist state systems to provide shelter, an education, and basic healthcare for most citizens. These spatial and temporal conditions, enumerated by Giedion as being critical for the development of modern architecture, can be viewed as being important for refugees too. Refugees experience *simultaneity* and *movement* in multiple places, and at the same time, these conditions characterise the diverse cities and homes in which they may live. While contemporary refugees continue to lose their sense of place and time as they transit through distant countries, reinforcing permanent housing and meaningful durations of time defined by work, school, and family ironically would restore a sense of identity to these individuals. Referencing the UNHCR Refugee Convention, 2020 is no longer 1951, and the legislation of the past has become outdated. It is imperative that our current international standards of legal protection respond to the global complexities of how refugees move and live. Such legal archives will continue to channel the voices of refugees as new waves of immigration and displacement reconfigure how state governments embrace—or deny—human rights to those who are most vulnerable.

01 *UNHCR Coronavirus emergency appeal report*, UNHCR's Preparedness and Response Plan (March-December 2020), 1.

02 For 2018 statistics on forced displacements, see the UNHCR figures at https://www.unhcr.org/ph/figures-at-a-glance, last accessed May 5, 2020.

03 Madhan Balasubramanian et al., "Migration and COVID-19," Sydney Policy Lab (May 2020), policy paper. Refer to https://www.sydney.edu.au/content/dam/corporate/documents/sydney-policy-lab/migration_and_covid-19-spl.pdf?mc_cid=799711ec19&mc_eid=6f18ef71f2, last accessed May 5, 2020.

04 Marcelo M. Suárez-Orozco, "Catastrophic Migrations," *Humanitarianism and Mass Migration: Confronting the World Crisis* (Los Angeles: University of California Press, 2019).

05 Alex Aleinikoff, *The Arc of Protection: Reforming the International Refugee Regime* (Stanford: Stanford University Press Briefs, 2019), 4. This revisionist analysis focuses on refugee rights and refugee autonomy, as well as how countries could effectively share the responsibilities of refugee hosting.

06 Sigfried Giedion, *Space Time, and Architecture: The Growth of a New Tradition* (Cambridge: Harvard University Press, 2008).

07 Our joint project with the Social Science Research Council (SSRC) "Crossing Legalities: Inter-Asian Sovereignty, Borders, and Infrastructures" is funded through a New Paradigms consolidation grant (2019-2020) and defines new methodologies between architecture, law, and space in regions like South-East Asia. This project includes the Swinburne Law School (Sven Gallasch and Jeremy Kingsley) and National University of Singapore, Department of Architecture (Kah-Wee Lee).

08 Elsadig Elsheikh and Hossein Ayazi, "Moving Targets: An Analysis of Global Forced Migration," *Haas Institute for a Fair and Inclusive Society* (July 2017), research report, https://belonging.berkeley.edu/moving-targets-analysis-global-forced-migration.

09 For the original 1951 document, see https://www.unhcr.org/3b66c2aa10. On the act of non-refoulement, see https://www.unhcr.org/4d9486929.pdf in reference to the International Refugee Convention and the 1967 Protocol, last accessed May 1, 2020.

10 UNHCR, 1951 Refugee Convention, 3.

11 Regarding Fridtjof Nansen's development of the Nansen passport as the first High Commissioner for Refugees, see https://www.unhcr.org/en-au/events/nansen/4aae50086/nansen-man-action-vision.html on the Nansen International Office for Refugees (or Office International Nansen pour les Réfugiés), last accessed 1 April, 2020.

12 "Palestine Refugees," UNRWA, https://www.unrwa.org/palestine-refugees, last accessed June 3, 2020.

13 Refer to the original document 1967 Protocol listed here: https://www.ohchr.org/EN/ProfessionalInterest/Pages/ProtocolStatusOfRefugees.aspx,last accessed April 1, 2020.

14 Report of the UNHCR, *Part II Global Compact on Refugees*, General Assembly, 73rd Session, Supplement no. 12 (2018), 1. Refer to https://www.unhcr.org/gcr/GCR_English.pdf, last accessed April 1 2020].

15 UNHCR, *Part II Global Compact on Refugees*, 1. Regional differences that deal with handling refugees are highlighted in order to acknowledge how different countries might assist local populations of refugees.

16 UNHCR Global Compact, 15.

17 On the refugee determination process, refer to "Refugee Status Determination in Australia," *UNSW Sydney*, https://www.kaldorcentre.unsw.edu.au/publication/refugee-status-determination-australia, last accessed April 1, 2020.

18 "Refugee law in Australia," *Australian Law Reform Commission*, https://www.alrc.gov.au/publication/family-violence-and-commonwealth-laws-improving-legal-frameworks-alrc-report-117/22-refugee-law-2/refugee-law-in-australia-2/.

19 Jennifer Ferng, interview with House of Welcome (HoW), Granville, NSW, November 2019. See also Jock Collins, et al., "Syrian and Iraqi Refugee Settlement in Australia," *University of Sydney Business School*, Working Paper No. 1, March 14, 2018.

20 Matt Katz, "The World's Refugee System is Broken," *The Atlantic*, February 29, 2020 at https://www.theatlantic.com/international/archive/2020/02/japan-refugees-asylum-broken/607003/.

CONTESTED STATES

CREATING AFFECTIVE ENCOUNTERS WITH SPACES OF CONFLICT AND IDENTITIES OF DIFFERENCE

Heather Mitcheltree & Mitchell Ransome

Strategically positioned in the Mediterranean, the island nation of Cyprus, has had a long and turbulent history of occupation and conflict. On the 16th of August 1960, after decades of resistance against British rule, Cyprus was finally granted independence. Newly afforded self-determination from colonial rule, it was a nation struggling to come to terms with its identity and governance structures in this new, post-colonial era. What ensued, stands as a dark chapter in Cyprus' history—a turbulent period of fierce ethnic fighting, military incursions and occupation, displacement, loss, United Nations interventions and the eventual deployment of Peacekeeping forces. It is a period that came to an uneasy pause through the creation of the Buffer Zone, a UN patrolled exclusion zone that divides the island.

Serving as a physical divide between the north and south of Cyprus, the Buffer Zone is a spatial manifestation of an ongoing state of conflict. Structuring the nation in terms of "boundaries and thresholds, all strongly linked to the construction and projection of identity," this divide stands as a symbolic representation and structural reinforcement of identities of difference.[1] Since the establishment of the Cypriot Buffer Zone in 1964, and the extension of the zone after the ceasefire in 1974, the UN patrolled demilitarised zone has remained largely untouched—a caesura between the north and south of Cyprus. Whilst in recent years several border crossings have opened up, the country remains divided and in a state of ongoing contestation—homes, buildings and urban fragments within the zone fixed in indeterminant stasis.

At the Gates

This is our fourth trip to Cyprus in six months. We have come to continue scanning parts of the Buffer Zone and to mount an exhibition as part of the Buffer Fringe Performing Arts Festival in Nicosia. Today, some quick additional scans of Paphos Gate before meeting with our UN escort to head into restricted areas of the Buffer Zone. Around Paphos Gate, cement block fortifications, 44-gallon drums, embrasures and sandbagged gunner stations sit on top of the Venetian stone ramparts that encircle the city, defensive fortifications that are part of the city's very foundations and that have been added to over the years. (Figs. 1-2) The stone ramparts and fortified city walls tell of a long history of conflict—of the different empires that have fought to control this strategic island outcrop, and of a more recent legacy of civil war. The temporary and haphazard nature of parts of the construction stand as physical reminders of intense periods of fighting—bullet holes and the deep scarring of mortar attacks still riddle the façades of many buildings throughout the city.

To our right are the crumbling remains of Spitfire Café, occupied now only by stray cats. Cordoned off by cyclone mesh fencing and razor wire, its roof and mudbrick walls have gradually succumbed to the ravages of weather. Oblivious to the ceasefire line that runs through the former café, the cats happily lounge in the shade of the vegetation that over the years has taken over the structure. The road that we are scanning passes through the battlements. On one side, the Republic of Cyprus, on the other, the ceasefire line, portions of the Buffer Zone, and the Turkish Republic of Northern Cyprus. On top of each of the battlements fly flags—reminders of competing claims of territoriality and national identity. Behind us stands a UN guard post, an urban allegory of the gaze—a physical presence that bears witness to the proximity of these opposing spatialities and the ongoing state of contestation. (Fig. 3)

We pass in between.

Fig 1 (Opposite): Gunner fortification on the Venetian wall, Paphos Gate, Nicosia, Cyprus. Image by Mitchell Ransome.

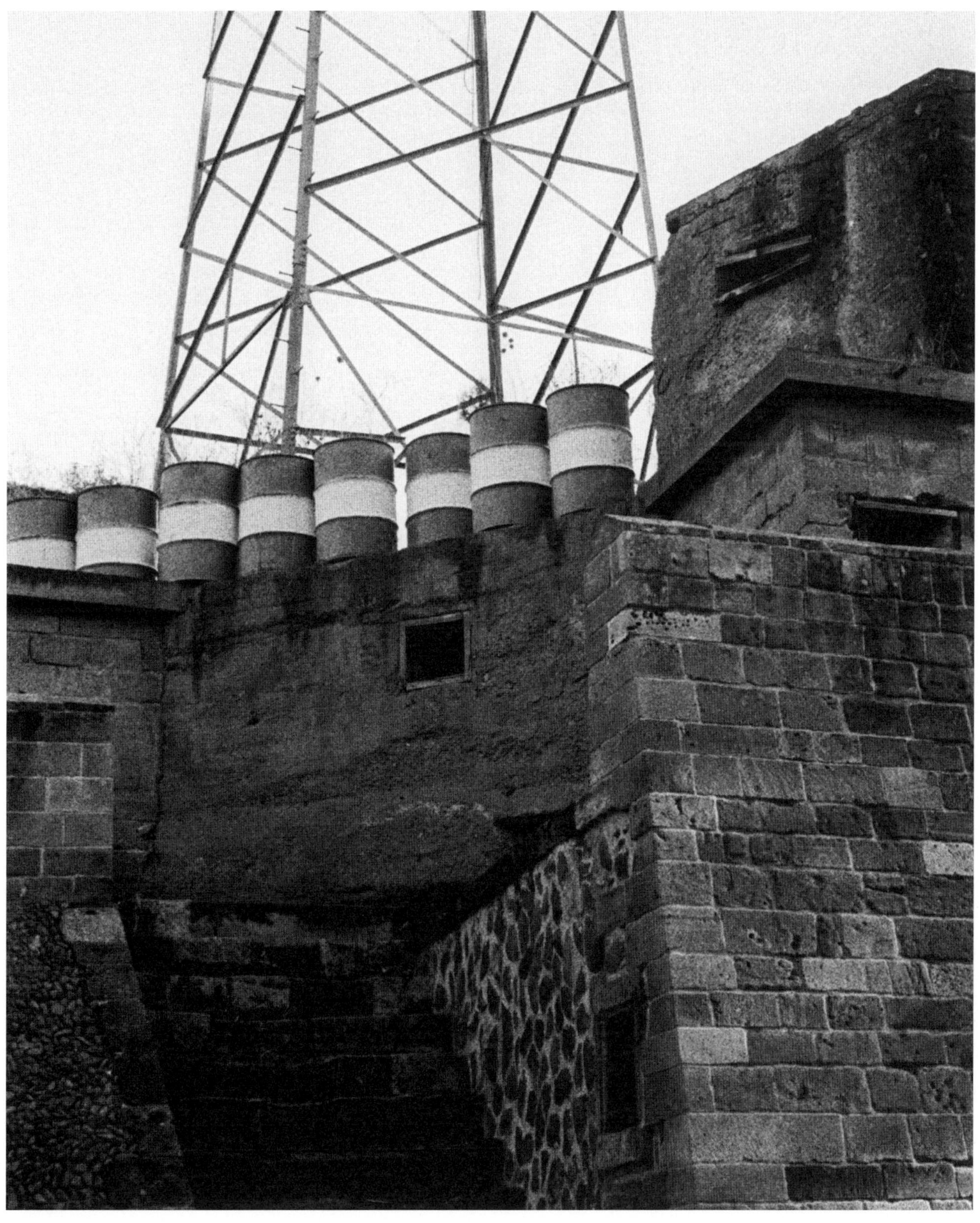

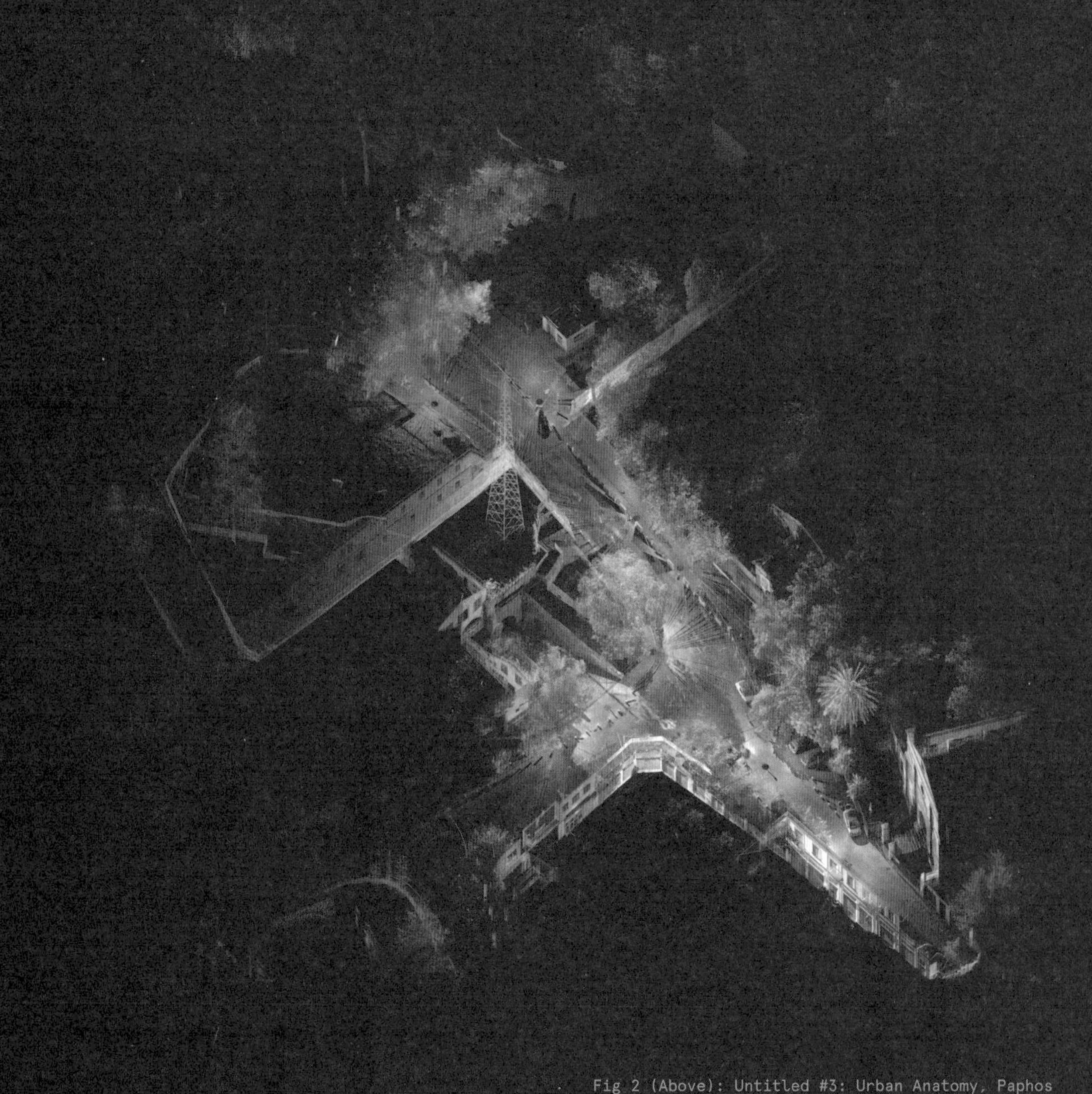

Fig 2 (Above): Untitled #3: Urban Anatomy, Paphos Gate, Nicosia, Cyprus. All following images by Heather Mitcheltree & Mitchell Ransome.

Fig 3 (Opposite): UN post, Paphos Gate, Nicosia, Cyprus.

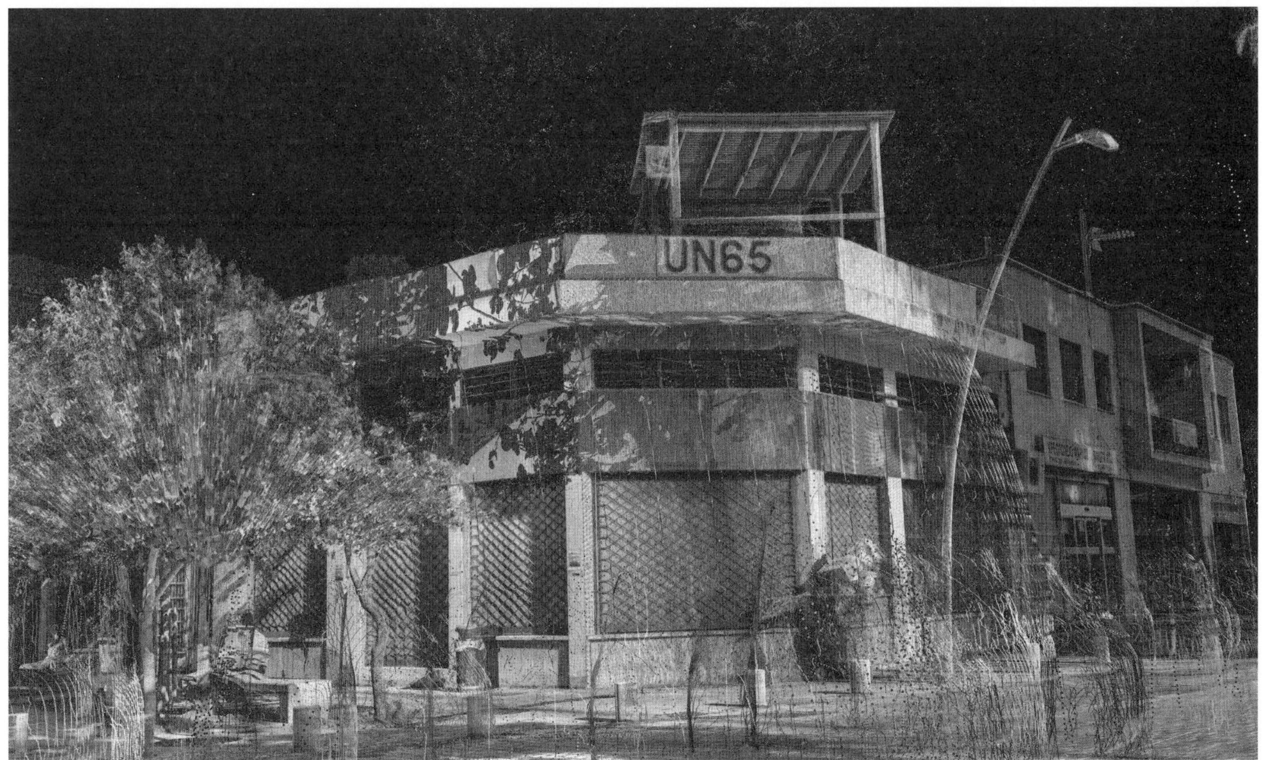

Scanning Sites of Conflict

Over the years, much of the heritage architecture within the zone has gradually deteriorated, battered by the elements and overrun by vegetation. Having been granted access to the Buffer Zone in Cyprus by the UN, we have been documenting and creating a digital archive of the architecture within this zone, and exploring the ways in which emergent 3D scanning can be utilised to create installations and affective encounters with contested spaces, the ephemerality of memory, trauma and the architecture of the in-between. In the context of ongoing conflict and division, these 3D digital scans and resultant audiovisual installations, reframe how we engage with boundaries, mechanisms of spatial control, and the dialectics of identities of difference, conflict and division.

Outside of the old US Embassy, we map out our scan points and workflow, taking care with where we position the scanner to get clear lines and overlap in the registration between scans. This building was hit hard during the conflict (Fig. 4), and we have to climb over rubble and prop up the tripod in between fallen building debris, before carefully levelling it to take our scans. It is hot, and still, and the only sounds are the birds overhead and the whoosh and whir of the phase shift scanner as the reciprocal two laser pulses fire, determining the distance each point is from the scanner through the difference in the reflected wavelengths. As the laser fires, and the wavelength distance is calculated, an image is slowly created. Millions of points of information are gathered and registered, a digital log of coordinates in space from which an approximate model of the site that we are scanning builds. It is a slow process, and this is just one of several buildings we are trying to scan while we have access and a Peacekeeper escort. The scanner beeps as the orbital rotation of the laser and camera slow to a halt. We move to the next scan point, taking care to allow for clear lines of sight and scan overlap, before starting the process again.

From our previous scans, we have found that it is often the threshold moments, transition points between rooms, from outside to inside, and changes in direction that can cause glitches in the scan registration—misalignments, shifts in frame, off-plane parallel replications, and odd ghostings in the final 3D image. (Fig. 5) Whilst part of what we are producing is pinpoint accurate 3D documentation of the buildings within the Buffer Zone—an archive of the remnant architecture and spaces in-between—it is these 'glitches' and the potentiality of this emergent technology to enable a paradigm shift in how we engage with and view space that interests us the most.

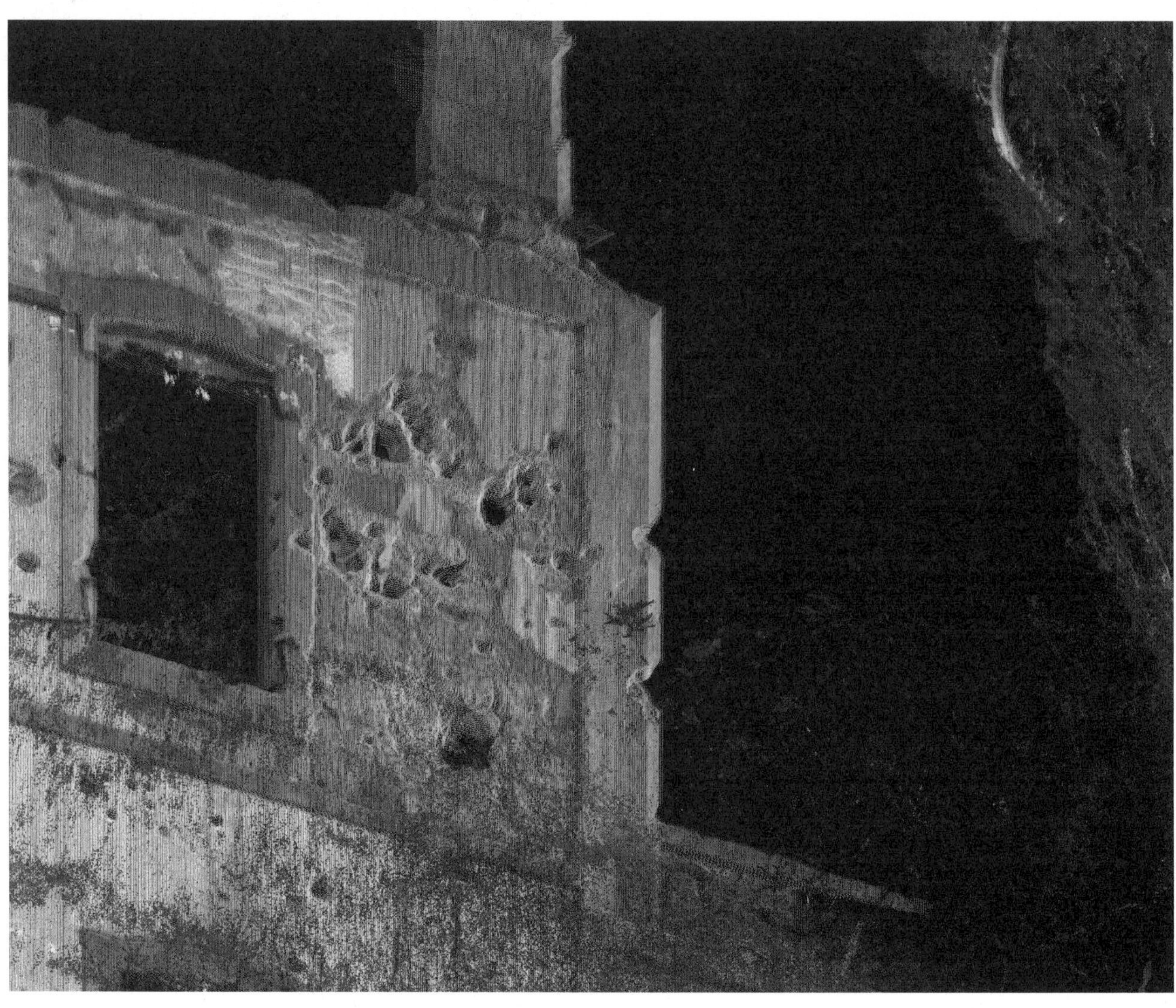

The spatial displacement and resultant ephemeral nature of the 'glitch' is something that we experiment with and accentuate in the installations and images that we create from our scans. The work is as much an interrogation of the limits of disciplinary borders, as it is an examination of the liminal and how we engage with sites of deep memory, conflict and loss.

Fig 4 (Above): Scan of damage to US Embassy south façade, UN Buffer Zone, Nicosia, Cyprus.

Fig 5 (Opposite): Scan of the old US Embassy, UN Buffer Zone, Nicosia, Cyprus.

Fig 6 (Next Page): Abandoned Nicosia International Airport lobby, Cyprus.

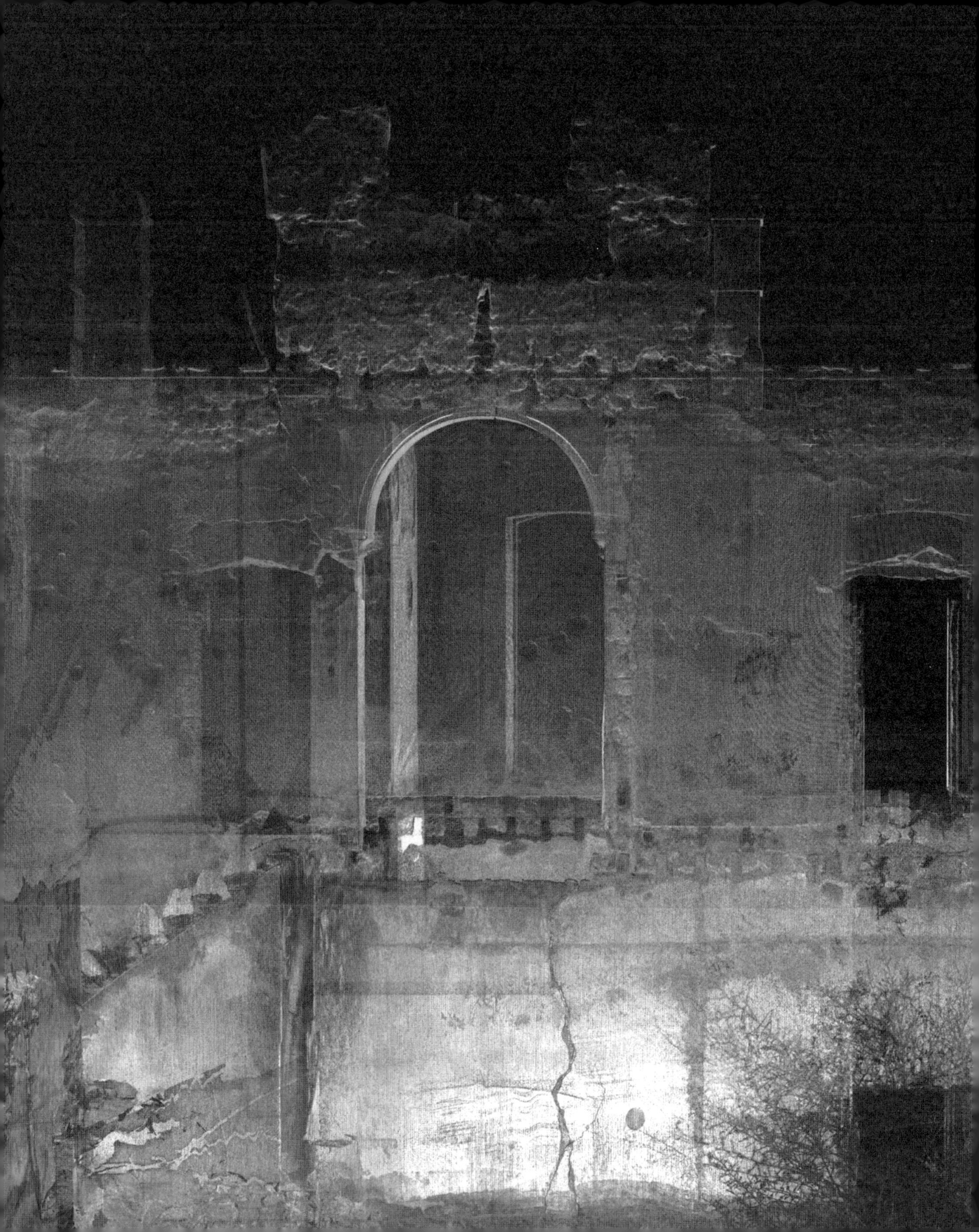

Creating Affective Encounters with Sites of Loss and Trauma

From the scans, we have been creating video installations. These are audiovisual assemblages that enable an affective engagement with these inaccessible sites of conflict—curatorial fly-throughs—that overlay, cut, break and shift between different sites and moments within the Buffer Zone. In creating the video installations from the 3D scans, physical boundaries, walls and barricades, appear as solid re-substantiations of their material counterparts, only to fragment, dissolve and then resolidify. Through shifts in scale and resolution, the grain and virtual nature of the point-cloud digital spaces shift between degrees of tangibility. The expansion and re-shaping of the spatial and tectonic experience within the digital sphere enables an interrogation of the edge. This is one of the reasons we have been drawn towards experimentation within these digital mediums. Like the socio-spatial and political boundaries, and sites of conflict and division that we are documenting, this digital sphere is ground in a constant state of flux—boundaries in continual reformation and dissolution.

Digital scanning technology, and the possibility for manipulation and creation of alternate modes of experiencing and representing space within a digital sphere, enables what Vidler has described as a new form of spatial warping—a pushing and pulling of boundaries.[2] Within this exploration of spatial practices, there is also a questioning of, and resistance to, disciplinary-specific standardised and legitimised modes of production and representation. The boundaries within which we operate—how we frame our disciplines and the fields of practice in which we navigate (and subvert), are boundaries that have been continually interrogated over the years. Most recently, this interrogation of disciplinary boundaries is evident in seminal works such as those of Rosalind Krauss and her 1979 critique of art practice and hybridised disciplinarity, Foster in his examination of the art-architecture complex, and Vidler's writings on the shifting nature of disciplinary boundaries and modes of architectural praxis.[3] Whilst the video installations created from the digital scans facilitate what Vidler has called a warping and "morphing of space through the rapid collapse of time,"contrary to Vidler's concerns about the potential loss of perspective within digital space, through the very mechanism of their formation, these installations are reliant on relationality and perspective.[4] The scanning and registering of millions of points of data, each of which on its own is simply a point in space, together combine to form a 3D digital representation, an image reliant on the relationship between different points. Within the installations, the images move, merge, and jump from one location within the Buffer

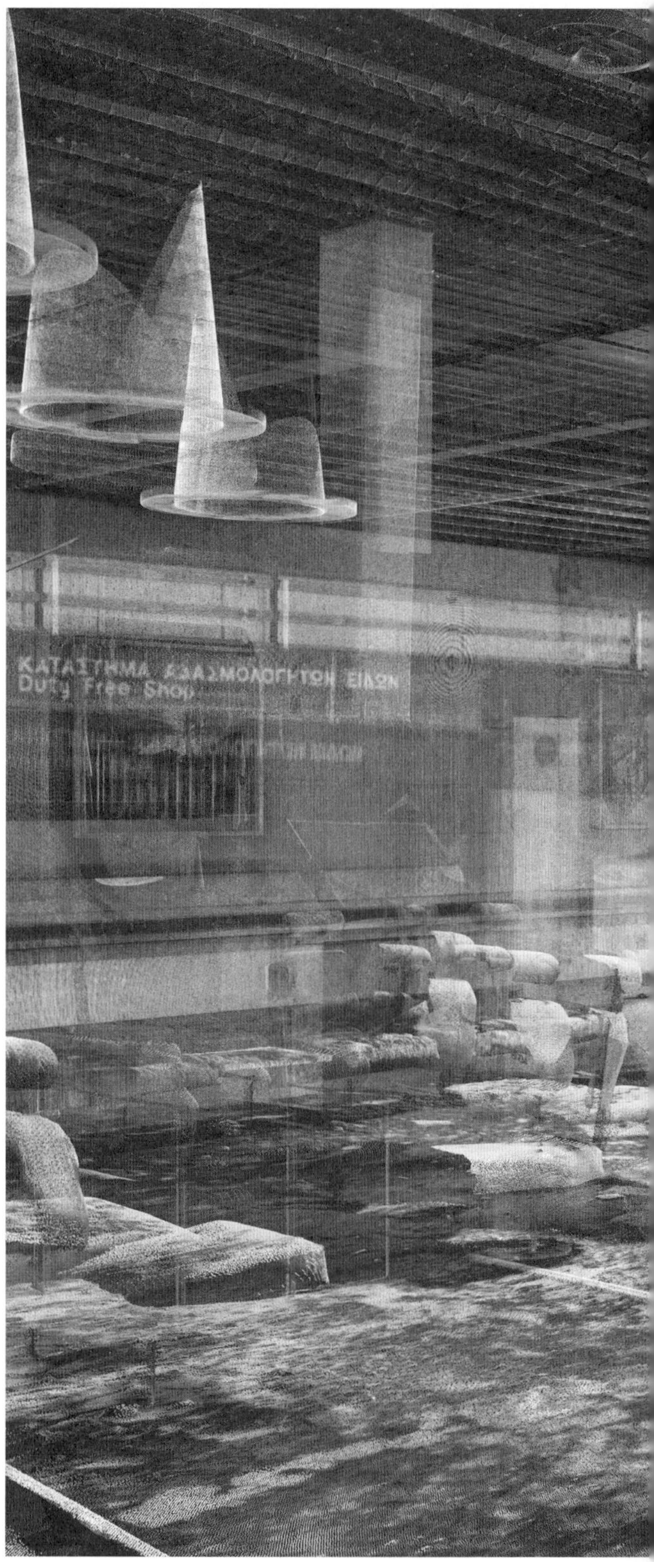

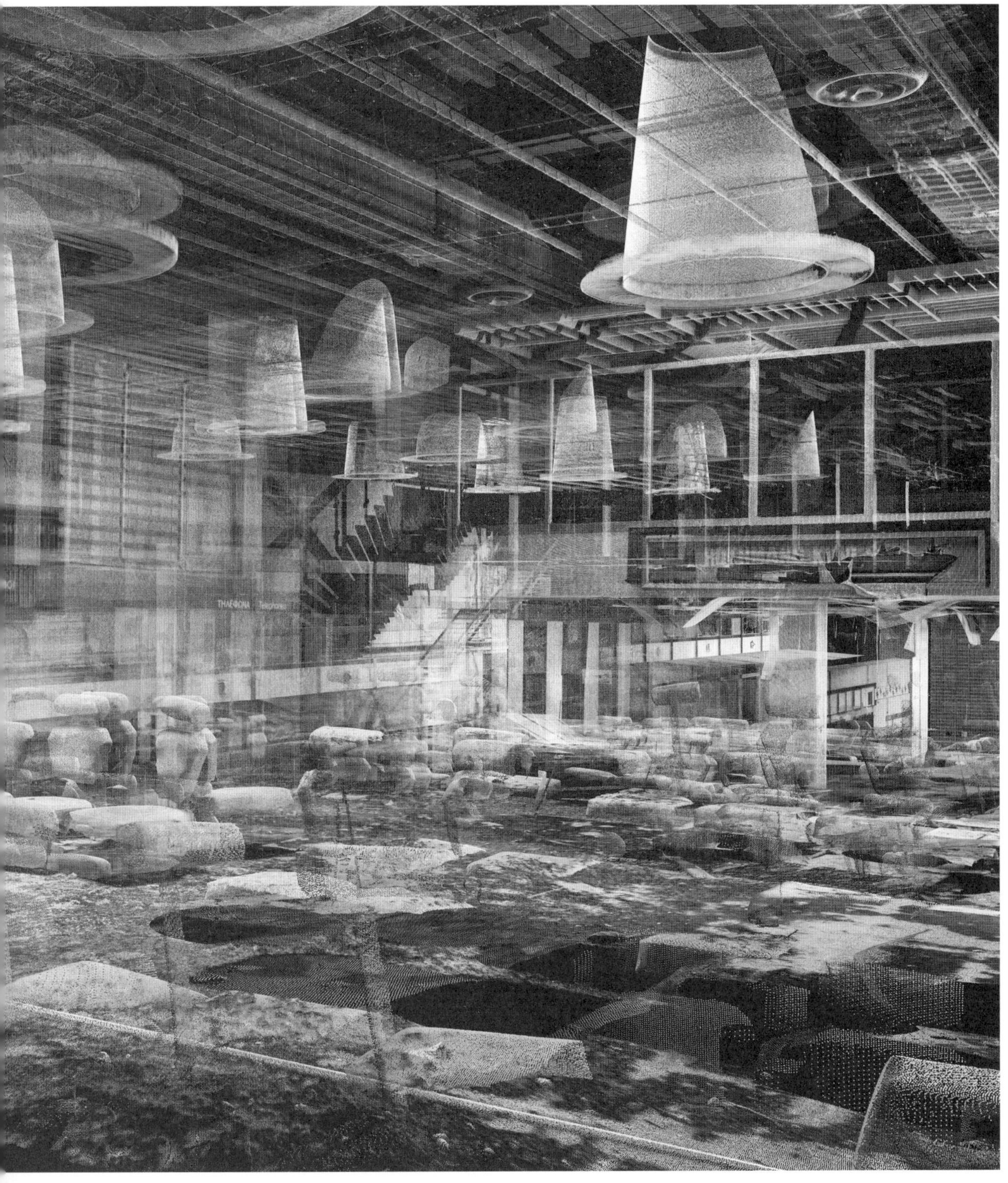

Zone to another. Disparate sites and scenes are juxtaposed in a curatorial reframing of the sites that we are examining, and the relationality of the point-cloud image and the mechanics of the scanning process, combined with the act of curatorial assemblage, creates new relationalities and a dialogue about the boundaries that we create and inhabit.

The film shifts from an x-ray effect, a distant pan across the airport (Fig. 6), to the intimacy of a domestic setting, and then shifts again.[5] Through editing, selective reframing, movement, changes in scale and audio overlays, the 3D lidar scans cease to be simply an act of mechanical reproduction—they are transformed into something 'other'—a transgressive act of production, that does not liquidate the physical or 'real,' but creates its own 'genuineness.'[6] The viewer is drawn into a tense, cinematic, digital space that shifts between the abstract and pinpoint accurate digital reconstruction of the physical spaces. These deliberate topographical shifts and juxtapositions create a curatorial assemblage—an evocative landscape of perpetual trans-temporality and semantic slippage. Within this digital landscape, spatial restrictions and boundaries shift and morph as the viewer passes through walls and seamlessly across disparate geographical locations, militarised borders and is granted access to the spaces in between.

Bearing Witness

Located within the Buffer Zone, our exhibition was set up as a series of walls within walls. Within the spatial confines of the exhibition, the viewer stands as both voyeur and participant in a performative act of bearing witness; a double reflexive act in which the viewer, cast in silhouette into the scene, simultaneously becomes both part of the spectacle of surveillance, and the gaze. (Fig. 7) Inserted and cast in negative into the liminal exclusion space of the Buffer Zone, the viewer temporarily occupies a space between borders, in defiance of the alienation of forcible displacement and militarily enforced exclusions. But this space in between is not the physical site of the scans themselves, it is a third space, something other, and in its transformed state, it is neither simulacrum nor simulation.[7] It is a space that does not result in a decay of the real, and despite the precision of the registration of points in space, it is not a purely faithful simulation of the real. It is a new territoriality, an expanded space, that both references the real whilst simultaneously creating an alternative real—an 'other.' This 'other' space does not delegitimise nor replace its referent, but rather seeks to articulate the narratives of conflict and loss that lie hidden in sites rendered inaccessible across the Buffer Zone. Within this hybridised reality, there exists "a tension between permanency and suppression, between presence and oblivion of space."[8] Paradoxically, the viewer is granted access to the Buffer Zone whilst simultaneously being aware of the spatial discord and dissonance between the representational and the real, and their inability to physically negotiate these bounded spaces. In viewing the installations, the virtual bridge between spatially disparate sites, and the conditional nature of the viewer's access, reinforce both an act of transgression and a questioning of how we access and occupy these spaces in between.

The spatial dissonance inherent in the digital topos that is created through the 3D scanning process, and digital manipulations of the point-clouds, facilitates engagement and affective encounters with the dialectics of boundaries. In applying 3D scanning and spatial visualisation methods to the restricted spaces within the Buffer Zone, we see a diaphanous emancipation of the physical that "decomposes and recomposes linguistic material [enabling an] infringement of code" and dialectic re-formation.[9] The liminal nature and emotive poignancy of sites of conflict charges these spatial representations of loss with an ability to transgress dialectical boundaries. Beyond the spectacle of surveillance and the voyeuristic aspect of the gaze, these contested spaces serve as a symbolic locus in which individual and collective memory, trauma, place and temporality coalesce.[10] (Figs. 8-9)

The resultant curatorial assemblages enable narrative plurality in relation to sites of conflict, bearing witness to the traumatic disruption of the linearity of time and space, in which time is simultaneously frozen, compressed and stretched. Through these audiovisual assemblages, space is created for the unscripted, and "within these unreadable lines and beyond any fixed meaning something else is created."[11] Digitised and rendered, the sites are liberated from their physicality and the boundaries and barbed wire that inhibit access. Within this digital sphere the spaces take on an ethereal presence. In tracing the memories and shadows of what was, what remains, and what might be, these works attempt to engage with the dialectics of conflict and loss, bearing witness to the spaces in between, the trauma and conflict of division, and the ways in which we construct narratives of self through the boundaries that we draw, maintain, and dissolve. Through the manipulation of 3D digital scans, and interrogation of the spaces in between that are constructed from the scans, there is a transgression and questioning of representational practice; a questioning of how we construct, experience and represent physical space through emerging technologies. Within this digital realm, dialectical schisms surface and moments of liminality are given voice, "enabling other possible meanings and practices to emerge."[12]

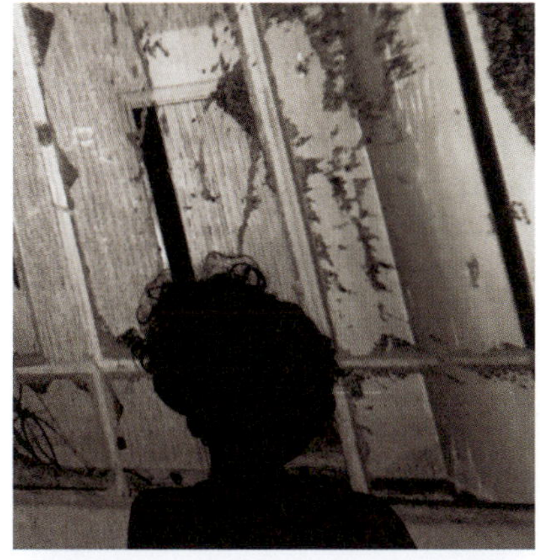

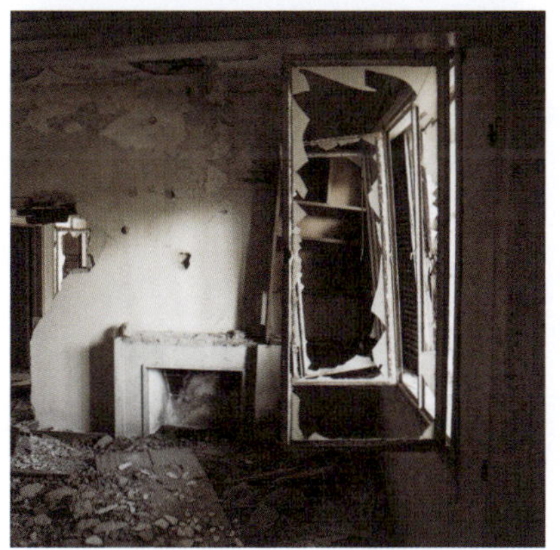

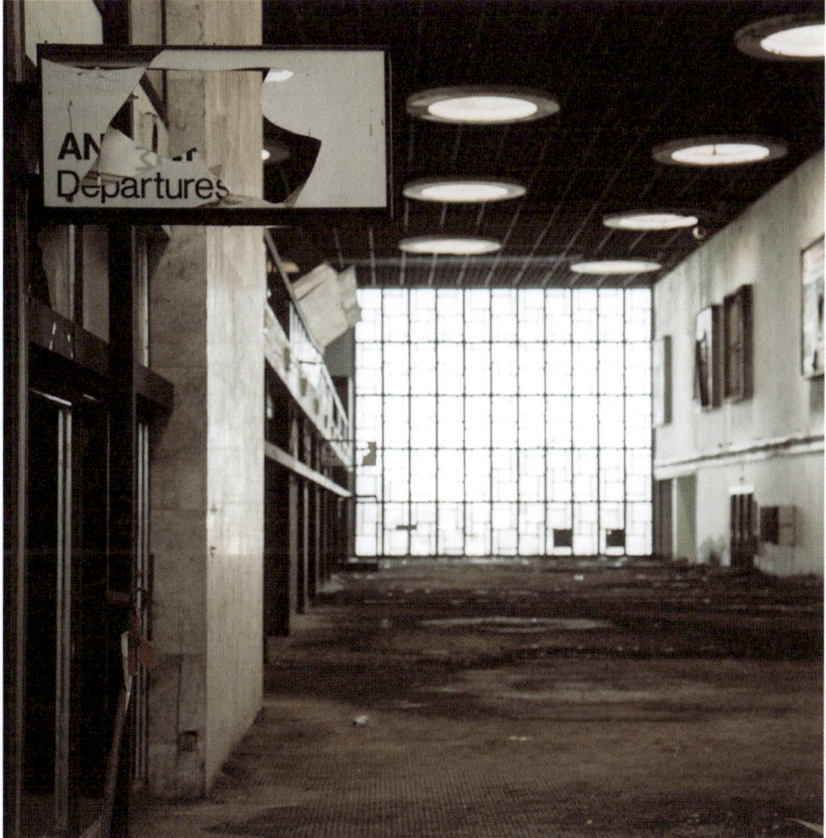

01 Kim Dovey, *Framing Places: Mediating Power in Built Form* (London: Routledge, 2008).

02 Anthony Vidler, *Warped Space: Art, Architecture, and Anxiety in Modern Culture* (Cambridge: MIT Press, 2000).

03 Rosalind Krauss, "Sculpture in the Expanded Field," *October* Vol. 8 (1979): 8-31; Hal Foster, The Art-Architecture Complex (London: Verso, 2013); Anthony Vidler, "Architecture's Expanded Field: finding inspiration in jellyfish and geopolitics, architects today are working within radically new frames of reference," *Artforum International* Vol. 42, No. 8 (2004): 142.

04 Anthony Vidler. "The Medium and Its Message, or 'I'm Sorry, Dave, I Don't Have Enough Information'," *Architectural Record* 189, no. 5 (2001): 71.

05 Heather Mitcheltree and Mitchell Ransome, *In-Between the Margins* (2019), Mp4 video.

06 Walter Benjamin, *The Work of Art in the Age of Mechanical Reproduction* (London: Penguin, 2008).

07 Jean Baudrillard, *Simulacra and Simulation* (University of Michigan Press, 1994).

08 Emilio Martínez Gutiérrez, "Memories Without a Place," *International Social Science Journal* 62 (2011): 19-31.

09 Peter Eisenman, "Autonomy and the Avant-Garde: the Necessity of an Architectural Avant-Garde in America," in *Autonomy and Ideology: Positioning an Avant-Garde in America*, ed. R. Somol (New York: Monacceli Press, 1997).

10 Guy Debord, *The Society of the Spectacle* (New York: Zone Books, 1994).

11 Kim Senior, "Incorrigible and Undisciplined Lines in Visual Social Research: Ways of 'Writing' and 'Drawing' at the Interstices," *Critical Perspectives on Communication*, Cultural & Policy Studies 30 (2011): 1.

12 Jean Baudrillard, *Carnival and Cannibal: Ventriloquous Evil* (London; New York: Seagull Books, 2010).

Fig 7 (Top Left): Silhouette of on-looker at Buffer Fringe Performing Arts Festival 2019 projection installation, In-between the margins, Cyprus.

Fig 8 (Bottom Left): UN Buffer Zone, House 14 main living area, Cyprus.

Fig 9 (Right): Mnemonic markers: Untitled #5-Departures Hall, Nicosia International Airport, Cyprus.

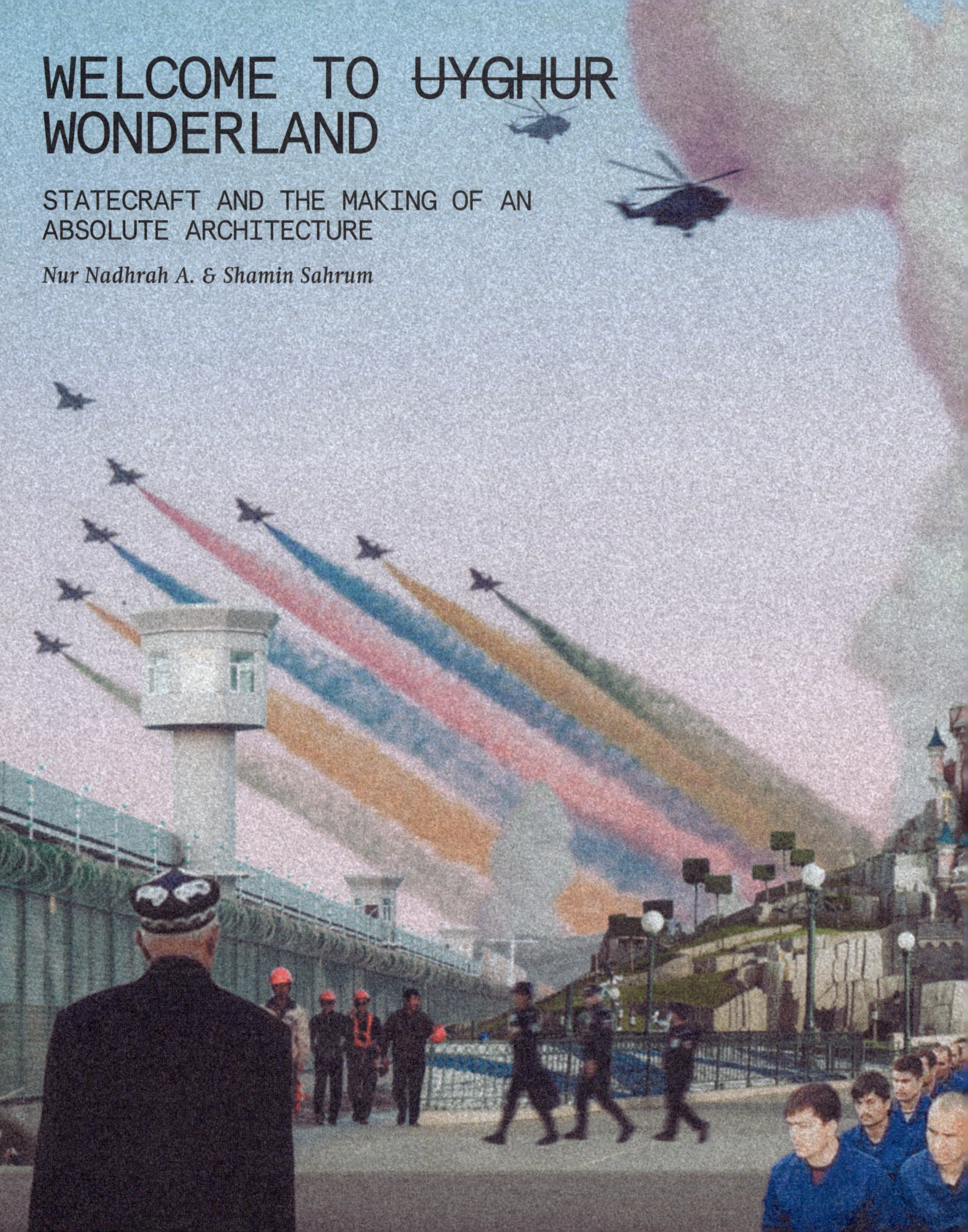
WELCOME TO ~~UYGHUR~~
WONDERLAND
STATECRAFT AND THE MAKING OF AN
ABSOLUTE ARCHITECTURE
Nur Nadhrah A. & Shamin Sahrum

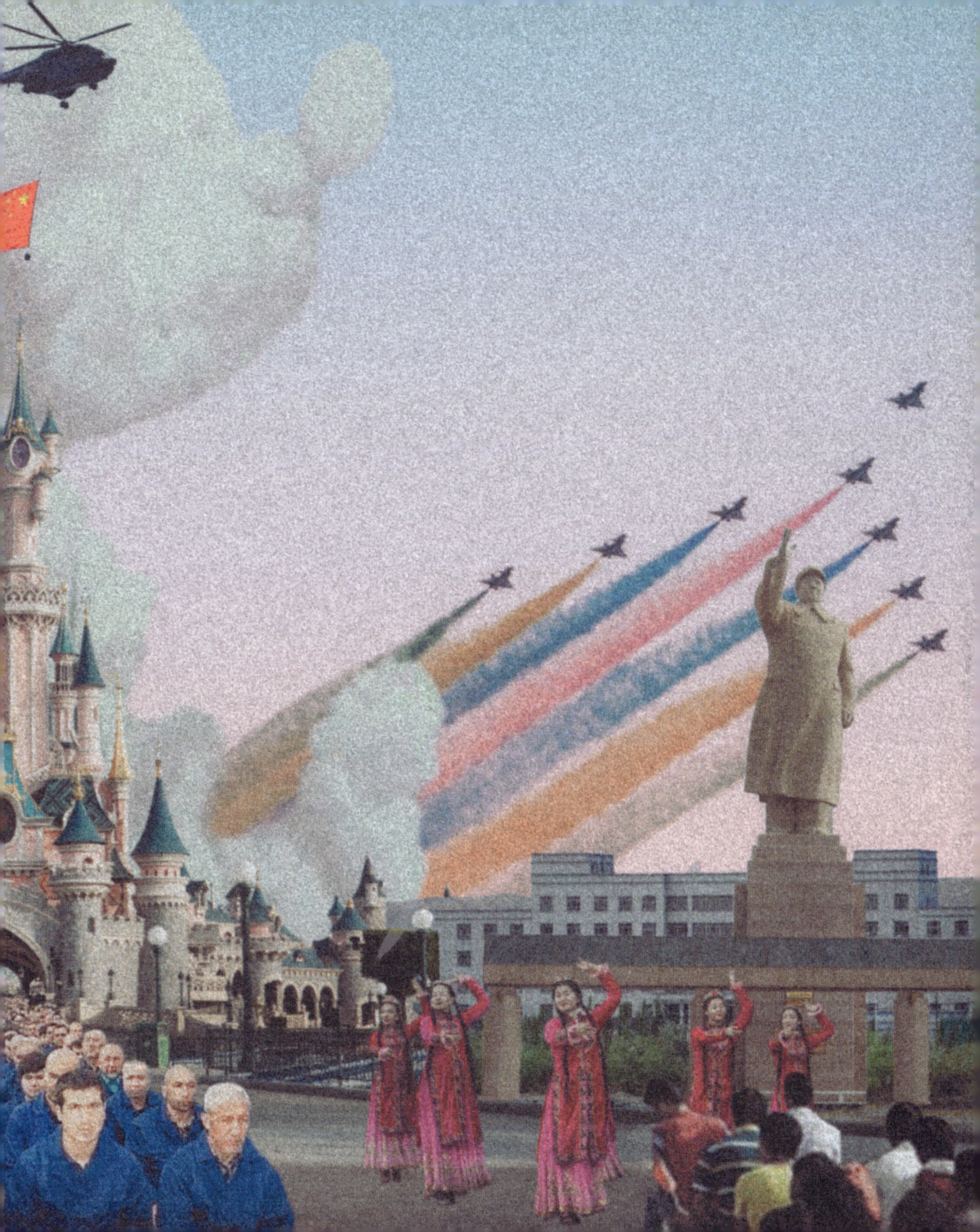

In a province in China, a vast network of 're-education' centres dot the Xinjiang landscape. Facilities within these 'schools' include a music and art room, classes where one can learn how to give manicures and another to learn to cut hair. Students that graduate are able to integrate into society with newfound skills. However, the highly secure facilities are a far cry from the average educational complex. Shrouded by secrecy and with heavy fortifications rivaling that of a correctional facility, these 're-education' centres continue to expand amid international outrage.

According to recent official reports from the United Nations and independent researchers, it is estimated that up to 1.5 million people have been detained without due process and consent.[1] Global outcry over the mistreatment of Uyghur people within these facilities has been expressed, often falling on deaf ears of the Chinese Government as they continuously deflect allegations of human rights violations by the international community. Despite the global outcry, the chairman of the Xinjiang regional government, Shohrat Zakir, declared that the re-education system was accomplishing its goal of eliminating radicalism and separatism.[2]

Yet the fate of those detained behind the Red Curtain remains to be seen . . .

Welcome to ~~Uyghur~~ Wonderland:
A tale of a fictional facility

A massive master plan for a 're-education' facility has been drawn up. The plan is envisioned as a phased complex of adjacent correctional facilities, and is projected to be complete in the year 2030. Positioning the self-contained facility in a strategic location proved crucial in setting up the narrative of the monumental infrastructure. The remote territory of Xinjiang Uyghur Autonomous Region, known for its vast natural reserves and scenic beauty, provides the perfect backdrop for this unprecedented facility. The name Xinjiang (新疆) means 'new frontier,' as it forms China's border with eight neighbouring countries. As such, Xinjiang is a crucial part of China's ambitious Belt and Road Initiative, which has a longstanding geostrategic role as a bridge between Mainland China, Central Asian countries, Europe and eventually, Africa.

Ethnically, the Uyghurs are Turkic people with Islam being their primary religion. The Uyghurs made numerous, though unsuccessful, attempts to regain independence and reject colonisation; culminating from major protests in Yining in 1997 to the 2009 riots in Urumqi. The tragic riots of 2009 ended with the loss of 192 lives, with a further 1,721 injured.[3] This led the Chinese Government to blame the Uyghurs for instigating the riots and label the incident as a terrorist attack. By clearly defining their actions of persecution as unrelated to ethnic cleansing, the Government assert that it is fully within their rights to stamp out acts of 'terrorism' within the pretext of national security. The creation of Uyghur Wonderland, a unified image of a 're-education' facility, will further strengthen the State's agenda of transformation through 'education.'

Four large quadrants separated by habitable walls form the basis of this urban-scale complex. Its large-scale infrastructure does not reflect that of the usual institutional learning facilities. Instead, its built components are more closely associated with carceral architecture; aligning with official requirements which outline the need for its 'education' centres to adhere to detainment and surveillance infrastructure. The complex is essentially a fortified and self-contained city, embedded into the surroundings of Xinjiang's nature reserves.

At the heart of this compound is a rotating, circular platform that separates the four quadrant walls. Its movement is hardly noticeable with the naked eye. From the vertical gaze of orbiting satellites, ever watchful over the State's every move, the facility is seen in a constant state of flux as it mediates activity between an entertainment and production complex, while blurring the distinction between carceral and non-carceral architecture. The Chinese State is fully aware that their previous facilities and their whereabouts were exposed due to observations via satellite imagery. Such observations provided valuable evidence for independent organisations and human rights activists regarding the rapid growth of the camps all over the country.[4] Indeed, the existence of nearly 1,000 massive, high-security compounds scattered throughout the region has been exposed. Unwanted satellite surveillance proved to be a flaw in the State's concealment of the correction facilities, prompting the aspect of the panoptic gaze to be controlled by means of perpetual flux via rotation.

This central platform rotates anti-clockwise at a speed of 30 degrees per hour, acting as an automated timekeeper for activities unfolding within the complex. Inhabitants of this complex are subjugated to the slow movement of the walls as their lives are directed from quadrant to quadrant, and their

All images by the authors.

Previous Page: The 'Cultural' Quadrant of the fictional facility.

Opposite: The central rotating platform which functions as a timekeeper for activities that take place in the facility.

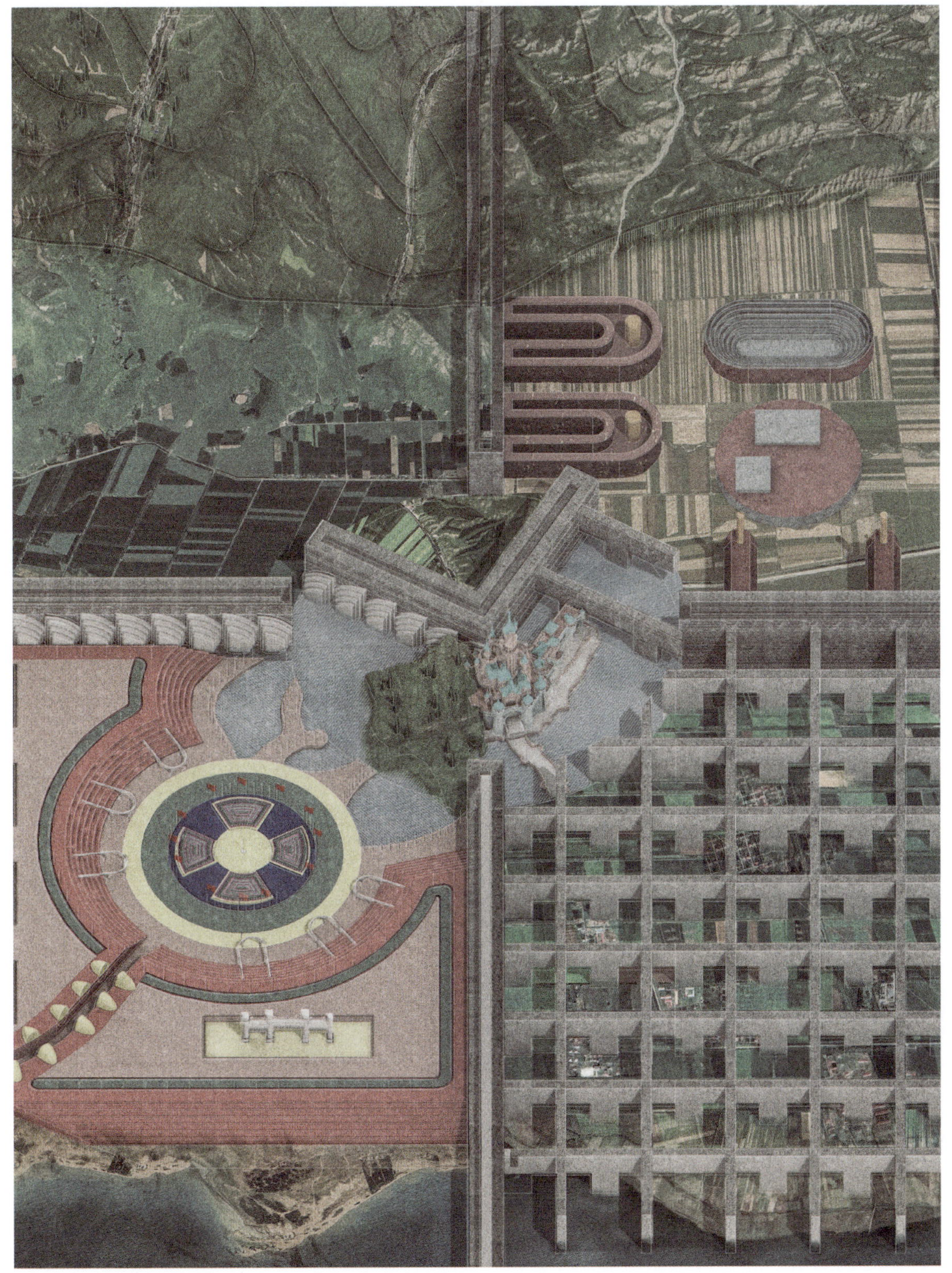

bodies become actors directed by the apertures of the rotating walls. Each of the enrolled individuals that live and work within this facility know their place as they take on multiple roles: as cultural envoys, citizens and factory-line workers. Individual freedom from the facility is earned by cooperating as a hard-working and patriotic citizen who conforms to the State's nationalistic agenda. The slow movement of walls opens up different views and passages each time a shift in quadrant occurs, indicating a visual-cue for the change in activities as certain quadrants are momentarily obstructed.

Days for the inhabitants start early in the morning as they leave their walled courtyard quarters, deceptively reminiscent of a rural-agrarian utopia. In alignment with the State's poverty alleviating measures, each family is allocated a plot of land that they are free to cultivate. Markets, sundry shops and public squares make up the micro-economies of the community. Life within the walls of the 'Living' Quadrant for the inhabitants seems ordinary but it is far from normal. There are no cries of children, no laughter heard in the streets—having been separated from their families since birth. Security is also invisible, embedded within the daily fabric of the living quarters; not unlike the kind deployed in various cities in the Xinjiang region. Certainly, Xinjiang is monitored by a complex web of surveillance technology and controlled through intrusive policing systems, creating a new type of civic infrastructure that revolves around fear tactics and punishment.[5] Uyghur Wonderland, in essence, is a fully integrated approach to such tried and tested surveillance techniques.[6] It wields architecture as a perfect totalitarian tool for absolute control over society, and is made possible in part by the complex wavering of legal rights from the discourse regarding the global 'War on Terror.'

An eerie silence follows the slow opening of the high, rotating walls: a cue for the inhabitants as they transition from the 'Living' Quadrant to the 'Education' Quadrant. The 'Education' Quadrant forms the core of this facility's program. For years the State has constantly justified the allegedly 'illegal' camps—criticised by the global community—as nothing more than poverty-alleviation measures providing opportunities for vocational skills training and language assimilation for the Uyghur ethnic minority. This is a fundamental component of their 'de-extremification' campaigns. The strictly regimented programs were intended to stamp out any deviant ideology and upon completion of the program would enable former 'attendees' to successfully integrate back into Chinese society. However, foreign media often looks at the depiction of students dancing in their customary ethnic outfits, happily participating in group-learning and vocational activities, as nothing more than State deception and propaganda, wishing to focus more on the ill-treatment of the Uyghurs to demonise the State.

As part of the 'Education' Program, knowledge of the State is prioritised, as is the athleticism through sports; the logic being that physical competition suppresses dissident urges. A large sporting event is held every two years, where the gold medal winner stands to take home the prize of their dreams: the chance to return to their hometown of origin, feeding into their longing to see a glimpse of 'home' that can only be recalled by memory.

In exchanging mind for matter, the inhabitants are then led from the 'Education' Quadrant to the 'Production' Quadrant. Here they spend their day being a part of any number of production lines available within this facility; as a cognisant cog in the national economy. To boost productivity and labour morale, factory floors are arranged on the perimeters of this quadrant, overlooking a scenic meadow field. Full-height glass panels bathe the production hall with ample natural light. However, the vast meadows are strictly off-limits, only afforded to the workers as scenic views. The meadow is merely there to improve working conditions 'within' the production facility.

At precisely 6 p.m., the State's national anthem plays out over the loudspeakers, signaling an end to the production hours. As the sun sets and the sky turns a glowing pink hue, inhabitants change into their customary ethnic costumes and make their way into the last quadrant for the day. A low murmuring sound of rotating concrete walls creates an opening towards Monument Square, an expansive podium situated in the 'Cultural' Quadrant. This last quadrant can be seen as a grand stage, showcasing all that is unique about Uyghur culture to foreign eyes. It is the only quadrant where outsiders are given access and is an entertainment complex meant to 'celebrate' Uyghur cultural performances, in which there are sing-alongs to patriotic anthems followed by all the glitz of a national day parade. This is a true celebration of ethnicity as propagated by the State, who is eager to display to the global community their efforts in acknowledging ethnic and cultural differences as part of its national identity. Unknown to the visitors, however, the performers will be re-enacting the same show for as long as they remain inhabitants at the facility, night after night after night after night.

As the last bus leaves Monument Square, the walls open up and direct the tired inhabitants back to their living quarters, where yet another day awaits in Uyghur Wonderland . . .

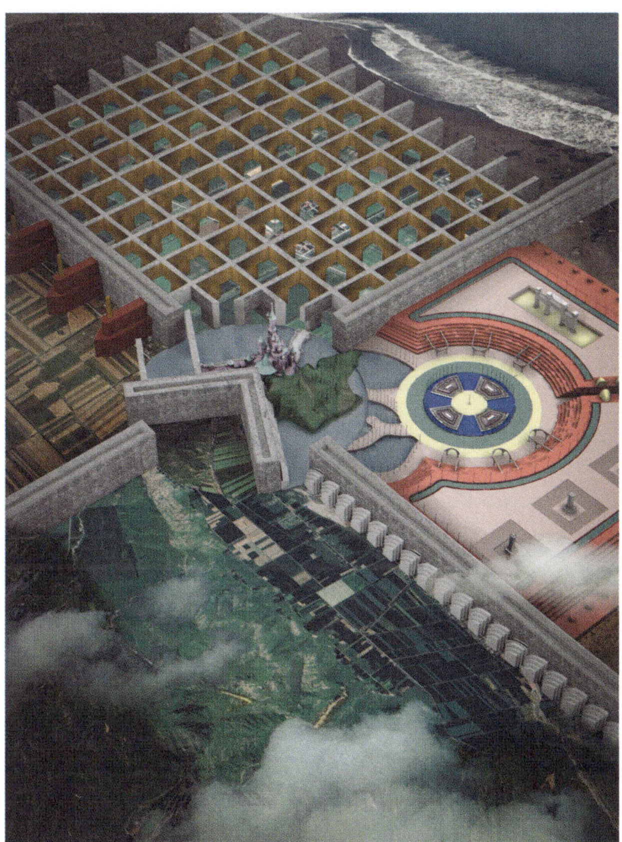

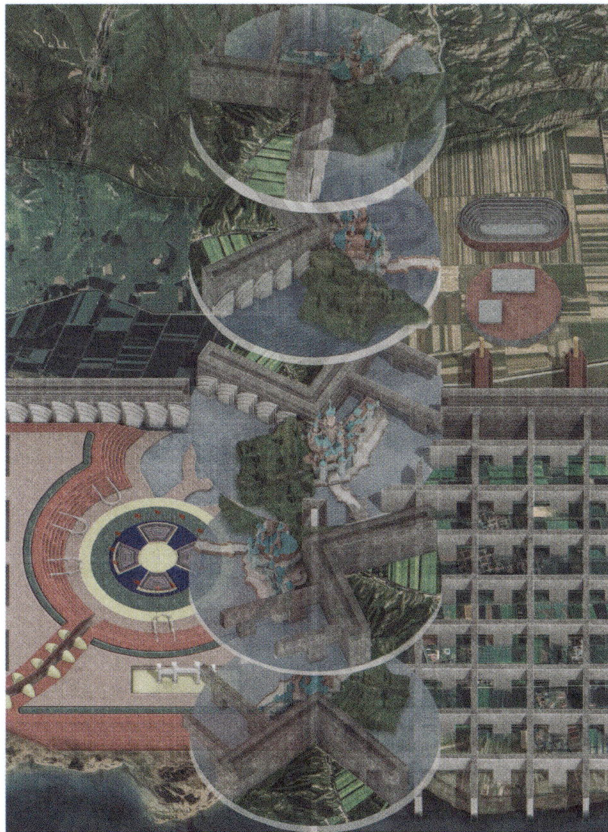

01 Danika Cooper, "Invisible Desert," *E-Flux*, April 6, 2019, https://www.e-flux.com/architecture/new-silk-roads/313103/invisible-desert.

02 Chris Buckley, Steven Lee Myers, "China builds more secret 're-education camps' to detain Uighur Muslims despite global outcry over global suffering," *Independent*, August 10, 2019, https://www.independent.co.uk/news/world/asia/xi-jinping-regime-han-chinese-threat-uighur-muslims-persecution-detention-camps-a9051126.html.

03 Katie Corradini, "Uyghurs under the Chinese State: Religious Policy and Practice in China," *Human Rights and Human Welfare* (2011), https://www.du.edu/korbel/hrhw/researchdigest/china/UyghursChina.pdf.

04 Fergus Ryan, Danielle Cave and Nathan Ruser, "Mapping Xinjiang's 'Re-education' Camps," *Australian Strategic Policy Institute*, November 1, 2018, https://www.aspi.org.au/report/mapping-xinjiangs-re-education-camps.

05 Léopold Lambert, *Weaponized Architecture: The Impossibility of Innocence* (New York: DPR-Barcelona, 2012), 18.

06 The integrated approach of its technological surveillance can be read more about here, "China's 'Re-Education' Camps: An Affront to Religious Freedom," *Muslim Public Affairs Council*, August 16, 2018, https://www.mpac.org/blog/policy-analysis/chinas-re-education-camps.php.

Left: The facility is isolated by the natural topography, with mountains to the North and a large lake to the South.

Right: At the heart of the complex is a central platform that moves anti-clockwise, functioning as an automated timekeeper for activities within the compound.

HYPERNATURE

Ma Yansong

Translated from Mandarin by Han Jiang and Jin Ye

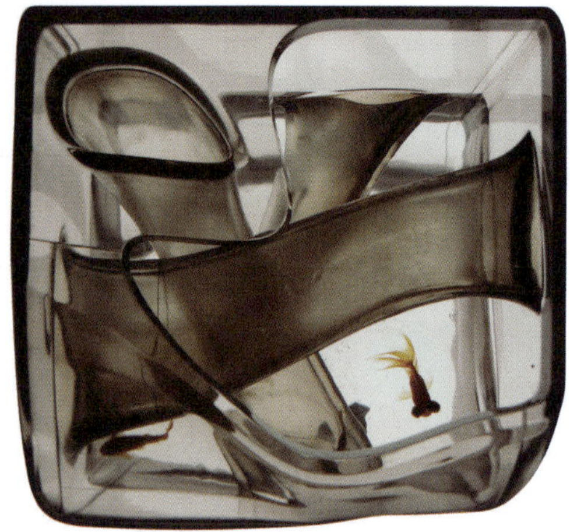

We are seeking
Living space for fish in the city,
But human beings and the fish
Must invert:
The fish dominate.

Space begins to spill,
Cubic boxes have melted.
Their collapse
Marks an end of the machine era.

The surface
Keeps melting,
Inner and the outer meet in obscurity.
Outer surface of the melt, inner surface of the water,
The fish frolics in
Intricate space.

Air and water agitates,
Inner and outer blurs.
It is an internet world:
Open.

Today, the 'Fish Tank' is still on a desk in the MAD office. It is a dwelling originally designed for fish, prioritising their lifestyle and the trajectory of their movements. This tank is no longer a simple cubic box. I would like to think that the fish feel happier in this environment, however, I cannot possibly tell as they do not speak to me.[1]

Nature has long been an interest of mine, as has the vividness of life. This is probably because of the environment I grew up in; I was born in Beijing and grew up in a *siheyuan* (courtyard house) located in a *hutong* (laneway) area, where I had the feeling of being free and full of life; in the courtyard you could see the sky and feel the land. Here there were trees, birds and most importantly my playmates to hang out with. The Old Beijing City is like a big garden: there is Beihai, Jingshan, Qiongdao, Zhongnanhai, Shichahai . . . A city where nature, culture and landscape are interwoven.

The influence of my childhood environment has subtly shaped my understanding of the city. I view many old cities in China as 'landscape cities'—the overall environmental layout is the priority, with function and technology receding behind artistic conception. This kind of urban space is somewhat more spiritual, a characteristic that today's cities are lacking.

In 2004, I returned to China from the US and founded MAD Architects. The old city of Beijing at the time made me feel somehow 'unreal.' The massive scale urbanisation driven by rapid economic development was imposing upon Beijing's traditional urban structure. The architectural system—mainstream Modernism—had fundamentally detached architecture from nature. In reaction to this, I hope my work can disrupt the boundary between nature and the city, reconnect them organically and establish a new urban response to nature. Consequently, a future city can emerge with the full spectrum of convenience that a modern city provides, but also with the poetic and artistic touch from the hearts of Chinese locals; thereby not only addressing functional aspects, but also celebrating human spirituality and cultural values.

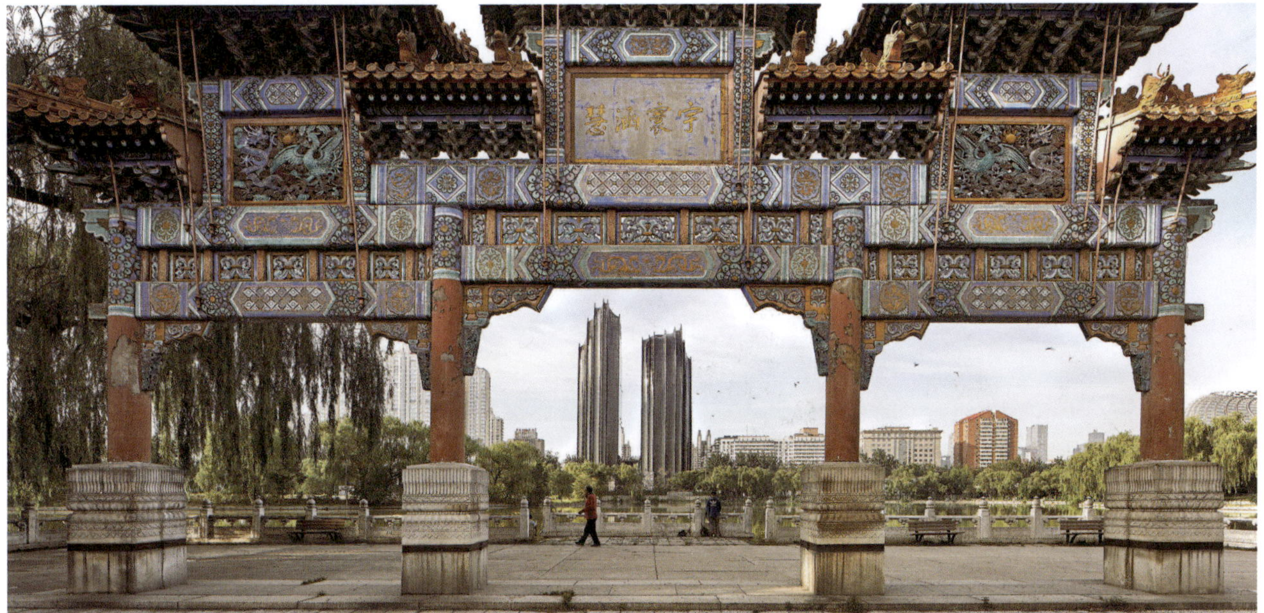

When I was studying modern cities, from Le Corbusier's *Ville Radieuse* to Rem Koolhaas' *Exodus*, I noticed the obsessive tendency to perceive a city from God's perspective; giving top-down attention to the holistic form of the city. Ironically, it is forgotten in modern models that the principal function of a city is to provide its residents with a good living environment. It is in fact common for people to feel oppressed and unsettled when living in a densified urban environment, where one's vision is constantly disrupted. Hence, MAD strives to break the repetitive and generic cubic box design in order to establish a firmer connection between the high-rise building and nature.

In 2006, MAD won a landmark design project overseas. We had the opportunity to build two high-rise residential towers in Mississauga City, located outside Toronto, Canada. This was my first attempt to break the common and stereotyped cubic box typology to create a more liberal connection between high-rise buildings and nature. Residential architecture itself is a response to and enhancement of its urban context and nature, while high-rise buildings are more likely to narrate their geographical and cultural environment. Since the beginning of the Absolute Towers design, we intended to give the architecture a feeling of being soft, in order to diminish its overwhelming presence. We wished to arouse people's yearning for nature by enabling them to sense wind and sunlight in their urban living experiences. Therefore, the vertical lines that emphasise height in traditional high-rise buildings were removed in this project. Instead, each entire building is twisted at various angles to formulate different landscape experiences at different heights. When the two buildings are projected together, the curves provoke interactions, and the architecture seems to be floating and moving.

Fig 1 (Opposite): MAD Architects, Fish Tank, 2004. Photo by Fang Zhenning.
Fig 2 (Above): MAD Architects, Chongyang Park Plaza, Beijing, 2015.

Following this, MAD had more chances to explore and enrich our concepts through projects conducted domestically and internationally. In 2008, MAD planned and organized a high-density urban design experiment with eleven young, international architects in Huaxi—the CBD of Guiyang. This collective project exhibited a new possibility for the city: a hybrid urban complex, where man-made constructions had a more intimate relationship with nature, and where residents were encouraged to selectively experience the urban and natural environment to uncover new perspectives. From then on, MAD was able to explore a more effective and comfortable method of urban design that allows for harmonious coexistence with nature; that is, to build clusters of architecture in response to geographical features and mountains, forming a brand-new urban landscape at the intersection between architecture and nature. During this phase, according to characteristics of each subsequent enumerated city, we practiced a series of projects: Cultural Island in Harbin, Chaoyang Park Plaza in Beijing, Huangshan Mountain Village, Nanjing Zhengda Himalayas Center, and so on. For each city, we applied the design methodology of blending architecture into the adjacent natural landscape.

I hope that these new urban spectacles which are deeply integrated with nature encourage people to rethink their connections with the world, in the same way that people and the universe converse with each other in the Old City of Beijing. Some believe that Chinese traditions represent 'the past' and the West equates to 'being modern'—and that combining both will synthesise something new. I am doubtful of this.

It is my opinion that only unprecedented approaches will benefit the future of architecture; a thing whose genes will inevitably be derived from certain traditions, but which does not repeat the past nor grow from hybridisation. Instead, its results are completely unfamiliar. In 2009, whilst designing the Yiwu Grand Theatre project I conceived the phrase of 'being at the place, but at different times.' Since then, my pursuit has shifted to a subject beyond natural landscape; it is based on certain cultural qualities but with a peculiar form. This pursuit was also practiced in the design of the Lucas Museum of Narrative Art, Quzhou Sports Centre, and so on.

A cultural landmark should firstly respond to the local environment. Furthermore, it should distinguish itself from surroundings in its evocation of time, so as to create distance between architecture and reality. Only when there is a comprehensive understanding of the local culture and environment, can the concept of 'being at the place, but at different times' be established.

The Yiwu Grand Theatre's concept was rooted in the perception of scenery in Jiangnan.[2] Yiwu is a city in the southern area of China, and its unique scenery is a composition of rivers, bridges and cloud-wrapped houses. Through the ages, people composed poems depicting the beauty and peace of these scenes of Jiangnan, which is an important spectacle in the Chinese cultural sign system:

> The inner lake, outer lake and the overlapping mountains are composed beautifully together. The September is suffused with the smell of osmanthus, while lotus sprawling miles on the lake, waving their flowers with the sweet breeze. Day to night, the songs along with the clarinet flutter around the water—the old and the kids are fishing and harvesting lotus roots happily.[3]

Black tiles, white walls, eaves and screens—built around water—the architecture of Jiangnan appears to be an ink painting if contemplated from afar. The architecture does not seek to attract attention but rather illustrates elegance and lightness.

MAD's Grand Theatre design responds to the landscape and nature of Jiangnan, making the distant mountain its background and the water its stage. Semi-transparent screening is layered in the formulation of a roof to mimic the traditional roof tiling of Jiangnan architecture. The Theatre floats on the lake gracefully, murmuring to its surroundings as though it has been there for thousands of years and yet may also have come from the future. Through the transparent and loose form, it blends into the temperament of Jiangnan but distinguishes itself from the context as a new way to sustain local culture.

Ultimately, MAD aims to create a specific time and place where the boundary between architecture and nature is blurred. In this way, architecture is no longer a three-dimensional machine constructed solely for human survival. It is expected to have the power to transit through time, linking the culture's past, present and future in a poetic way, and to use this pure poetry to enrich our minds and spirits. This is what we call 'HyperNature conception,' and this is our imperative for architecture.

01 The fish here is an analogy for a designer never fully knowing or understanding the people that she or he designs for. MAD's fish tank is an attempt to explore the feelings and experiences from a 'fish' perspective, and refers to a discussion from 3rd century BC-The Bridge of Hao-where Huizi says "You were not the fish. How could you know the fish is happy?"

02 Jiangnan, literally means 'South of the Yangtze River,' is a geographic area referring to lands immediately to the south of the lower reaches of the Yangtze River, including the southern part of its delta. The region encompasses the city of Shanghai. It's also a political and cultural regional identity parallel to Jiangbei, 'North of the Yangtze River.'

03 Watch the Tidewater, Liu Yong, the Song Dynasty. Chinese is a scenic language, where words always represent some signs in the cultural context. For example, chengyu is using, normally, four characters to lay the current situation with a story in the historical past. This phenomenon that a Chinese word or a short phrase is understood as a scene in the language users' recognition is defined as the 'sign system.'

Fig 3 (Opposite): MAD Architects, Yiwu Grand Theatre, Yiwu, 2019.

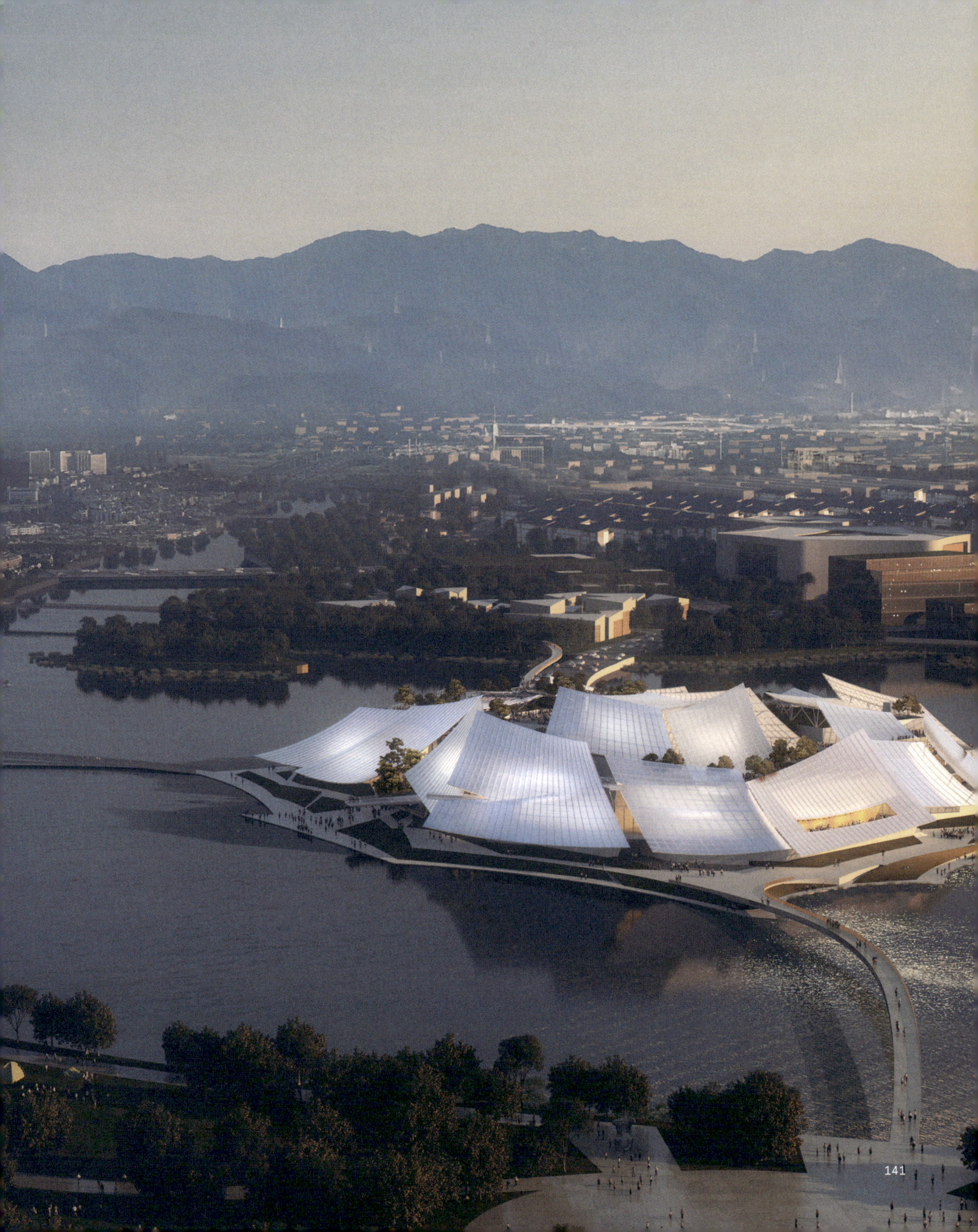

SUPPORTERS OF THE MELBOURNE SCHOOL OF DESIGN

The Faculty of Architecture, Building and Planning is grateful to the generous individuals, families and companies listed below who have donated to provide better opportunities for our students and staff over the period from the 1st of January 2019 to the 18th of June 2020.

We have made our best attempt to ensure the list is correct, but we are aware that our records may not be complete. If you notice any errors or omissions please contact Andrew Middleton, ABP Development Manager, on (03) 8344 3111 or miaj@unimelb.edu.au.

Joseph Reed, Façade of The Bank of New South Wales; John Wardle Architects, Melbourne School of Design, University of Melbourne. Point cloud scan by Ben Waters of Siii Projects. Image reproduced with author's permission.

Lord Mayor's Charitable Foundation
Grant F Marani
Faith Baker & Brian Baker
Late William C W Chen & Betty V W Chen
Vera Moore Foundation
Regalia Group
Beulah International
SGS Economics & Planning
Hansen Yuncken Pty Ltd
& The Peter Hansen Family Fund
Hans Varney & Carolyn Varney
Bates Smart
Warren and Mahoney Architects
SJB Planning
SJB Architects
SJB Urban
Peter Williams AM & Trish Williams
Mandy Yencken & Ted Yencken
John Wardle Architects
Richard Falkinger AO
Dato' Peter C H Tan & Phillip C Tan
Tony Isaacson

Gwenda Thomas
Julie Willis
Andrew Lee King Fun
Ron Billard
Kang Family
Raghav Goel
Hansen Yuncken Pty Ltd
& The Peter Hansen Family Fund
Yi Siang Ooi
Alexandra T Chu
Rebecca L Bond
Justin A Bokor
George A Michell AM
The Teng Family
George Hatzisavas & Jennifer Warburton
Kelvin J Steel
Robert McGauran
Douglas K Y Lee & Joaquina Lee
Steven L Pell
ABP Commencing Class of 1964
Architects Registration Board of Victoria
Haripriya Rangan

Christopher A Heywood
Andrew Middleton & Clare Harper
Dominique Hes
Philip Goad & Anna Johnston
Tom Eames
Chris Harvey
AnnMarie Brennan
Patricia Morton & Bruce Morton
Robyn Dalziel
James M Macneil
Fred Coates & Faye Coates
Daniel W Haskell
Charles R Freedman
Dario Nordio
Craig C Wilson
Thomas Y Lui
Jeffrey J Turnbull
Chris Smith
Maureen X Wu
Alan L Nance & Rhyll M Nance
David Beauchamp & Lynette Howden
Alasdair N Fraser & Jenny Fraser
Andrea Macdonald
Jacqui Remond
Matthew Bell & Melinda Wong
The Tibbits Family
Karl Brown
Elisabeth F Grove
Peter Epaminondas Tsitas
John Hasker AM & Jennifer F Hasker
Barry J Matthews
J H Holdsworth
Late Robin M Edmond &
Elvira S Edmond
David N Moore
Roger B Beeston
Mary Traitsis
Elizabeth Ridge
Jeff Robinson

INFLECTION

JOURNAL OF THE MELBOURNE SCHOOL OF DESIGN

Reflecting on 7 years

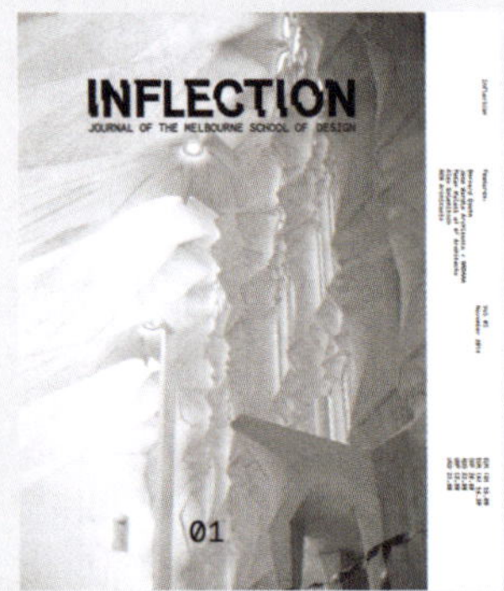

Vol. 01
Inflection (2014)

Ariani Anwar, William Cassell
and Jonathan Russell

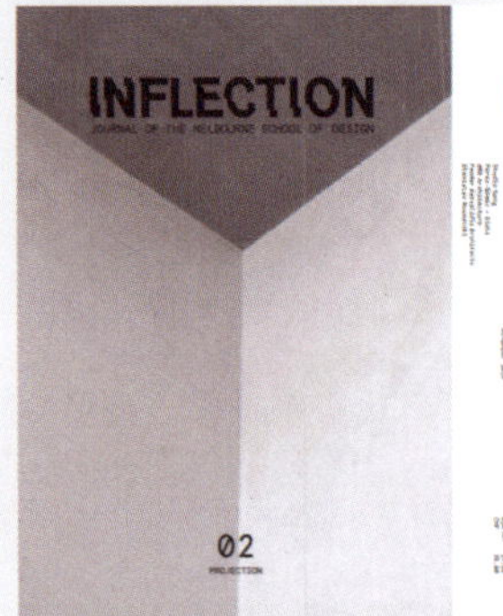

Vol. 02
Projection (2015)

Ariani Anwar, William Cassell
and Jonathan Russell

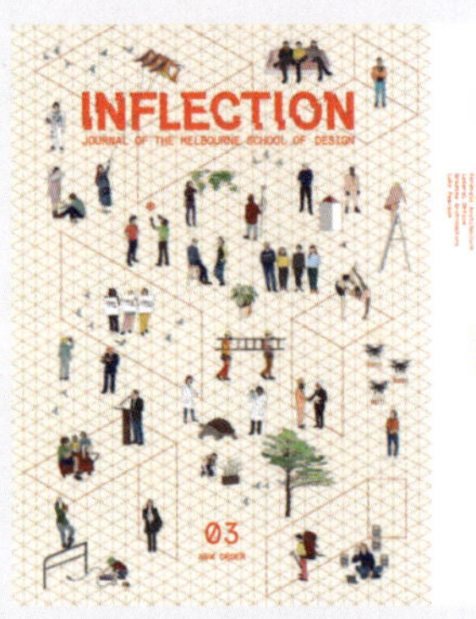

Vol. 03
New Order (2016)

Courtney Foote, John Gatip
and Jil Raleigh

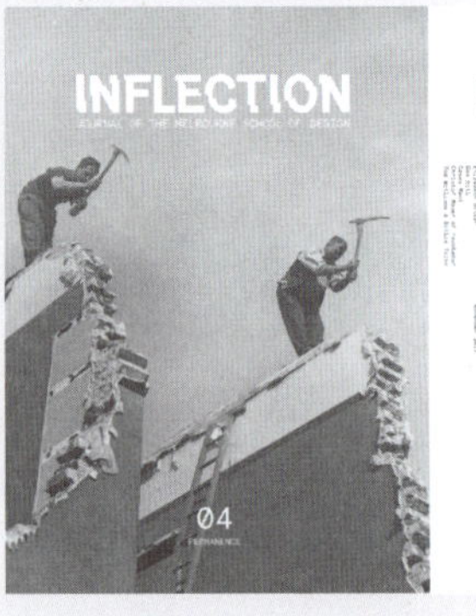

Vol. 04
Permanence (2017)

Dominic On, Nina Tory-Henderson,
Jessica Wood and Stephen Yuen

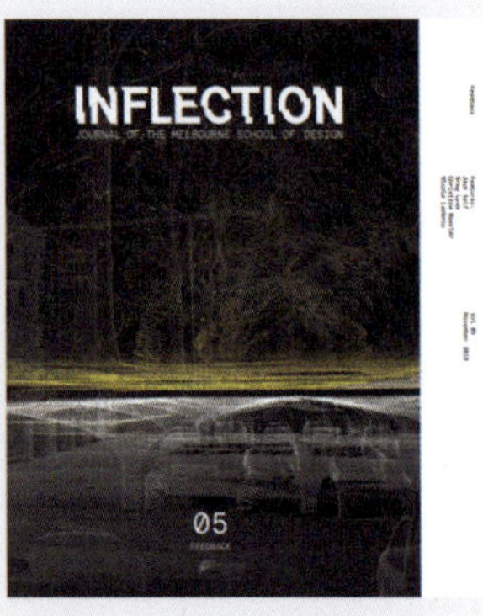

Vol. 05
Feedback (2018)

Lucia Amies, Olivia Potter,
Samuel Chesbrough, Sarah Mair
and William Ward

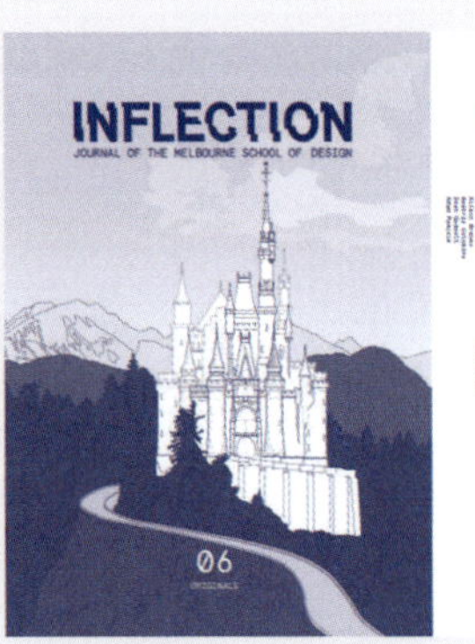

Vol. 06
Originals (2019)

Harrison Brooks, Anna Petrou,
and Brittany Weidemann

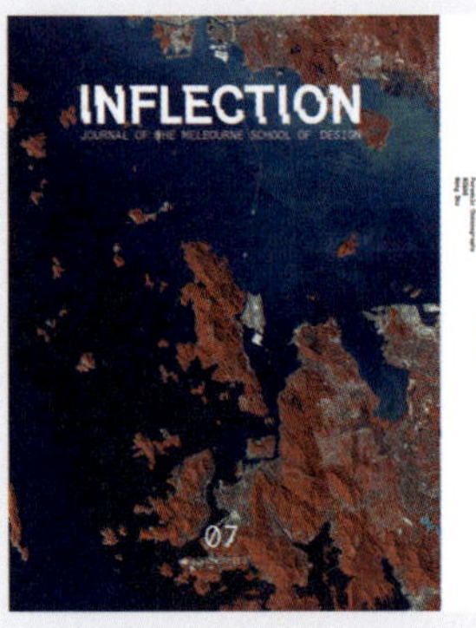

Vol. 07
Boundaries (2020)

Han Jiang, Louis O'Connor
and Arinah Rizal

Inflection starts here,
we leave the change to you.

To purchase this and other copies of *Inflection*,
please go to Melbourne Books at https://www.melbournebooks.com.au/